ESSAYS,

PHILOSOPHICAL AND THEOLOGICAL.

By JAMES MARTINEAU.

BOSTON:
WILLIAM V. SPENCER.
1866.

CAMBRIDGE:
STEREOTYPED AND PRINTED BY JOHN WILSON AND SON.

CONTENTS.

PUBLISHER'S PREFACE.

The publisher takes special pleasure in offering this volume of Essays selected from the much-admired writings of Rev. James Martineau, Professor in Manchester College, London. Mr. Martineau is considered one of the profoundest thinkers and most brilliant writers of this century. His contributions to the Prospective, Westminster, National, and other Reviews attracted the attention of the best minds in both England and America, and produced a marked and favorable impression upon men of all denominations. He has done more, perhaps, than any other writer of our time to detach religion from its historical accidents and accretions, and to defend its essential elements from the destructive assaults and tendencies of the positivist and critical schools. He is by far the ablest exponent and champion of religious faith in its contest with the scepticism and materialism of the age; and his criticisms of Mill, Spencer, Comte, Mansel, and Bain are almost necessary to a complete understanding of the positions these men severally occupy, and leave scarcely any thing to be desired on the other side. The subjects discussed in these Essays have awakened a general and growing interest among all classes of thoughtful readers; and the publisher esteems himself fortunate in being able to collect them from inaccessible magazines, and in presenting them to the American public in a permanent and elegant form.

BOSTON, March 31, 1866.

ESSAYS.

ESSAYS,

PHILOSOPHICAL AND THEOLOGICAL.

COMTE'S LIFE AND PHILOSOPHY.*

FROM the day of a man's death seven years must elapse, so this Catechism informs us, before he can be "*incorporated in the Supreme Being;*" *i.e.* registered among the worthies of humanity, and honored with a commemorative bust. We neither belong to the priesthood, nor are within six years of the date that must decide the question of Comte's apotheosis. Leaving so great a verdict to the council of the future, we avail ourselves of the labors of his translator and the recent close of his career to notice a few characteristics of his genius and system. Neither the puerilities of his later writings, nor the self-exaggeration pervading them all, cancel his claim to recognition as the most powerful and constructive thinker of the modern scientific school, and as a half-pious believer in the dreary visions of a philosophy held by many, though avowed by few. The

* The Catechism of Positive Religion. Translated from the French of Auguste Comte, by Richard Congreve. London: Chapman, 1858.

National Review, 1858.

difficulties over which his influence has triumphed attest his intellectual force. In his survey of particular sciences, not excepting his own (the mathematics), he has incurred the reproach of serious errors and misconceptions. Even among *savants*, his temper and personal pretensions are as unique as are Ewald's among critics and theologians. His style is an oppressive miracle of tediousness, benumbing the vivacity of the cleverest translator, and taxing the patience of the most practised student. His chief reputed merit — the creation of Sociology — he proclaims with the airs of a *μάγος*, instead of committing it to the test of time and thought; and men like Mr. Mill, who had accepted his baptism, and been initiated into his gospel, excuse themselves from his apocalypse. And no sooner do "Secularists" indulge their gratitude for his abolition of theologies and hierarchies, than he publishes himself Supreme Pontiff of humanity, and sets up a theocracy without a God. Yet, in spite of every weakness and offence, he has found his way to the thought of the present age. A few vigorous minds he has moulded to an extent unknown, perhaps, even to themselves; and many more owe no slight obligation to the pregnant hints everywhere scattered through his first great work. His main attempt — viz. to destroy the antithesis between the physical and the moral sciences, and draw them out in one continuous series, by ranging man and his life among natural objects — has established itself as a characteristic of our time, and exhibits more signs of vigor than the older forms of anthropological and social doctrine. If the most marked intellectual tendency of the age be to advance the lines of every science into a domain hitherto distinct — to press physical conceptions into chemistry, chemical into physiology, physiological into morals and politics, and by the energy of inductive law to shoulder metaphysics and theology over the brink of the world altogether — it is largely due to the action, direct and indirect, of the *Philosophie Positive.*

The doctrines of Comte can scarcely be appreciated without some reference to his personal career. On this point, indeed, he himself lays no little stress; and he has accordingly supplied, in a series of prefaces, an autobiographical sketch of his mental history. It appears that during his earliest years he was exposed to two singularly inharmonious influences, whose struggle must have affected his whole development. His family belonged to the Catholic and monarchical party in the South of France; to conciliate which the first Napoleon had surrendered to ecclesiastical *régime* the young revolutionary schools, in which, at the same time, the exact sciences constituted the preponderant discipline, and the political sentiments of the crisis still remained. No amalgamation could well take place between elements so discordant. From the first, the theological influence seems to have found no entry into our author's nature; and his whole problem was to bring his political and social ideas into some systematic relation to his mathematical and physical knowledge. In this respect his genius and character bear the true Napoleonic type; and as the exiled Emperor at St. Helena shows himself still the officer of artillery, and regards the world from the engineering point of view, so Comte betrays the same tendency to push dynamics into the conquest of history and mankind, and coerce the universe of life and persons into the formulas applicable to *things*. The French tendency to large and neat generalization, so tempting to the love of order, so dangerous to the paramount feeling of truth, does not appear to have been checked in him by any considerable devotion to the *literæ humaniores*. No trace appears of the *scholarly* habits of mind, and that peculiar balance of faculty, to which philological and moral studies seem to be indispensable. Though his view over history is wide, and supplies him with many original reflections, yet the tact of sympathetic criticism is nowhere found, and the dominance of the natural philosopher's rules of thought is always conspicuous. His mathematical training was completed in the Polytechnic School; and during its progress he seems to have fallen under the influence of St. Simon, and caught the inspiration of his socialistic dreams. This influence he himself professes to have been "disastrous;" inasmuch as it suspended his purely philosophical activity in favor of schemes of direct political experiment. But the disciples of this singular enthusiast have always reproached Comte with intellectual plagiarism from their master; and certainly the historical generalizations of Comte continually remind us of the principles and methods of the earlier school. After long dissatisfaction with the disorderly condition of all political and social speculation, and an eager desire to carry the exactitude of physical science up into the phenomena of life and humanity, he at last realized his hope in 1822, at the age of twenty-four, by the discovery of his great law as to the three successive phases of human evolution. This law is as follows: that, both in the individual and in the history of mankind, thought, in dealing with its problems, passes of necessity through (1) a theological stage; (2) a metaphysical; before reaching (thirdly, and finally) the positive: resorting, in the earliest instance, to the idea of living and personal agents as the motive-power of nature; then proceeding to substitute abstract entities, such as force, substance, &c.; and only at last content to relinquish every thing except the study and classification of phenomena in their relations of time and place. In 1825–6, he sketched in some minor essays the mode of applying this law to the re-organization of the body politic; and in the latter year commenced an oral exposition of his discovery in its entire range of application. His course was unhappily interrupted by a *profond orage cérébral*, in other words, a temporary attack of mental disorder; for their mismanagement of which he fiercely attacks his physicians and the usages of their profession. His recovery enabled him to complete his lectures in 1829. This *vivâ-voce* exposition forms the basis of his great work *Cours de Philosophie Positive*, the publication of which extended over twelve years, from 1830–1842. It consists of six very thick volumes, divided into sixty *leçons;* during the course of which he reviews, by the light of his law, the *ensemble* of human knowledge, beginning with the purely quantitative sciences, as the most simple; and having taken the inorganic studies in the order of retreat from this primitive base, advancing to the province of physiology. The laws won in that field he carries up into anthropology; and by adding on the effects of combining men in associated numbers, he seeks to establish a special and crowning science of *Sociology*. It is on his ability to accomplish this final object that he stakes the whole credit of his method; and whatever is prior to this he regards as the mere vestibule to his great structure. The better to secure a trial of his claims upon this issue, he has made his sociological system the subject of a separate work, *Système de Politique Positive;* in which the natural sciences are entirely left behind, and his law is applied exclusively to the relations of human nature and history. The second title of this work, *Traité de Sociologie*, being borrowed from his essay of 1824, resumes, in 1851, the thread of his early career.

In the mean while a complete revolution had taken place both in his inner character and in his external relations; cutting his life into two dissimilar periods, the identity of which in the same person his original disciples must find it difficult to realize. The severe mathematician, the rigorous philosophic censor, the scornful materialist, is now converted into the "High-Priest of the Religion of Humanity," the chief of the "Occidental Republic," the type of the "Regeneration of the Affections," sending missionary despatches to Russian emperors and Turkish viziers, and surrendered apparently to the visionary enthusiasms of a St. Simon or a Robert Owen. He speaks of himself as the founder of a new, final, and universal worship. He claims an annual subsidy from his disciples, in support of his sacerdotal character, and addresses the yearly circular which demands the tax to all the Western lands. He repudiates our chronological era and the

Roman calendar; makes 1788 his zero of human history, which begins for him with the French Revolution; gives us thirteen months in the year, and a day over for commemorating all the dead; and dates his productions in a way horrifying to Quakers, and questionable even to Hero-worshippers; finishing one preface on the 23d Aristotle, year 63, another on 12th Dante, a third on the 25th Charlemagne; writing to the Emperor Nicholas on 19th Bichat, and to Reschid Pacha on the 7th Homer, &c. Whence this extraordinary change in a man trained under the austere discipline of the exact sciences? Skilful observers of human character might perhaps notice in his first great work symptoms of great personal peculiarity, but certainly nothing which could prepare them for his later exhibitions. An overbearing dogmatism and astounding self-appreciation appear in all his expositions; and the personal preface in which he takes leave of the last volume of his *Philosophie*, besides betraying frequent soreness and bickerings towards the Académie and the *savants* of the day, querulously turns upon the authorities of the Polytechnic School for not appointing him to one of the higher professorships, and almost dares them to dismiss him from the subordinate post he held there. His contemptuous estimate of the reputations of the hour and the intellectual spirit of his time would have more effect but for the manifest admixture of disappointed feeling; for threnodies on the "decline of science" are heard with impatience when deriving their inspiration from personal grievances. There may have been grounds for the complaints of persecution so frequently insinuated against Arago; but there is enough in Comte's teaching and influence, notwithstanding his incontestable genius, to explain some indisposition on the part of the directors of public education to trust him with distinguished functions, without supposing malignant cabals against him, prompted by jealousy, and working by mean intrigue. Having publicly proclaimed his real or supposed injuries, and challenged dismissal, he was almost unavoidably taken at his word; and in 1843–4 underwent what he terms his "polytechnic spoliation," followed by seven years of persecution from the "pedantocracy" of Paris. It was during this interval that the agency presented itself which created his "second career." He had been thrown back entirely on private life; he had just completed his "immense elaboration," and his six volumes were before the world; and he had attained, in some involuntary way, another kind of freedom, not specifically defined, but termed an "irreproachable moral freedom," — a phrase which, interpreted by its connections, evidently means a dissolution of the marriage-tie. Disengaged in so many senses, he is no way claimed by the past, but open to new impulses; and just at this opportune crisis, by a destiny which might be called providential, were it not that "theological ideas are cerebral infirmities," he fell in with "an incomparable angel," similarly separated from matrimonial obligations, Mme. Clotilde de Vaux. Drawn to sympathy at first by "the sad conformity of their domestic destinies," they soon find that each nature is constituted to give what the other wants; she knowing nothing of Positivism, and he nothing of love, and neither unwilling to learn the lesson of the other. Comte attributes the previous sleep of his gentler feelings, first to his early withdrawal from the domestic circle into a scholastic seclusion; and next, to a marriage which he had contracted on purpose to repair his deficient affections, and which, thus taken as a prescription, very naturally failed to produce any new symptoms. It was not too late, however, at the age of forty-five, for the "better human sentiments" to be awakened in him; their energy, indeed, was all the greater for their previous exceptional repression; and when appealed to by a type of feminine nature unequalled in the past and present, and unsurpassable in the future, they effected in him a moral resurrection, became the source of new positivist inspirations, and completed the conditions of his great mission — to re-organize entirely the whole of human existence on the principle of giving ascendency to the heart over the understanding. Of this lady, though he speaks of her in all his prefaces as an object of interest to the whole world, we know nothing except that she was unhappy, and converted Comte from philosophical vigor to puerile sentimentality. She had begun, it seems, a fiction (*Willelmine*) intended to correct the mischievous influence of the doctrines of Mme. Dudevant; and her admirer makes it a topic of special praise, both of her and of himself, that notwithstanding their own unfavorable experience, they always inculcated the sacredness of marriage, and resisted the laxity of domestic morals too prevalent in France. When, however, he tells us that the heroine of the unfinished tale was to "have passed successively through the chief actual aberrations," preserved through all by natural purity and elevation, so as to end at last in domestic felicity, it is difficult to recognize the superiority in moral conception to the novels of George Sand; nor can we wonder that the authoress's family were unwilling, after her death, to give effect to her wish that the Ms. should be left in Comte's hands. A single year was the term of that "incomparable objective union" which was to alter his whole future career; her early death then restored him to his solitude, and left him, as he says, to the fainter though more assiduous exercise of "subjective adoration." Had any remnant of religious belief still clung to him, this event would have swept it away: "Were it possible," he says, "for my reason ever to go back to that theological condition which is adapted only to the infancy of humanity, this catastrophe would suffice to make me reject with indignation the providential optimism which affects to console our miseries by enjoining on us a stupid admiration of the most frightful disorders. Ever-innocent victim as thou art, scarcely knowing life but by its deepest griefs, thou art laid low at the very moment when at length a worthy personal happiness commenced, closely connected with a human social mission! And I too, though less pure — did I deserve, after so many unjust sufferings, to have thus frustrated the long-delayed felicity reserved for a lonely existence constantly devoted, from its opening, to the fundamental service of humanity? Does not, moreover, this twofold private calamity constitute a public loss in a way to exclude all idea of compensation?" With this sentiment he seems to have completely imbued her own mind, little as it seems to breathe the feminine tenderness which he ascribes to her; for she died repeating again and again the strong-minded protest that she did not deserve so to suffer and be cut off.

The philosopher's heart, however, once softened, scarcely knows how to make enough of its newly-discovered susceptibilities. Not only did the image of his mother, whom he acknowledges to have inadequately loved during her lifetime, — terminated fourteen years before, — now appear to him in a more affecting light; but his servant-maid, — "the incomparable Sophie," endowed, as he observes, with the fortunate inability to read, which the more strongly brings out her rectitude and penetration, — becomes a model of womanly perfection, and completes his triad of guardian angels. He celebrates them all as concerned in the tardy realization of his emotional life, and wishes it to be understood that their inspiration is silently present in the whole execution of his great mission. But Madame Clotilde is still the dominant influence; and the terms in which the influence is described are most extraordinary, exhibiting the extravagance of passion without its poetry, and reduced to a mere affair of quantity, and uttering its devotion in tones that seem rather to mock at other religion than to breathe their own. What Dante has done for Beatrice, Comte will more effectually accomplish for his "holy Clotilde;" whose name, associated with his own, is to go down and be preserved in the most distant and imperishable memories of a grateful humanity. And it is highly characteristic, that her title to this eternal distinction is always her influence upon *him*, and therefore her instrumentality in the development of Positivism: *his* system, his discoveries, his genius, constitute the grand permanent essence; as connected with his public life an importance belongs to his private life, and this importance is shared by her who so powerfully moved him. The impression throughout is simply this: "When the Himalayas fall in love and make sonnets of thunder, the most distant hamlets of the plain will ask 'Who is it?'" It was through her angelic agency that he has become a really double organ for human nature, the representative at once of its intellect and of its soul; and without her he would never have been able, in his own person, to append to the career of an Aristotle that of a St. Paul! He certainly awards to the "new Beatrice" titles which have no parallel in the immortal verse that celebrates the elder one; for she is at once his "*subjective mother*," the source of his second and regenerated life, and his "*objective daughter*," the docile pupil of his first and intellectual life. Nor do merely human analogies and relations suffice to express and satisfy his feeling. This lady is to be recognized, not by him alone in his three daily prayers, but by all truly regenerate people, as "the best personification of the Supreme Being." Candor, however, requires us to acknowledge that, in claiming this highest distinction, he is by no means exclusive in his affection; for within a few pages he says, that to the positivists *every* worthy woman habitually furnishes the best representation of the true *Grand-Etre*, and that the affective sex is, in his system, set up as the moral Providence of the human race. In his annual circular of 1853, addressed to the tributaries who furnish his subsidy, he explains how it is that he spends so much more of his moderate income in house-rent than in maintenance; he admits that his lodgings, strictly speaking, exceed his actual material wants, but urges that they were the "scene of his moral regeneration under the angelic impulse which commanded his second life;" and, considering the decisive blessings which the West has already received from this source, he would charge with ingratitude all those who, sharing the public and private benefits of the new religion, would let him be torn from the scene of their origin. These holy walls, with the adored image for ever imprinted on them, are a daily help in developing an intimate worship of the best personation of the Supreme Being; and have proved so "during all those years, already not a few, in which her glorious subjective eternity has taken the place (alas, too soon) of her sad objective existence." There, under this resistless patronage, such a harmony establishes itself between his private and his public life, that the advances of each may soon extend to the other; so as to make him feel the true theory of their unity long before putting it into expression. Thus the same environment which witnessed his first regeneration will soon find itself consecrated by many decisive celebrations of the chief social sacraments. "I have just completed," he says, "the principal part of my religious structure, and the decisive little work in which the subjective participation of my holy eternal companion is already unanimously recognized. How else shall I be able to achieve, with equal advantage, the remainder of the principal elaboration, and even the less important works that will follow? I have already reached the age when I must scrupulously administer my time and my means of executing, with full cerebral vigor, all that I promised at the end of my fundamental work. It is for this reason that I shall always repudiate the stupid material economy which would deprive me of a powerful spiritual assistance." The fantastic forms under which, here and elsewhere, the author's egotism and self-exaggeration present themselves; the elaborate minuteness with which for the benefit of the "West" and the "Future" he publishes his sickliest feelings; the pomp with which he claims "eternal veneration" as well as temporal maintenance for his "noble services," — might induce a suspicion that he is playing a part, and practising on the simplicity of his disciples. Nor is it easy, in estimating minds of this peculiar constitution, to draw the psychological, or even the moral, distinction between self-flattery and artful misuse of the confidence of others. But Comte's dogmatic self-assertion, whether it speaks in maudlin softness or with hieratic grandeur, we believe to be perfectly sincere; the homage which a nature barren of every superhuman reverence, and paying only a provisional respect to the past phases of mankind, necessarily turns in upon itself. Of Divine and permanent in the universe he admits nothing; and of its progressive phenomena he himself is the newest and ripest, — the blossom shaped at length from the rising sap, and tinted by the growing light, of history. There was a grand fate concerned, he intimates, in his encounter with Madame Clotilde; the rebirth of his heart was indispensable; and "the *ensemble* of human destinies commissioned an incomparable angel to deliver to him the general result of the gradual perfectionating of our moral nature." He evidently looks on the whole past as a mere prelude to his own labors, and having no significance except as ushering them in; all its products, like the nodding sheaves in Joseph's dream, are to stand round upon the field and bow to him. If any thing lingers on the world that is too stiff-necked and refractory for this, it will simply have to disappear; and the only force that remains to older modes of thought is just sufficient for the process of mutual annihilation, that Positivism may enter upon the cleared field without a blow. For example, throughout the area prepared by the Roman empire, two incompatible forms of monotheism, Islam and Catholicism, have for upwards of a millennium aspired to universality; at last they are exhausted; for five centuries the Crescent has renounced its pretensions to the West, and the Cross surrenders to its "eternal antagonist" the very locality which it first consecrated. The ancient territory of the civilized world is nearly equally divided between the two; they have no longer any energy that is productive and conquering, but only enough to neutralize and extinguish each other in favor of the Positive Philosophy. For this hour the philosophy, through its antecedents, has been all the while preparing itself. Remounting by the steps of a noble filiation, Comte claims Hume as his chief forerunner in philosophy, with Kant as an accessory, whose fundamental conception waited for true development in Positivism. In relation to political doctrine, he was preceded by Condorcet, in conjunction with De Maistre, whose principles first became fruitful in the positive school, and are nowhere else appreciated. Add to these Bichat and Gall as his predecessors in scientific physiology, and you have the six recent names that connect him with the three systematic fathers of the true modern philosophy, Bacon, Descartes, and Leibnitz. Higher still, he finds *himself* again in the middle ages, under the cowl of Thomas Aquinas, the cloak of Roger Bacon, and the wreath of Dante; and thus directly reaches his true precursor, the prince of genuine thinkers, the incomparable Aristotle. Though *the world* was not ready till now for the final retreat of monotheism before the positive philosophy, all capable thinkers instinctively felt their relative merits, however imperfectly they expressed their feeling. Tacitus and Trajan, it is now admitted, were right in pronouncing "inimical to the human race" a religion which consigned perfection to a celestial isolation, disowned the dignity of labor by deducing it from a divine curse, and made woman the source of all evil. Those eminent men did but anticipate the ultimate judgment of matured humanity. They could not be aware of the provisional benefits of which, during the infancy of a new civilization, this faith was to be the medium; and they pronounced what the ripened reason of our age at length confirms. And when the Christian priesthood and influence had finally become effete and retrograde, it was reserved for M. Comte, by fully satisfying the intellect and sentiments of these last days, to assume the Pontificate of Humanity, and vindicate the ancient instinctive antipathy of philosophy to Christian or other theology. It is worthy of remark, however, that while, in his survey of old times, his sympathies resort to the judgment of philosophic emperors and historians against a faith of the common and even the servile class, it is his cue, in dealing with the present day, to invert this order of preference, to speak slightingly of the educated and ruling orders of society, and to pay special court to the proletary class, especially the women among them, and above all, if they have the "fortunate inability to read." Among these alone, he says, can be found the openness to real truth, and the reverent docility necessary to true discipleship; the freedom from pre-occupation by either retrograde or anarchical ideas; and more particularly, the mind unspoiled by pretended private judgment on political and other matters quite beyond them. Already has the proletary class suffered in this way from the exercise of universal suffrage; and only in women, through their happy exemption from political rights and interests, has the requisite submissiveness of spirit been preserved. To them, therefore, he especially appeals; not without a consciousness that he has some resistance to expect from their feeling in favor of certain doctrines on which he throws contempt, in particular the doctrine of a future life. But this repugnance, he assures them, is quite a mistake; and if they will only reflect that he makes *them* the true personification of the *Grand-Etre*, and through their influence on the affections of men gives them a *subjective* immortality in the minds of others, they will be convinced that his system is far from being dry and cold, and will be ashamed to regret the loss of a mere egoistic futurity. Does not positivism lay down the law of "eternal widowhood" (*i.e.* forbid second marriages)? How, then, can it be said not to provide an honorable homage to feminine affection? In all this bidding for support from particular classes, there is surely something little worthy of either a philosophy or a faith. And when we connect with it the assertion, in the fifth volume of his first great work, that probably up to that time he was himself his only disciple, it can scarcely fail to appear like the expression of morbid disappointment. The more and more eccentric displays of pretension which characterize his later volumes, are painful to all who appreciate his earlier genius. But they are too curious as psychological studies, and too vitally connected with the distinctive type of his doctrine, to be left out of sight. Indeed, he so constantly insists on the inseparable connection of his subjective experience with his public action on the world, that it is impossible, by his own rule, to characterize his system without tracing the manifestations of his idiosyncrasy.

The episodical treatise in which are found the most peculiar exhibitions of his later mode, is the *Catéchisme Positiviste*, announced, as translated by Mr. Congreve, at the head of this article. It was published towards the end of 1852, and forms a kind of *excursus* from the second volume of his *Politique*. It is in the form of dialogue, between himself, as sacerdotal instructor, and an "angelic interlocutrix," who is no other than Madame Clotilde. The conversations unfold the mysteries of the positivist "religion;" the attributes of the "incomparable goddess" of humanity; the "institution of guardian angels;" the three daily prayers; the organization of the priesthood, and the whole ritual and calendar of this new anti-faith. The date of publication was purposely fixed near the commencement of Louis Napoleon's dictatorship. That crisis, the author intimates, had imposed a salutary silence on all babblers (*i.e.* had extinguished journalism, political association, and discussion); and he avails himself of the sudden stillness to obtain a hearing, and to "direct especially the feminine and the proletary thought to his fundamental revolution." His previous scientific expositions address to the popular mind too antipathic a treatment to win the indispensable success; and to meet the conditions of active propagation, he turns outward the moral and effective side of his doctrine, asking leave to use only two pairs of strictly scientific terms, which he cannot do without, viz. "*statical and dynamical*," "*objective and subjective*." Here, then, if anywhere, we may expect to find the results on which he dwells with greatest pride; and if we must seek in his larger works the logical root and evolution of his system, here is the depository of its choicest fruits. Yet, strange to say, the book is inconceivably absurd; and it is only in the literature of Mormonism that any thing more childish and dismal can be found. Mr. Congreve's affectionate reverence for his master is undoubted; and the aim of this translation is certainly to glorify, not humiliate, the new hierophant. People have always differed about monuments; and Madame Tussaud is known to believe that the saints and heroes look best in waxwork and their own old clothes.

Since the publication of the books of Exodus and Leviticus, no more elaborate system of "religion" has appeared than M. Comte's. It has its *cultus*, private and public; its organization of dogma; its discipline, penetrating to the whole of life; its altars, its temples, its symbolism, its prescribed gestures and times; its ratios and length of the different parts and sorts of prayer; its rules for opening or shutting the eyes; its ecclesiastical courts and rules of canonization; its orders of priesthood and scale of benefices; its adjustment of the temporal to the spiritual power; its novitiate and consecration; its nine sacraments; its angels, its last judgment, its paradise: in short, all imaginable requisites of a religion, — except a God. Were it not for this omission, we should feel an interest in examining a structure so curious and careful. But in presence of this blank, any serious estimate of the scheme would be as idle as for the geographer to discuss the climate and flora of his dreams, or the architect to measure the spires of the frost-work and criticise the castles in the clouds.

It may well be asked, what possible principle of coherence, what inner meaning at all, there can be in a system professing atheism, yet propagating a "religion." With the answer to this natural inquiry we shall be content, and then proceed to a less repulsive side of our author's doctrine. His originality is sometimes too great for his conservatism; and he wants now and then some equivalent for what he has been ruthlessly cancelling. Having superseded "monotheism," he finds it necessary to invent a "new Supreme Being;" and such Being he has accordingly provided, and ordered to be represented in statuary by "a woman of thirty with a child in her arms." This *Grand-Etre* is "the aggregate of co-operative beings endowed with nervous systems of three centres;" * the sum-total of the civilized or progressive part of our race, whether

* Réflexions synthétiques, au point de vue positiviste, sur la Philosophie, la Morale et la Religion; court Aperçu de la Religion positive, &c. systématisée ou fondée par Auguste Comte, p. 65.

past, present, or future; the picked clay of humanity, that falls kindly into an idealizing mould. The greater portion of mankind's ἄριστοι having become historical, and each generation adding its quota to the noble dead, "the Supreme Being is not yet fully formed," but receives "new component parts" so long as our planet remains habitable by men. "In the composition of the Great Being the dead occupy the first place, then those who are yet to be born. The two together are far more numerous than the living, most of whom too are only its servants, without the power at present of becoming its organs. There are but few men, and still fewer women, who admit of being satisfactorily judged in this respect before the completion of their objective career" (p. 89). After death, however, — so it is said with shocking burlesque, — there comes to each the judgment, that is, the verdict of his fellow-citizens whether he is worthy to be contributed to the *Grand-Etre;* and should he be voted into so sublime a place, his presence thenceforward in the recognized ideal of humanity constitutes his "future life," — his "subjective immortality."

We need not proceed further. What the worship of saints would be, if the King of Saints were dead, — nay, what the sceptic Euhemerus actually supposed the Hellenic mythology to be, — such deification of mortals in default of an Immortal is the avowed religion of positivism. The minutest prescriptions are given for conducting the whole process, both mental and ritual. At your altar in the morning, for instance, you are to adore your mother, — probably (if you are adult) "become subjective" to you, and requiring to be brought before your secret vision. To help the effort and express the inwardness of the object, you must shut your eyes. This done, you first set up the *place* on which the figure is to enter; next, fix her intended attitude; thirdly, choose her dress; and then, at length, permit herself to glide into view; taking care to idealize by subtraction only, not by addition. In due order, the prayer to her ensues; consisting for the first half of the hour in "commemoration" of her goodness; then, for the rest, in "effusion" of the feelings thus awakened. The evening prayer is to be said in bed, and to be only half as long; and the midday devotion may limit itself to recitals of a quarter of an hour. The wife and the daughter (or, for a woman, the husband and son) are to be conjoined as guardian angels with the mother, and to have their turn of homage. The public worship only applies the same principle to a wider circle of relations, running through and celebrating all the great social ties, the several stages of human progress, the natural classes of the body-politic; and forming an ecclesiastical calendar, with special services all through the year. The temples are all to face towards the metropolis of humanity, — Paris, of course; but meanwhile the positivists will not object to use the churches and cathedrals as they are, and occupy them as they fall into disuse. Even the Madonnas may pass well enough, with altered name, for the Goddess of Humanity. But instead of the cross (or of the crescent) must be substituted, as sign of the faith, the curve described by the hand in touching the three chief cerebral organs. There are no elements too incongruous to blend in this strange "religion." The dissecting-room, the high altar, the lover's bower, all subscribe their proportion to its ceremonial and sentiment; not without an ever-recurring preponderance of the last, significantly expressed in the saying, that "soon the knee of man will never bend except to woman." *

It is dreary enough, yet pathetic too, to stand by and see the great materialist elaborately mimic the Catholic Church, which had surrounded his youth with its forms without holding his manhood by its faith. The meaning was gone, but the picture remained, and looked in at every deeper and gentler hour with a lingering charm. The sacrament of early life was disenchanted; yet he could not withdraw his eye. He forgot that the wine of the Real Presence was poured out, and adored the empty cup. His plagiarisms from Catholicism are not confined to the details of external ritual. He owns, and tries to imitate, the vast moral power it exercises through its biographical traditions, its gallery of martyrs and saints; and to embody this education by ideals is one of the chief ambitions of his system. He missed the deeper truth, that these lesser pieties depend upon a greater; that the human reverences constitute a true hierarchy, which falls into confusion when the Supreme term is gone; that though lower men may give veneration to a higher, he is higher no more if in his heart he accepts it; and that only when the whole heart of humanity is habitually drawn upward in trust of a Living Perfection, can we safely apportion homage to one another. Once or twice, indeed, the suspicion seems to cross him that, if indeed we stand at the head of living natures, the conditions of any collective

* Politique positive, vol. i. p. 259.

humility must fail, and that it would be better for aspiration could we retain the sense of "our inferiority to angelic beings." But there will ever "appear above us" (so he answers his own misgiving) "a type of Real Perfection, below which we must still remain, though it invites our persevering efforts to continual approximation." May we not ask, *Where*, then, do you find this "type of Real Perfection above us?" Is it indeed *Real* to you? Or is it *Ideal*, — and that in the poor sense of being merely *imaginary?* If we stand at the summit of the hierarchy, the space "above us" is a blank, and has neither "type" nor attraction any whither. The angels and God being removed, no concrete personal living "perfection" exists beyond our humanity, and what you substitute is an abstraction feigned by our forecasting fancy — not an *actual Being other than ourselves*, but a *potential state of certain future selves.* Is not this poor ghost, which counterfeits the "Real" object of faith and trust, an involuntary testimony to the indispensable energy of that religious aspiration for which Comte's universe is empty of all provision?

From this desolate side of positivism we gladly turn to estimate some of its distinctive features as a theory of human knowledge and a classification of the sciences. Its leading positions are these:

Theology and Metaphysics are two successive stages of nescience unavoidable as preludes to all Science.

We can know nothing but phenomena, their co-existences and successions; and the test of our knowledge is prevision.

By "phenomena" must be understood objects of *per-*

ception, to the exclusion of psychological change reputed to be self-known.

The idea of Causality, efficient or final, is an illusion which should be expelled from philosophy.

The sciences logically arrange themselves in a certain series, according to the growing complexity of their phenomena; and their historical agrees with their logical order.

The first and the last of these positions involve *historical* assertions, as to the actual procedure of the human mind, of the most sweeping kind. To test them satisfactorily would require a survey of the whole march of civilization, and a critique upon its springs of movement possible only to the regular historian of knowledge. It is easy enough, over so wide a field, to gather and group examples in confirmation or in disproof; but the evidence of a general law depends on the balance of the whole, and can only be estimated on the large scale. We shall not attempt, therefore, to explain the grounds of our prevailing dissent from Comte's historical rules, or the connections which might perhaps save whatever truth they have. We address ourselves in preference to the three intermediate positions, which are the real key to the whole system.

A question, however, arises *in limine* as to the *name* of this "philosophy." Why call it "*Positive*"? From what is it discriminated by this epithet? The terms with which it stands in contrast, and which mark what it would exclude and replace, are "*theological*" and "*metaphysical*." But neither of these is its proper correlate, or would ever occur to the mind in connection with it. Each of them might be thrown into various antitheses: "theological" might be opposed to anthropologic, to atheistic, to naturalistic, &c.; "metaphysical," to physical, to historical, to logical, &c.; but cannot, in virtue of its own meaning or definition, be made a contrary to "positive." The only opposition into which this word can be thrown is expressed by the term "*negative;*" and what Comte really means to intimate by this phrase is, that there is *nothing at all* in either theology or metaphysics, and that his procedure is distinguished from them both by *having all the reality to itself.* He is quite at liberty to think so, and to make good the boast, if he can; but to embody it in his nomenclature, and adopt it as the base of his classification, is in the highest degree unphilosophical, an offence at once against logical precision and moral propriety. To arrogate merit under the guise of a scientific division, is quite inadmissible, except in the code of quack-advertisements and ecclesiastical polemics. It is as if we were to divide human studies into politics, poetry, and *sense;* or to classify men as merchants, farmers, and *fools.* If we take away the coloring of self-praise involved in the word "positive," the attribute which we require to mark is simply this, — *the limitation of research to phenomena, in their orders of resemblance, co-existence, and succession;* an idea which the word *positive* has no tendency whatever to convey. *Phenomenological,* as opposed to *ontological,* indicates the character which Comte requires to express; and had he stated it thus, we should have recognized an old and well-established antithesis, and perceived that the theology and metaphysics which he separates into two states are essentially one; conjointly, indeed, opposed to *his* exclusiveness, but only on principles common to them both. The recognition of *reality* behind appearance, of *causation* as well as manifestation, is that which they assume and Comte denies. The nature of the controversy is disguised, and its issue taken for granted, by the substitution of a threefold for a twofold classification, and the appropriation to the final form of a laudatory predicate instead of a neutral definition.

Beyond the *petitio principii* involved in this choice of a word, nothing whatever is advanced to show that phenomena and their laws are the only accessible objects of human thought. The principle is diligently reiterated without end; but its evidence is never adduced, and the difficulties attending its admission are nowhere appreciated. The axiom being laid down that phenomena are all in all (and further, as we shall see, that perception is the sole medium of intelligence), it is clear that there can be no knowledge but physical; and it is only stating this proposition from the other side, to say that all theological and metaphysical conceptions which go beyond phenomena are invalid; they must be negative, if only the other be positive. Tried by the tests of physical knowledge, ontological cannot but fail; its genius being wholly different, and its criteria not the same. It is the perpetual boast of Comte that positive science gives *prevision*, a triumph never won by its rivals. True, but not very conclusive; for *pre*vision, — the perception of what is to turn up hereafter, — is an apprehension of *phenomena*, and naturally must arise from the study of phenomena, and not from reflection on *realities other than phenomena.*

So far forth as theology and metaphysics have presumed to obtrude themselves into any science of observation, and usurp its proper work, so far have they mistaken their province, and deserved the reproach of failure. Nothing that they can teach respecting the causation and meaning of things will enable us to determine beforehand the particular course of cosmical or human events, or in the least dispense with the necessity of inductive research. It is one thing to have true faith and insight respecting the infinite sources of all possibilities, and quite another to be familiar with the order of concrete actualities. But this rule reads both ways; and if there be no right of road in one direction, neither is there in the other; and Comte can no more disturb the theologian's truth than the theologian can interfere with his. If prevision is impossible, if we cannot operate forward from the absolute to the relative, conversely we cannot operate backward from the relative to the absolute; and the positivist should as little pretend to deny upwards as the theologian to affirm downwards. As no theist professes that God is a phenomenon, the failure of phenomenological research to meet Him contradicts no one's faith; and the boast of one investigator that he found no God at the end of his telescope, and of another that the cerebral dissecting knife comes across no human soul, misconceived altogether, though quite in the spirit of Comte, the fundamental conditions of the problem. *Ὄντα* are known, not as the corollaries, but as the postulates, of phenomena; and if not recognized at the beginning, will never be found at the end. The two orders of apprehension, though each is the complement of the other, have no common measure; and endless contradiction arises from confounding their functions and methods.

Above all, is it absurd to test the validity of theological and metaphysical conceptions by their power of movement and "progress"? Why, the very sameness with which they are taunted, — their patience from age to age, — is precisely the sole conceivable evidence they could offer that they are what they profess to be, the representation in us of the constancies of the universe. And nothing could more effectually discredit them, as the steady shadows of eternal entity, than a history of growth and change. If they indeed be, as they pretend, the background of cognition answering to the abiding realities which hold all phenomena, it is their business and function to keep still. Their vindication lies in their permanence. They are the conservative elements of all knowledge; the base and condition of movement, but not the moving thing; the vital atmosphere that sustains it, but not its beating wing. Do you complain that the ideas of Causality, of Soul, of God, of Substance, never get on, but are essentially what they always were? Instead of damaging them, you give the highest possible testimony to their veracity and authority. Did they sweep forward, as you desire, they would belie their word, and be detected as belonging to the tide of physical change, not to the infinite deep below. If on account of this stationary character any one denies to these ideas the name of knowledge; if this word, as implying distinction and plurality, be refused to the self-identical and simple, — we shall not object, provided it be understood that they are, if not knowledge, the conditions of knowledge; if not the object seen, the light by which we see; that reliance on them is indispensable to reading the universe as it is, and that the enlarging field of phenomena and law finds them still equal to their all-comprehensive function, though needing revision in their special form and application.

And to what, after all, amount the alleged "unprogressiveness" and "barrenness" of all conceptions except of phenomena and their laws? If by this be meant that we spin no theological cotton, and lay down no metaphysical telegraphs, that our breakfast-table displays our electro-plate, but not our creed, — the remark is true, but trivial enough. If it asserts that men's private temper, and family administration, and political aims and social sympathies, are unaffected by their religious and philosophical convictions; that those convictions have ceased to influence what the poet writes, the historian tells, the artist paints, what the schoolmaster teaches, what the merchant does with his wealth, what the patriot and the statesman endeavor to achieve by law, — the statement is as false as it is startling. Much as we are in the habit of hearing about the old "ages of faith," when nobody doubted and everybody obeyed, they never put in an appearance in real history, but shrink away like a golden age from the illumination of direct evidence, and retire into an elder darkness. Beyond the select enclosure of the Church order, there have always been hardy and defiant spirits, or thoughtless and indifferent, or subtle and refined, that have yielded their inner life but little to theological authority; and wherever opportunity of expression has been given, as in the earliest poetry of

France and Italy, this fact has unambiguously displayed itself. There seems no reason to suppose that theological and philosophical ideas ever had more power in the world than they have at this moment; though their scattered and unorganized condition precludes them from embodied and hierarchical manifestation of authority. M. Comte has no appreciation of the freedom and variety of movement which the human mind in its modern development demands. With the French tendency to idolize the "unity of power," and to see in distributed and individual forces nothing but "*anarchy*," he treats the insurrection against Catholicism as a dissolution of faith; and considers all the private and personal substitutes for the theocratic *régime* of the Church as merely provisional disguises of irretrievable decay. Nor does it occur to him that it is illogical to demand from the theological and abstract convictions of men the same direct and visible application to the business of the passing hour of which their technical knowledge is susceptible. In our practical work we have to deal with phenomena and modify them; and here the instruments of our power can only be found in right apprehension of the laws of phenomena. Theology and metaphysics do not profess to teach us these; but to go behind them, and enable us to think truly of their ground and source; supposing this promise realized, it can evidently give us no new arts, no rules by which either to predict or to command any particular succession of external facts. But the influence upon our tone of sentiment and affection, upon the interpretation we put on life and nature, on the admirations we feel and the ideal we follow, is profound and powerful, although indefinite. It is always difficult, indeed, to fetch out this power into actual life, and give it concrete application; to bridge over the interval between our faith respecting real being and our manipulation with transient phenomena; to incorporate a spiritual religion into a working church: and of this confessed difficulty Comte avails himself to persuade us that the "positive sciences" contain the only practical order of human ideas. But the same argument would equally discredit all our ideas of beauty, harmony, and sublimity; whose expression is, in like manner and from like causes, difficult to create into palpable forms, and when so created, is equally inoperative in the prediction and command of phenomena. If the merchant does not keep his books by his theology, neither does the artist bake his bread by his æsthetics; and in either case the reproach of inefficiency is equally idle.

But Comte not only restricts the intellect to phenomena, he restricts the word "phenomena" to the *changes perceptible by sense*. They must be *external* to us, presented to material observation, in order to become "facts" at all. Successions of *feeling*, *idea*, and *will*, known to us by consciousness, are to be thrown out of the account, and furnish nothing upon which intelligence can work. *Psychology*, accordingly, resting as it does upon *self-observation*, is a mere illusion; and logic and ethics, so far as they build on it as their foundation, are altogether baseless. This repudiation of all *reflective knowledge* is due chiefly to Comte's acceptance of phrenology, — a system which has always taken an infatuated pleasure in knocking out its own brains, by denying *ab initio* the validity of that self-knowledge on which all its own evidence directly or indirectly depends. The arguments on which Comte relies in his criticism on the psychologists are the stock objections of Gall and Spurzheim and Combe, viz. that the mind observing and the mind observed being the same, the alleged fact must be gone and out of reach before it is looked at; that a mental state is not a whole fact, but only a part or function of a fact, being as much a mere outcoming of some cerebral state as the feeling of indigestion is the sensational side of deranged action in the stomach; and that psychologists have never found any thing out, or reaped any scientific fruit. The inadequacy of this argument has been felt and acknowledged by J. P. Mill, whose superior knowledge of psychological literature, and disciplined habits of reflection, enabled him to appreciate far better than the French metaphysician the real value of this class of pursuits.

It is necessary to protest *in limine* against the representation which Comte gives of the "psychological method." He places it in false contrast with a mode of procedure against which it has nothing at all to object, and which its votaries have, in fact, been the chief agents in advancing. Availing himself of De Blainville's remark, that the phenomena of every living being may be regarded either *statically*, *i.e.* with reference to the conditions essential to their occurrence, or *dynamically*, *i.e.* with reference to the products in which they embody themselves, he lays it down that the mental functions must be studied under one of these two aspects: we must either engage ourselves with the *organs* requisite for their manifestation, in which case our work is purely physiological; or we must attend to the construction and course of scientific theories, and compare and analyze the ways of thinking by which the human mind has actually won its knowledge and achieved its progress, — and in this case our task resolves itself into a critique on the intellectual history of mankind. To these two processes he opposes the psychological, which, he says, pretends to discover the fundamental laws of the human mind by contemplating it in itself, *i.e. wholly apart from either causes or effects*. The rivalry thus set up on behalf of the physiologists (to take their case first) every scientific psychologist will entirely disown. He does not in the least object to the most searching investigation of the organic conditions under which the several orders of mental phenomena arise: he only maintains that, besides the relations in which they stand to their bodily antecedents, they also have certain relations *inter se;* that, as felt by us, they are variously like and unlike, so as to be susceptible of classification, and present themselves in determinable sequence so as to be reducible to laws. To effect *these* classifications, and ascertain these laws, is certainly the primary aim of the psychologist. He thinks it possible to attain it by comparative self-knowledge; and even were it proved that the whole series of phenomena were loose among themselves, produced not one out of another, but each separately from its own prior organic condition, he still deems it a legitimate and useful service to bring into order these derivative uniformities; for there is no reason why in this particular instance the general rule should fail, that order among the effects is a clue to corresponding order in the cause. But in assuming this as his centre of work, the psychologist passes no slight on the physiologist's investigations into the nervous and cerebral conditions of sensation, thought, and emotion. He is well aware that the light of discovered order radiates forward as well as backward, and that if uniformities of succession or co-existence can be detected in the physical conditions, they will become exponents of similar relations among the mental facts. He simply leaves this indirect method of classification to the physiologist, and himself resorts to the direct; willingly availing himself of every help supplied by researches into the vital organism, and giving no countenance to the narrow-minded assumption that the selection of one order of relations for special attention is a disparagement of another. It is not to the *discoveries*, but to the *fictions* of phrenologists, that intellectual philosophy objects; nor can any one familiar with the writings of Descartes and Locke, of Spinoza and Berkeley, of Reid, Mill, and Hamilton, deny its habitual eagerness to use to the utmost the results placed at its disposal by the zeal of the anatomist. The antagonism, therefore, supposed by Comte is all his own.

It is equally so when he accuses psychologists of *substituting self-examination* for study of the *realized products of human thought*, — such as scientific hypothesis, the history of civilization, and development of ideas. Not a book of modern psychology can be found, not a dialogue of Plato, not a treatise of Aristotle, in which the logical laws of human reason are not continually illustrated, if not directly deduced, by reference to the organism and method of the sciences, and the recorded procedures of human thought. The value of these historical materials for determining the principles of cognition is not more appreciated by Comte than by the objects of his criticism; the only difference is, that while they consult individual consciousness, in addition to the recorded development of the race, and for their power to read and interpret the monuments of intellectual history profess themselves indebted to sympathetic self-reflection, he denies that we can know ourselves, yet insists that we decipher the world. His position, therefore, is simply destructive; and we have not the invidious office of depreciating his proposed methods, which are of admitted value, but only of defending the philosophical competency of our own.

"The chief consideration proving clearly that the mind's practical self-contemplation is a pure illusion," is the following. Whatever the mind knows, is its *object* of knowledge; every *object of knowledge* is other than the *knowing subject*, therefore what the mind knows can never be itself. "By an invincible necessity, the human mind can immediately observe all phenomena except its own." "The thinking individual cannot divide himself in two; let one reason, while the other looks at the reasoning. The organ observed and the organ observing being in this case the same, how is it possible that observation should have place?"

This argument curiously reverses a celebrated maxim of James Mill, — and, indeed, of Hobbes, — to the effect that *to have* a feeling, and to *know that you have it*, are *identical*. Comte tells us that to have a feeling, and to know that you have it, are *incompati-*

ble. e.g. I fall into a frozen pond; I know the water and the ice, but I cannot possibly know that I am cold. Or, I go a sea-voyage under bilious conditions; I observe the swaying water and the lurching ship; but "an invincible necessity" conceals from me the fact that I am sick. Of the two things given in the act of perception, viz. the percipient consciousness and the perceived object, it has usually been supposed possible to doubt the second, but not the first; the very doubt itself bringing, as another state of the conscious self, its own refutation. And accordingly, though we have numerous forms of idealism which construe all outward phenomena into mere appearances within the mind, we have hitherto had no strictly corresponding materialism, cancelling from our knowledge all mental states on the ground of their *being ours*, and claiming certainty for the outer world *precisely because it is foreign to us.* This, however, is the strange position taken up by Comte. The argument by which he supports it is a mere appeal to the mystery which belongs to all cognition, whether of external or internal facts. How is it possible, he asks, that we should know our own state, since we must cease our mental activity in order to observe it? In other words, reflection upon our inner experience must *follow upon* that experience itself, and be separated from it by a certain interval of time. Be it so; why is this more inconceivable than the perception of an outward fact which stands off from me by a certain interval of space? If our intelligence can bridge the chasm of *local separation*, what hinders it from uniting the termini of succession? What is *memory*, if the *present self* can never know any thing about the *past self?* Its distinction is, that it reports to us, not simply outward things in themselves, but outward things (or inward) as they affect us; so that — it has even been contended — there is properly no memory but of our own former states. If now its reports are *good for nothing*, there is an end of the matter, and human acquaintance with the past is an illusion. But if they be accepted as valid, the knowledge which they supply is either *immediate* or *mediate*. Is it immediate? Then are we immediately cognitive of our own past states, in spite of Comte's maxim. Is it *mediate?* Then do we, as *now* remembering, know something past, as having *then* perceived it; the truth in my present remembrance is just what there was in my former perception; and without immediate cognition of my own state at the percipient moment, no mediate knowledge of it could be given by memory. In fact, the act of perception is necessarily and equally an act of self-consciousness, objective no more than subjective; and to claim for it authority for phenomena without, is in itself to concede to it like authority for phenomenon within; nothing being an outward phenomenon at all except what appears on the double field of *thought* and *things*, and is known as *being* and as *felt*.

And if we be incapable of knowing our own experiences and thoughts, we cannot perform on them any act of comparison, separation, or combination. Yet what is *human language* but the crystallized form of countless discriminations and analogies, so clearly felt, and frequently referred to, as to demand the means of permanent expression? Comte refers us to scientific theories and logical processes as the only possible means of reaching logical laws. But how could these intellectual methods speak to us intelligibly at all, were it not for the parallel movement of our own thought, carried into the study as interpreter and test? To beings not self-conscious, or not able to rely on their reflective insight into their own ways of intellectual action, the record of other men's reasonings could awaken no responsive intelligence; only through our sympathetic self-knowledge do they find us out and teach us any thing. All grammar, all philology, all scientific language, are in fact *psychological deposits;* not less certainly testifying to the perpetual action of self-reflection, as one factor of human knowledge, than the geological strata bear witness to the operation through ages past of the very elements that work upon our homesteads and on the beach at our garden-gate to-day. Comte's advice is excellent, if addressed to those who can open their vision upon their own nature and intelligence; but has no sense or application for the sort of blind chimera or one-eyed cyclops that he imagines, with pictures of the universe glazed upon the surface, and never taken home to any known self within. No doubt our *self-knowledge* is dependent to an incalculable extent on the living in a human world, and standing before the face of *other men:* the manifestations of their nature, whether by natural language of the moment or by the historical record of past processes of thought, are conditions necessary to the development of our reflective faculties; and if we were to insist on insulating the self-consciousness from all these data, that it might spin a science out of its own viscera, we should but impose upon an empty power a self-consuming task. But, on the other hand, our ability to decipher the expression of other minds depends, in its turn, on converse with our own; and to bid us study the fruits of their research and meditation, while despairing of all acquaintance with our own, is to place a banquet before the sleeping or the dead. It is impossible to make *either* of the reciprocal conditions prior to the other; their efficacy lies in the balance and alternation of action and re-action; and so close is the inter-dependence of psychological and objective knowledge of human nature, that a theory which despises either excludes both.

The objection, however, which Comte is most zealous in urging against the psychologists is, that their method has never been crowned with any success, great or small, and that their labor has been absolutely barren. Even if this statement be tried by the test present to the author's own mind, viz. the amount of direct discovery respecting the processes of the mind, it is a monstrous exaggeration. The logical doctrine of Aristotle, the modern theory of vision, the ascertainment of laws of association and abstraction, Butler's exposition of the moral constitution of man, — deserve to be ranked among positive achievements of a high order, and are recognized as such by the vast majority of competent judges on these points. If perfect unanimity is not attained even on these doctrines, neither is it secured at present in regard to any of the corresponding parts of biological science; and the only advantage which the positivist has over his predecessors in intellectual philosophy is in his liberal promises for the future; his disparagement of the past not being justified, so far as yet appears, by the detection of a single law of our mental or moral nature. These reproaches of backwardness should at least be reserved till they can be uttered from a point of real advance. Perhaps, too, the test by which the fruitfulness or sterility of a pursuit is estimated by Comte may not be altogether admissible. His demand obviously is for some new field of "prevision" special to psychology: the demand is disappointed, because intrinsically unreasonable. From objective studies we expect objective results; from subjective studies it is natural to look for subjective results: not so much for a *fresh sphere brought into knowledge*, as for a more refined *knowing power*, for quickened faculties self-protected from beguiling errors, for intellectual implements of more ethereal temper and disciplined skill. That this appropriate effect of reflective studies has been their habitual attendant, is undeniable; every period of intense speculative activity being the precursor of the next advance of even physical science, and educating the faculties up to the point when the discovery of new laws becomes possible; setting the previous gains of human research in due order and relation, and preparing language and method for new service. Alternately acting and studying its action, the mind, whether by *systole* or *diastole*, sustains the pulsation of its living thought; and to demand the one operation without the other, is not less absurd than to complain that the heart does not always propel without resilience. Nor is it only in the successive periods of human culture that this need of reflective studies is observable. No fact is more conspicuous in individual biography and the comparative experiences of education, than the systematic superiority, in pliancy and balance of faculty, of men not strange to metaphysical and moral studies, over those who never quit the circle of mathematical relations and physical laws. Were the methods of intellectual and moral philosophy altogether illusory, it is inconceivable that a certain habituation to them should be an indispensable gymnastic for the mind, and a needful check to the narrowing tendency of the "positive sciences," when exclusively pursued.*

Closely connected with Comte's contempt for the psy-

* In spite of Comte's contempt for psychology, he is one of the most resolute of psychologists himself; and freely appeals, when convenient, to that very self-consciousness which at other times he declares to be quite blank and dumb. Thus we find him announcing that the "phenomena of life" are "*known by immediate consciousness*" (*Phil. Pos.* vol. ii. p. 648, vol. iii. p. 8); an assertion standing in accurate contradiction to the doctrine on which we have been commenting. Nay, so completely does he forget his denial of any possible self-knowledge, as to affirm, when required for his purpose, that "*man at first knows nothing but himself*," — so as to apply his self-knowledge as a universal formula for the interpretation of nature. But how could man erect his self-consciousness into a rule for explaining all phenomena, if no inward fact were cognizable by him at all? Perhaps, however, it is only since monotheism came in, that psychology has become impossible and absurd; for, while denying it to modern metaphysicians, Comte is full of admiration of its use among the ancient augurs. He claims for polytheism the honor of instituting the first careful observation of nature; laments that we have to put up with our poor meteorological registers in place of the far superior weather-tables of the Etruscan soothsayers; and affirms that, with a view to the interpretation of dreams, the intellectual and moral phenomena were made the subject of the most delicate observations, pursued day by day with a perseverance not to be again expected till the positive philosophy has reached its final development (*Phil. Pos.* vol. v. p. 135). It is to be presumed that, as dreams are altogether inward facts, this marvellous store of scientific observation accumulated in their service, and throwing light on the intellectual and moral life, could be no other than *psychological capital.* How is it that it may be invested in Divination; but must be inaccessible to Science, at least until Positivism finds a profitable use for it?

chologists is his disrespect for certain ideas and beliefs whose only guarantee is in our self-consciousness. Thus he treats as an illusion our idea of *Causation;* requiring us to dispense with it altogether, not merely in its theological form of *Will*, but no less in its scientific equivalent of *Force*. "Every proposition," he says, "which is not ultimately reducible to the simple enunciation of a fact, particular or general, must be destitute of all real and intelligible meaning." Again: "*Forces*, in mechanics, are only *movements*, produced or tending to be produced; but although this is happily pretty well understood now-a-days, yet an essential form is still required, if not in the conception, at least in the habitual language, in order to cancel altogether the old metaphysical notion of *force*, and present more accurately than hitherto the true point of view." And he shows the same jealousy of any properly *dynamical* notions when complaining afterwards of Bichat's speculation respecting "vital *forces*," and proposing to return to the true path by substituting the word "properties" for "forces"! His definition of the word "*Law*," as an "invariable relation of succession or resemblance among phenomena," together with his severe restriction of the human mind to the investigation of "Laws," demands of us an entire disuse of all belief or even idea of Causality.

Now if he had been content with saying that causes lie beyond the field of observation, and that scientific induction, even in its highest generalizations, can never carry us further than the order of co-existence and sequence among phenomena, he would have stated only an important truth, — the one great truth on whose clear apprehension depends the whole difference between ancient and modern investigation of nature. All knowledge which finds its test and triumph in accurate *prevision*, or, more generally, in the determination of absent facts by means of present data, does require exclusively an attentive study of the relations of events in time and place. Though we were endowed with no other power than the ability to register, compare, and analyze series, without any suspicion of a purpose, or wonder about origination, we should want nothing (except, indeed, an indispensable moral incentive) to complete the conditions of scientific discovery. It stands to reason, indeed, that, in order to *foresee*, we need only to know the *sequences* to which events, beginning from the present, are limited; and that, in order to fill-in the absent half of a cluster of phenomena by suggestion from what is at hand, we have but to learn the groupings in which they uniformly occur. And the rule, thus rational in its principle, is confirmed by the actual history of natural knowledge. No scrutiny, it is true, ever succeeds in laying hold of a *new force*, and fixing it in its distinction before our view: all that can be done is to detect some unsuspected *effects*, which are but a fresh disposition or succession of phenomena; and behind that veil no astuteness can carry us. We are apt to be deceived on this point by the habitual employment, in scientific treatises, of *names* for reputed forces of different kinds, — chemical, electric, magnetic, vital, &c. We naturally suppose that the votary of each department of research has something to tell us of the force prevailing there, and of the characters which distinguish it from its dynamic neighbors. On closer inspection, however, we shall find that of the force itself, apart from what it *does*, he has nothing special to say: he defines it by the *appearances* it puts forth; he separates it from *other* forces by stating the *dissimilar effects* which they severally exhibit; nor has he any other means of referring to the ranks of δυνάμεις than by marshalling the perceptible phenomena under their appropriate heads. The name "*magnetism*" stands for the viewless cause of all those movements in certain metals (iron, cobalt, nickel) which occur in the vicinity of particular ferruginous ores, or of iron brought into similar conditions: the movements may be induced under considerable variety of prior conditions, through which it would be impossible for us to trace any identity of originating power; and the assumption of unity rests entirely on the termination of all these conditions in one result, viz. the polar disposition or deflection of the needle. It is the specialty of the phenomenon that is honored with the *hypothesis* of a special force. *Heat*, again, is the name of an equally unknown cause of certain phenomena, — such as a given animal sensation, and the expansion of bodies, and their change from solid to liquid and liquid into gaseous, — which are entered under this category for no other reason than that they cling together, and though not alike in themselves or appreciable through the same sense, arise under the same physical conditions. The concurrence of these effects having tied them into a group, the rise of any one of them becomes a sign of the possibility of the rest, or of the presence of the supposed cause: but of that cause, *per se*, as apart from its effects, — of its unity, except in their concurrence; of its difference from magnetism, except in the unlikeness and separation of the effects, — we have assuredly no cognizance. Thus much, then, must be freely granted to Comte, — that all investigation into *natural forces* is delusive, unless understood to be mere *phenomenological research*, prosecuted under the disguise of dynamical language; and that its only real result must be to ascertain the analogies and the order of perceptible facts. If this be true, we must materially alter our ordinary conceptions of the operations of nature. We must no longer attribute any reality or efficient existence to gravitation, electricity, cohesion, &c.; but, treating them as mere fictions of thought subservient to classification, must resolve the universe, *under the eye of science*, into a legion of phenomena, irregular to begin with, but susceptible of being regimented and disciplined by due attention to their likeness and affinities. If our language is to be regulated exclusively by the resources of the natural sciences, and nothing to be admitted into it but what they can undertake to guarantee, nothing short of a clean sweep of every dynamical form of phrase can satisfy the obligations of truth. And yet this is manifestly impossible; and has been found so by Comte himself.

How are we to reduce this apparent inconsistency? Inductive science gives us no access to causes behind phenomena; yet we cannot expound it without speaking of them, and assuming them. Is fiction, then, the indispensable vehicle of truth? And must a false postulate underlie the whole fabric of our knowledge? So would it assuredly be, if every idea were to be discarded as invalid for which inductive science declines to be responsible. But when we have confessed that, by the way of perception, and in the study of laws, causation cannot be reached, it by no means follows that the idea is to be expelled the service of the human mind. The question arises, whether, as it evades us at the *end* of science, it may not, perhaps, be found at the *beginning:* the spectacle-case may well be empty, if the glasses are already on the nose, helping us all the while to see the very emptiness itself. If the idea of causality be a metaphysical datum, it is no wonder that we miss it as a physical quæsitum; nor is it difficult to understand why it presents no variety to our mind, however various be the phenomena behind which it is planted, or the corresponding changes of name it may assume. By an irresistible law of thought, *all phenomena present themselves to us as the expression of power*, and refer us to a causal ground whence they issue. This dynamic source we neither see, nor hear, nor feel; it is given in *thought*—supplied by the spontaneous activity of the mind itself as the correlative prefix to the phenomenon observed. By the general acknowledgment of philosophers, this idea is so strictly "a necessary idea" as to be entirely irremovable from the conception of any change; to cut the tie between them, and think of phenomena as *not effects*, is impossible, in fact, even to the very writers who propose it in theory.

What value, then, are we to put upon this belief? Either we must take it as a natural revelation, or reject it as a natural lie; in the case of an original datum of thought contradictory to no other, a third course is impossible. If we are to rely on the veracity of our constitution as thinking beings, we must accept the subjective postulate as giving a valid rule for objective nature. If we are to suppose our *intellectual* constitution mendacious, and deem causation a mental fiction, no reason will remain for trusting our perceptive constitution any more; and our observation of facts and quest of laws will perish by the contagion of uncertainty. It is impossible, except by arbitrary caprice, to save the one part of our cognitive nature while sacrificing the other, and vain to pretend that the depositions of the first are in any sense opposed to those of the other. That the "power" given to us in *thought* is apprehensible by no *perception*, avails as little to disprove its reality as the *inaudibleness* of light to convict the eye of false reports. Yet this is the only argument by which Comte justifies his contempt for causes. We freely surrender to him all search by scientific methods after a *plurality of forces* distinguishable in themselves: but he confounds this illusory aim with the recognition, on the authority of a law of thought, of *universal causation*, inserted by the mind, without any change of type, behind all sets of phenomena in turn. Start up what may to arrest our attention, one and the same homogeneous idea of *power* occurs to us; and whether it receives the name of chemical, or physical, or vital, the dynamical background of the conception remains unvaried, and the momentary representation alone is exposed to change. The trustworthiness of this belief has the same guarantee as the self-evident predicates of space and time: it is the indispensable condition of our thinking of phenomena at all; they are just as absolutely unpresentable to the mind apart from causality, as motion without duration and extension. Indeed, it is remarkable how these two great data, Space and Time, rescue us from the scepticism of the materialist school. They stand as eternal barriers to forbid our final exit from the natural faiths of reason; or as a bridge that spans the gulf between metaphysical and physical apprehension, and has a bearing upon each; so that, destroy which you will, the whole roadway of human knowledge falls, and neither of the interdependent realms remains accessible or habitable at all. Will you take your stand on the entities of Reason alone? Then, as Comte truly says, your knowledge will never advance a step; you will find no law, and win no prevision. Will you try the other side, and say that Perception of phenomena is the only source of knowledge? Then you must throw away from your belief both space and time, which, as eternal, are not phenomena, and as infinite, you cannot have perceived; and with them must perish all that they contain, so that your solid realism goes off into absolute Nihilism. Will you attempt a compromise, and let natural faith have its way unquestioned respecting these two necessary receptacles of phenomena? Then the postulates of thought, by no means stopping there, are not only good for these, but good for more; and causality slips in by the plea that makes room for Law.

Final causation, not less than efficient, our author imagines to be contradicted and disproved by "positive" knowledge; and he is fond of turning aside from his exposition to mark the points where science appears to exclude the notion of providential design.

Thus astronomical discovery, in his opinion, completely overthrows the doctrine of divine purpose in the arrangements of the solar system: 1. Because design, whenever alleged, is conceived of as relative to *man*, whose nature gives the only measure we have of good and evil; and though he might plausibly be supposed the object of divine care so long as his station was assumed to be central, the idea must vanish with the disclosure of the earth's dependent and planetary position. 2. Because it is demonstrated that the order and stability of the solar system, and the fitness of its several bodies for the residence of living beings, are necessary consequences of purely mechanical laws. 3. Because in many respects the system might be greatly improved, and by no means deserves the admiration wasted on it.* This last argument we may leave to those who feel themselves able to pronounce on the relative merits of possible universes, as compared with one another and with the actual. The belief in design is by no means pledged to the doctrine of optimism. The readiness with which every theist admits the existence of evil, the frequency with which he speaks of imperfections in life and nature, and his habitual reference to a future and ideal world, show that his faith can co-exist, without prejudice, with the conception of more "advantageous conditions" of being than he wit-

* "With persons unused to the study of the celestial bodies, though very likely well informed on other parts of natural philosophy, astronomy has still the repute of being a science eminently religious; as if the famous words, 'The heavens declare the glory of God,' had lost nothing of their truth." In a note Comte adds, "Now-a-days, to minds familiarized betimes with the true astronomical philosophy, the heavens declare no other glory than that of Hipparchus, Kepler, Newton, and all those who have contributed to the ascertainment of their laws."—*Philosophie Positive*, vol. ii. p. 36.

nesses where he is. For ourselves, we confess Comte's censorship over the universe affects us very much in the same way as many religious writers' patronage of it. *They* undertake to show how much better, *he* how much worse, it is than it might have been. If this sort of argument is open to the one, it cannot be closed against the other; and we may leave them to settle it between them as best they may. Whether the stomach is made on the best principles; whether the sea is not a little too salt; whether the isthmus of Panama is not to be regretted; whether the ice may not be rather overdone about the poles; whether, if M. Lesseps had been consulted, the shortcomings of the Red Sea might not have been avoided; whether the two sides of the moon are fairly treated; whether Jupiter is all right without a ring, or Venus would be improved by diminution of light and levity, — are matters for those who know every thing and a good deal more. Such questions are as a flood let loose, and spreading without use and without bound, covering the landmarks of all fruit-bearing truth and turning thought into a desolating waste. Mend the world as you will, there must always remain ideal standards, measured by which it will be liable to criticism as before. The body of man, for instance, is variously frail, and can scarcely stand, without fracture, a ten-feet fall; but give him cast-iron ribs, and a railway accident will contrive to crush him; and the more you harden him, the greater the forces into which he will venture. In short, the critique of nature in detail is quite beyond us; and whether we find there little providences or monstrous blemishes, we are alike in danger of seeing only the reflection of our own egotism.

Praising or censuring the arrangements of the world, we equally set up certain ideal ends of our own imagining, which we assume that it was or ought to serve; by the test of these we try nature, and, according as her structure realizes or falls short of them, we pronounce it perfect or imperfect. Comte and the divines are therefore both within the same school of teleological criticism; both speak of a good or a bad way of realizing a presupposed conception; both are equally far from confining themselves to the study of *actual* phenomena and effects, uncompared with others that *might have been*. Forming as we do part of the scheme of nature, limited as our power of conception is to the resources of the universe that bounds the horizon of our minds, we cannot pretend to be judges of the skill or clumsiness of the world's laws; and the moment we pass beyond the simple admiring perception of order and relation, and begin to imagine how much better or worse matters would have stood under other conditions, we entangle ourselves in a thicket of ever-growing problems, from which extrication is impossible. The faith in divine purpose will persevere through all; but the critique of that purpose in special instances is variable and insecure, and was properly excluded by Bacon from the business of science.

Thus the particular thought from which the creation of the world has been supposed to spring, viz. to be the moral centre of the universe, and the scene of a drama fixing the gaze of all higher beings, does really, as Comte's first argument remarks, lose its hold of probability by the Copernican discovery. The plurality of worlds, be they inhabited or uninhabited, is fatally at variance with the scheme of moral symmetry that makes man the hero of all time and nature. But to discredit this particular idea is one thing; to disprove the presence of design altogether is another. The tendency of the Copernican discovery, is quite in the opposite direction, to give enlargement, instead of curtailment and extinction, to the significance and purpose of the world. The old theory of the divines proving too small to suit the magnificence of the facts; its chief object, man, finding himself in presence of a scene so unexpectedly august, — *which* is the more natural inference, that therefore this scene must have a *greater* cause than we had conceived, or that it can have *none at all?* And so perhaps it will ever be. In one instance after another *ad infinitum*, it will be found that the idea we had planted at the heart of a thing is too small, and is transcended by the scale of the reality. To make this the excuse for substituting a smaller or a blank, is perversely to justify a logical retrogression by a scientific advance, and to say that, the more glorious the creation, the less thought must it contain. No less a paradox than this is Comte's reasoning that, because a particular idea of the divine intention gives way, Final Causation in general is exploded.

The only considerable argument in the passage on which we are remarking is the second, — that the physical forces and arrangements being known, to which the order and stability of the solar system is due, the phenomena are exhaustively explained without any intervention of purpose at all. Now what is the nature, and wherein lies the plausibility, of this reasoning? It is simply a playing-off of *physical* causation against *moral*, or, as it is called, *final* causation; the forces of matter are adequate to produce all the movements and all the equilibrium, and so no force of mind is wanted. But have we not just learned from Comte that we know nothing of any *forces of matter*, nothing of any *production* of one phenomenon from any other, or from causation at all? that our investigations and discoveries are absolutely debarred from passing beyond the grouping and succession of phenomena? Then what does he mean by here finding in physical causes a substitute and equivalent for the volitional action which he excludes? They cannot shut out and supersede that action, unless they are competent to do the same thing; if they claim to stand in its place, they must undertake to discharge the required office instead of it. Either, therefore, gravitation must be equal to the task hitherto given to the Divine Will, *i.e.* must be a real efficient force, and not a mere generalized phenomenon; or else it cannot make good its rival pretensions, or enter at all upon the field which is at present occupied by final causes simply on the merit of this qualification. In other words, our author may take his choice of two positions: he may limit the possible achievements of our minds to the ascertainment of laws, and say that causal problems are inaccessible; or, admitting causal problems, he may pronounce one solution true and another false, declaring *e.g.* in favor of physical forces as against spiritual agency. But he cannot do *both*, and slip about from the one to the other at will; he cannot fight a particular causal hypothesis with a mere law of phenomena which is not causal, and say in the same breath that we can know nothing of this matter, and also that we know the matter to be not so-and-so, but otherwise than that. Cause against cause, law against law; but no cross-fire is possible; and, slam the heavy gate of gravitation as you may in the face of Living Agency, still if its bars are only ranges of co-existence and succession, and its chevaux-de-frise only bristling clusters of phenomena, causation will slip through and round and over, and feel no obstruction to be there.

As to the choice which Comte practically makes between the two positions just described, there can be no doubt. He assuredly thinks of nature, not simply as the theatre of phenomena, but as the residence of *forces*. In what sense can he affirm that periodicity of planetary perturbation, and the consequent equilibrium of the solar system and its orbitary movements, are *necessary consequences of gravitation*, if he does not conceive of gravitation as a cause? From the two great conditions of every Newtonian solution, viz. projectile impulse and centripetal tendency, eject the idea of *force*, and what remains? The entire conception is simply made up of this, and has no sort of faintest existence without it. It is useless to give it notice to quit, and pretend that it is gone, when you have put a new name upon the door. We must not call it "attraction," lest there should seem to be a *power* within: we are to speak of it as "gravitation," because that is only "weight," which is nothing but a "fact;" as if it were not a fact that held a power, a true dynamic affair, which no imagination can chop up into incoherent successions. Nor is the evasion more successful when we try the phrase "*tendency of bodies to mutual approach.*"

The approach itself may be called a phenomenon; but the "tendency" is no phenomenon, and cannot be attributed by us to the bodies without regarding them as the residence of force. And what are we to say to the *projectile impulse* in the case of the planets? Is that also a phenomenon? Who witnessed and reported it? Is it not evident that this whole scheme of physical astronomy is a resolution of observed facts into dynamic equivalents, and that the hypothesis posits for its calculations, not phenomena, but proper forces? Its logic is this: *if* an impulse of certain intensity were given, and *if* such and such a mutual attraction were constantly present, then the sort of motions which we observe in the bodies of our system *would follow*. So, however, they also would *if* willed by an Omnipotent Intelligence. Both doctrines are so far hypothetical; both hypotheses are dynamic; both are an adequate provision for the facts; so that on this ground neither can exclude the other. There is, however, this difference: we know that the doctrine of composition of forces is an artificial device, by which, in innumerable cases, we treat *as if plural* a spring of motion which, like our own volition to a given muscular action, is *really simple;* the *quasi-plurality* being a contrivance for bringing the phenomenon under dominion to the calculus, and finding its equivalent. If it be maintained that the phenomenon is *really composite*, antagonist muscles and numerous levers being set in motion, we reply, that the complexity is at all events in the *mode of execution*, not in the principle of origination, which, being our own conscious volition, we know has none of those parts, but goes straight at the resultant. It appears, therefore, that the composite doctrine betrays its fictitious character where the volitional origination is an indisputable fact; and that, even allowing it in such case to represent reality, it is a mere executive reality, wielded as an instrumental medium by the immediate power of Will behind. In the same manner, the hypothetical composition of the Newtonian forces does nothing to exclude the primary causation of a Divine Mind.

In this connection it is curious to notice, in so acute a mind as our author's, the logical inconsequence produced by incompatible antipathies. He commits the inconsistency, — which would be extraordinary were it not ordinary with his class, — of excluding all Will from the universe because there is nothing but Necessity, yet insisting on Necessity as an attribute of all Will. It is evident that whichever of these two positions is established destroys the other; yet it is scarcely possible for the atheist to avoid holding both. "Look at this whole frame of things," he says, "how can it proceed from a mind, — a supernatural will? Is it not all subject to regular laws, and do we not actually obtain *prevision* of its phenomena? If it were the product of mind, its order would be variable and free." Of mind, therefore, it is a mark, that its phenomena are unsusceptible of prevision; of volition it is characteristic to be free; and the absence of these attributes negatives the presence of voluntary agency. Here, then, the atheistic argument itself not only concedes liberty to will as possible, but reasons from it as the one essential. Yet no sooner do these writers begin to treat of the only will which we directly know, viz. our own, than they contend for the contradictory of all this; affirming that the will has no freedom whatever; that it follows determinate and ascertainable laws; that its products are not variable or irreducible to rules of prevision; and that if we cannot yet foresee them, the fault is not in the indeterminateness of the facts, but in the imperfect conquests of our knowledge. From this it would seem that necessity and determinateness of sequence, being not less predicable of will than of other orders of facts, may as well be a sign of *it* as of any thing else, and cannot at all be taken to disprove it. Either, then, the will is free, or else theism is unharmed; and the attack on either of these propositions saves the other. The fact is, the atheistic reasoning is an involuntary testimony to the inextinguishable faith in the freedom of the will, — a testimony the more impressive because unconsciously given by a hostile witness. When the problem practically comes before him, how to get rid of *supernatural volition* from the universe, he can find but one mode, viz. to get rid of every trace of *freedom*, and enthrone everywhere *natural necessity*. In this he follows a perfectly correct logical instinct; he tries the issue upon the antithesis of two notions that are truly contradictory. But if they are mutually exclusive in the universe, so are they in man; and it is the secret consciousness of this that suggests and sustains the whole argument. When, after this radical acknowledgment, Comte condescends to the assertion that any man who fancies himself free, may undeceive himself by standing on his head for a few minutes, and trying what becomes of his clearest thoughts and strongest resolves, we cannot fail to see how much deeper is his involuntary wisdom than his superficial polemic. As well might you urge it as a disproof of free-will, that you cannot put the moon in your pocket, or contrive to live five hundred years, or write an epic in your sleep. Be the limitations of our power prescribed by nature, or self-imposed, or a mixture of the two, no one ever denied or questioned them; no one ever contended for a freedom in man unfettered by organic conditions. To do so would be to pronounce him omnipotent and absolute. In truth, free causality is so far from requiring the absence of all limiting conditions, that it cannot be conceived of except as in their presence. Its activity is in its very essence *preferential*, — the adoption of *this* to the exclusion of *that;* and to empty out all data, to cancel the finite terms, is to destroy the problem and preclude the power. All mental action is intrinsically *relative*, and when predicated as *absolute* becomes entirely inconceivable. It is therefore mere trifling to argue against free-will by pointing out the dependence of moral phenomena on organic conditions. These conditions are the very data of the whole problem; they may exist in every variety of number and intensity; by increasing which the range left open to determination may be continually narrowed, till, in the extreme case, it wholly disappears, the quæsitum is among the data, and the problem is self-resolved. The real question is, whether this extreme case is universal.

But we must release our readers from an unconscionable detention. We should, however, have been unfaithful interpreters of our author, if we had not made them feel a little of the tedium he inflicts. Our interest in him being chiefly from the moral side, we have addressed ourselves exclusively to the dogmatic groundwork of his system, and especially to the assumptions by which he discredits psychological science, appends ethics to biology, and dismisses religion into limbo. It is in this, his *Prima Philosophia*, that we find it necessary to contest every step. When, advancing from this abstract ground, he begins to construct his hierarchy of the sciences, we acknowledge for the first time the true style of a master-hand. Two things only provoke remark in this part of his work: (1) The principle of arrangement by which he gives order to the sciences, advancing from the more universal properties to the more special, is by no means original; and in the hands of Dr. Arnott had already, in 1827, been employed to raise in outline precisely the symmetrical pyramid of knowledge which Comte contemplates with so much pride. Our author's additional rule, that with this logical order the historical growth of the sciences agrees, will not, in our opinion, bear examination. (2) This linear arrangement of the sciences, all around the same axis, appears to us absolutely untrue, both to their inner logic and their outward history. We deny that the knowledge of human nature and life waits for an antecedent biology, chemistry, physics, and astronomy, or uses their conclusions, when obtained, as its presuppositions. We maintain the essential independence of its evidence and method, and the possibility, nay even necessity, of its beginning at the same moment, and advancing *pari passu*, with our apprehension of the outward world. We assert that the sciences dispose themselves round *two* great axes of thought, parallel and not unrelated, yet distinct; — the natural sciences held together by the one, the moral by the other. In practice our author himself proceeds as if it were so; and in his review of political and social doctrine, leaves his physiology and chemistry entirely behind. His notices of both groups of sciences, taken separately, abound with original criticisms and striking generalizations; but it is especially in the sphere of physical knowledge that his habits of thought render him an instructive and suggestive guide.

As for his celebrated threefold law, we will only point to the distorting effect it has had on his great historical survey. In obedience to its cruel exactions, the natural organism of European civilization has been torn to pieces. As the third, or positive stage, had accomplished its advent in the author's own person, it was necessary to find the metaphysical period just before; and so the whole life of the Reformed Christianity, in embryo and in manifest existence, is stripped of its garb of *faith*, and turned out to view as a naked metaphysical phenomenon. But metaphysics, again, have to be ushered in by theology; and of the three stages of theology Monotheism is the last, — necessarily following on Polytheism, as that, again, on Fetichism. There is nothing for it, therefore, but to let the mediæval Catholic Christianity stand as the world's first monotheism, and to treat it as the legitimate offspring and necessary development of the Greek and Roman polytheism. This accordingly Comte actually does. Protestantism he illegitimates and outlaws from religion altogether; and the genuine Christianity he fathers upon the faith of Homer and the Scipios! Once or twice, indeed, it seems to cross him that there was such a people as the Hebrews, and that they were not the polytheists they ought to have been. He sees the fact, but pushes it out of his way with the remark, that the Jewish monotheism was "premature"! The Jews were always a disobliging people: what business had they to be up so early in the morning, disturbing the house ever so long before M. Comte's bell rang to prayers?

It is unfortunate that Comte, like many men at once capable and vain, rests his chief pretensions on precisely what is weakest, least original, and most misleading, in his modes of thought: whilst he drops unconsciously, and leaves unmarked, his strongest and most fertile reflections. The consequence necessarily is, that his first reputation, conferred by disciples in answer to his own demand, will have to shift its ground; that a prior polemic must prepare the way for ultimate appreciation; and that before he can be wisely heard, the louder half of him must be forgot.

JOHN STUART MILL.*

BOTANICAL students, more than thirty years ago, turning over the leaves of the English Flora, encountered the frequent name of J. S. Mill, as an authority for the habitat or the varieties of flowers. Before the earliest of these papers was written, the author, stripling as he must then have been, was already known to distinguished men as a faithful observer of nature. A holiday walk through the lanes and orchards of Kent, which would have yielded to most youths a week's frolic and a bag of apples, filled his tin box with the materials of a naturalist's reputation. Nothing short of the same method of severe earnestness, carried through the whole intellectual training, and interpolating nothing between the child and the man, can well have formed the most elaborated mind of our age, and presented it almost complete at its first appearance. These volumes, indeed, bring to our recollection many an essay which, though not thought worthy to be included in their contents, would bear biographical testimony to the early richness and variety of the author's attainments. Nor was he thrown into this wide and heterogeneous culture without an organizing clue. In the analytical psychology of the elder Mill he inherited an instrument of great power for the logical reduction and systematic grasp of all knowledge: and his belief in it and mastery over it were complete. Limit as we may the pretensions of the Hartleyan doctrine, it affords an incomparable discipline for the first stage of philosophical reflection; and, from the fascination which it invariably exercises over young intellects, its discipline is unsparingly and spontaneously applied. Its first principles easily pass unchallenged in the sensational years of life, ere the finer and deeper shades of inward consciousness have emerged. Its chemistry of ideas actually explains so many marvellous transformations, and seems potentially competent to so much more, that we readily go into captivity to it at an age when ingenuity of process is more impressive to us than truth and precision of result. It has often exercised a profound influence over minds that, at a later stage, have been determined to violent re-action against it: as in the case of Coleridge, who named his first son after Hartley, and slept with the *Observations on Man* under his pillow. And of all the writers of this school, the most enchaining and irresistible is James Mill, whose *Analysis of the Phenomena of the Human Mind* has always appeared to us a masterpiece of close and subtle exposition, to be dissented from, if you please, in its assumptions and conclusions, but rarely to be broken in the midst. Did the facts of consciousness stand as he represents them, his method would work. He satisfactorily explains — the wrong human nature. The mental gymnastic, however, involved in the study of such a work is invigorating, and gives command over a kind of psychological calculus to which innumerable problems yield. Furnished with this, our author tried its application over the widened field of his own generation and the richer resources of his own nature: and we are recalled to his first tentatives in the present republication.

The cold rigor of the elder Mill concealed from the world the extent of his literary knowledge; and when, now and then, he supported his political doctrines from the Republic of Plato, or dropped a tributary phrase to the genius of that philosopher, people attributed it to some freak of pedantry, and almost disputed the right of a "Benthamite" to such an uncongenial admiration. What was begrudged to the father was freely conceded to the son, whose susceptibilities were believed to have an ampler range, who was known to have scholarship as well as science, and whose Platonic studies told not on his dialectic only, but on his style. He encountered, and to his true honor he vanquished, the greatest trial that can meet the young philosopher at the outset of his career, viz. the extravagant expectations and loud-whispered praises of an intellectual coterie, accustomed to abuse and confident of triumph. Elderly prophets who had been stoned in their day fixed their eyes upon him as a sort of Utilitarian Messiah, who would take away the reproach of the school. Could he not gracefully discuss poetry with the poet, and art with the artist? Had he not an appreciative insight into the earlier philosophies, which Bentham could only laugh at and caricature? Was he not surely destined, by his high sympathies with heroic forms of character, to give the hereditary doctrine a nobler interpretation, and rescue it from the ignorant imputation of selfishness? That a young writer, in whose hearing these things were continually said or implied, should disappoint no prediction contained in them, is a rare evidence of moral as well as intellectual strength. The narrowness and perversities which had brought the Utilitarian Radicals into disrepute, never, from the first, appeared in him. There was even, we should say, a conscious revolt from them, an over-anxious care to avoid them, and a deliberate set of the will to apprehend the opposite point of view, and feel whatever truth and beauty lay around it. It was from some feeling of this kind, and especially from a determination to disown the Bowring type of Benthamism, that the *London Review* arose in 1835, under the guarantee of our author's intellect and Sir William Molesworth's purse; and the review of Professor Sedgwick's Discourse with which it opened, though unsparing — not to say arrogant — as a manifesto against the rhetorical ethics of the Cambridge geologist, makes not a few concessions on the other side; it cheerfully surrenders Paley, and cautiously guards its defence of Locke; and shows a sensitiveness equally alive to the nonsense of opponents and the shortcomings of friends. So strongly are the papers of the next four or five years marked by the apparent resolution to escape from party one-sidedness, that they have almost an eclectic character, — with its usual accompaniment, an actual overbalance of candor in favor of rejected schemes of thought. The masterly article on Bentham certainly occasioned not a little flutter of displeasure among his thorough-going admirers, while the corresponding paper on Coleridge was welcomed by his disciples as a conciliatory and generous advance. Both of them, it is true, were written for the benefit of the author's own party: and the former therefore naturally became a criticism, cor rective of what was amiss at home; the latter an exposition, reporting what truth might be fetched in from abroad: and the balance cannot be expected to hang as even as if he had been teaching each party how to take the measure of its own hero. Still it is evident that he rose from the study of Coleridge's writings with an admiration powerfully moved; that they first transferred him from an abstract to an historical theory of politics; and that, in exhibiting the speculative outline of these writings, he felt half-ashamed of the radical allies for whose instruction he performed the task. This schooling of himself into appreciation of a Conservative philosophy was not altogether acceptable to the veterans of his party; but it obtained for him a hearing where their voices could not effectually penetrate, and established literary communication between lines of thought previously closed against each other. And his influence as a writer, measured in its intensity and its kind, was singularly complete at once — none of his larger productions having produced, it is probable, a deeper impression than the three great essays to which we have referred. This, indeed, is no more than the tribute due to the early balance and maturity of his powers. There is something almost preternatural in the singular evenness of these *Dissertations and Discussions*, — the produce of a quarter of a century, — scarcely betraying growth, because requiring none; and indicating not less severity of logic, and sharpness of statement, and authority of manner, in the first pages than in the last. And a higher quality than any of these, and equally apparent throughout, the more honorably distinguishes our author because personal to himself, and by no means habitual in his school, or indeed in any party connection, — we mean a deliberate intellectual conscientiousness, which, scorning to take advantage of accidental weakness, will even help an opponent to develop his strength, that none but the real and decisive issue may be tried. That our author is always *successful* in this we cannot indeed profess to believe; but we are convinced he always *means* it, and never misses it, unless through the involuntary limits of his mental sympathies.

These limits, however, cannot fail to assert them selves, in spite of the most elaborate culture. A catholic intellect is not to be created by resolve; and, notwithstanding his wish to interpret between "Benthamites" and "Coleridgians," Mr. Mill has still left the chasm between them without a bridge, and found neither wing nor way for bringing them together. He effected the exchange of one or two *political* ideas; borrowed the vindication of a "Clerisy," or endowed speculative class; enlarged the radical definition of the functions of the State; favored, with St. Simon as well as Coleridge, the search for "Ideas," as well as Facts in History; qualified the austerities of Political Economy with a tinge of Socialistic humanities; and balanced the conception of Progress with that of Order. But these modifications were torn from their connection and taken over to the Bentham side without their root: fruits, as it were, plucked from the orchard of the Highgate philosopher and stowed away in the store-closet of St.

James's Park, sure to be consumed in a season and to be reproductive of no more. Accordingly, the sociological doctrine, whose first elements were taken from Coleridge, completed itself under the inspiration of Comte. We do not say that this interweaving of opposite ingredients prejudges the truth and unity of the doctrine; but if the parts do cohere in one vital organism, it can only be by grafting anew: and one or other has left its stem, to grow apart no less than before. In fact, it was only in particular results, never in fundamental principle, that our author deemed approximation possible. For himself, he surrendered no inch of his footing on the old ground of the "Experience-philosophy" and the "Utilitarian Ethics," and only aimed to enlarge its imperfect survey, and complete the edifice which had been partially raised upon it. This he has accomplished over a vast portion of the field, and his labors (with those of Mr. Austin in another department) have so far, we believe, consummated the possibilities of the system which they represent. It has attained an unexampled completeness and refinement; its subtlest corrections have been applied; its inmost resources have been strained; and now, more than ever, it ought adequately to meet the intellectual and moral exigencies of life. That it really covers the whole breadth of human want our author doubtless believes; yet the tone of his writings leaves a singular impression of melancholy and unrest. He seems rather to be making the best of the human lot as it is, than to find it worthy of a wise man's welcome. With a firm hand he draws the prohibitory circle which limits our knowledge to the field of experience, and concentrates a steady eye on his survey within it; yet not without glances of thought, — pathetic in their very anger, — towards the dark horizon of necessity and nescience around. Balanced and courteous as he is, it is always with a certain sharpness and irritation that he turns in that direction, and says, "Why look there? there is nothing to be seen." And his moral discontent with the world is still more marked and more depressing than the speculative: his admirations spending themselves, and with fastidious scantiness, on what is wholly out of reach — on Greek polities, that have passed out of reality, and on socialistic, that are doubtfully destined to arrive at it; and his dislikes increasing as the objects are nearer home — England being more stupid than France, and the decorous middle class the meanest of all. Out of sympathy with society as it is, and with languid hopes of what it is to be, our author seems to sit apart, with genial pity for the multitudes below him, with disdain of whatever is around him, and in silence of any thing above him. No one would believe beforehand that a writer so serene and even, not to say cold, could affect the reader with so much sadness. You fall into it, without knowing whence it comes. All the lights upon his page are intellectual, breaking from a deep reserve of moral gloom.

The great mass of Mr. Mill's labor has been devoted to what may be termed the *middle ground* of human thought, below the primary data which reason must assume, and short of the applied science which has practice for its end. At the upper limit shunning the original postulates of all knowledge, and at the lower its concrete results, he has addressed himself to its intermediary processes, and determined the methods for working out derivative but still general truths. Does he treat of the investigation of Nature? he takes it up to the highest *laws of phenomena*, irrespective of the hypothesis of an ulterior source. Does he define the range of Logic? it is the science of *proof*, dealing only with the inference of secondary truths, not the science of *belief*, which would include also the list of first truths. Does he explain the business of Ethics? it is to appraise and classify voluntary actions by their *consequences*, not to scrutinize them in their springs. This avoidance of the initial stage, this banishment of it into another field, is perfectly legitimate, in order to bring each inquiry within manageable limits; and leaves in every instance a body of researches which, in their independent prosecution, yield results of immense value and interest. A perfectly serviceable logic of the inductive sciences may be constructed, without settling the metaphysics of causation; and of the deductive procedure, without determining the original premises of all thought. And a treatise on morals, which should establish methods of estimate for human actions and dispositions, founded on their personal and social tendency, would contribute, if not the more important, at least the larger half of a complete body of Ethical doctrine. Political Economy is not even in contact with any ultimate metaphysics at all, and can only be taken up and treated as a mid-way science, worked out, indeed, deductively, as our author has most ably shown, but only from hypothetical premises, special to itself, and not pretending to any unqualified, much less *a-priori* truth. It lies, therefore, unreservedly within the grasp of Mr. Mill's habitual method; and has accordingly been treated by him, we should say, with mastery more indisputable and complete than any other subject which he has touched. That he has somewhat relaxed the severity of abstract deduction maintained by James Mill and Senior; that he has gone beyond the rigid border of the science, and laid open to the eye and heart some neighboring fields of social speculation; that in demonstrating natural laws he so amply dwells on the conditions of their adjustment to human well-being, — may be complained of by closet *doctrinaires*, may actually render his book less fit for a student's manual; but, in our opinion, gives a wise latitude to researches whose interest will always lie chiefly in their applications. The problems of Political Economy are peculiarly amenable to an intellect like our author's, whose characteristics are rather French than English; — sharp apprehension of whatever can be rounded off as a finished whole in thought; analytic adroitness in resolving a web of tangled elements, and measuring their value in the construction; reasoning equal to any computation by linear co-ordinates, though not readily flowing into the organic freedom of a living dialectic; remarkable skill in laying out his subject symmetrically before the eye, and presenting its successive parts in clear and happy lights. No one has more successfully caught the fortunate gift of the French men-of-letters, — the art of making readers think better of their own understanding and less awfully of the topics discussed. It is seldom possible to read many pages of a German philosopher without suspecting yourself a fool: and even if you conquer your first despair, if you struggle and climb on, and make good your footing as you ascend, you are desired to look down so many frightful precipices and abysses on either side, that the thin ridge of science seems but precarious protection across the yawning nescience. French politeness takes far better care of your nerves, smooths and rolls your path into a gravel-walk, beguiles you into every ascent above your level, plants the abysses out of sight with a laurel screen, and persuades you that you are at the top just where the landscape is clearest and you are still far below the clouds. This exclusive taste for the positive and wholly visible, this ingenuity in conducting to the best points of view, and this faculty of lucidly exhibiting it, our author preeminently possesses; and in the treatment of Political Economy these aptitudes are available with all their benefits and without the slightest drawback.

Logic and Ethics, however, lie at a much less distance from metaphysical reflection; and, indeed, can be cut away from it only by an artifice of arrangement. So far as they admit of the separation, and their body of doctrine stands unaffected by the metaphysical assumptions which are left outside, so far we think Mr. Mill's strength as great here as elsewhere; and it is great precisely in proportion as his *middle ground* is more or less nearly adequate. In Ethics he has aimed at no more than the rescue of the "principle of utility" from misapprehension and obloquy. The *positive* side of his vindication, legitimating the use in morals of a canon of "consequences," he has made good. The *negative* side, excluding appeal to the authority of any internal rule, and resolving conscience into a reflection of the accidental sentiments of others, appears to us entirely to fail. In Logic, his exposition, considered as an *organon*, an analysis of method, a conspectus of rules for the interpretation of phenomena and the discovery of laws, is almost an exhaustive manual of procedure for the present state of science. But considered as a *philosophy*, giving the ultimate *rationale* of the intellectual processes it describes, it leaves us, we confess, altogether unsatisfied. Could he really have maintained a metaphysical neutrality, — could he have simply cut off and dropped out of view the *a-priori* top of logic, the causal postulate of nature, and the inner datum of morals, — could he have carried out his work lower down without reference to them, — our obligation to him would have been scarcely qualified. But this was impossible. There are certain points of his field at which the omitted topics cannot be ignored; and here, unfortunately, our author's original silence is exchanged for direct denial: we know no *a-priori* truths; no causation beyond phenomenal conditions; no inner moral rule. Not only do these negations necessarily descend upon our author's middle ground, and affect a portion of his conclusions in detail, but they express in him, as they must in every man, the grand lines in the whole configuration of his mind. Some of the directions which they take we will attempt to trace.

First, then, Mr. Mill is faithful to his antecedents in the fundamental question of all philosophy: "What is it possible for us to know?" His answer is, "We can know nothing but phenomena." In his article on Coleridge, he both presents the problem and records his reply:

"Every consistent scheme of philosophy requires as its starting-point a theory respecting the sources of human knowledge, and the objects which the human faculties are capable of taking cognizance of. The prevailing theory in the eighteenth century, on this most comprehensive of questions, was that proclaimed by Locke, and commonly attributed to Aristotle — that all knowledge consists of generalizations from experience. Of nature, or any thing whatever external to ourselves, we know, according to this theory, nothing, except the facts which present themselves to our senses, and such other facts as may, by analogy, be inferred from these. There is no knowledge *a priori;* no truths cognizable by the mind's inward light, and grounded on intuitive evidence. Sensation, and the mind's consciousness of its own acts, are not only the exclusive sources, but the sole materials of our knowledge. From this doctrine, Coleridge, with the German philosophers since Kant (not to go further back), and most of the English since Reid, strongly dissents. He claims for the human mind a capacity, within certain limits, of perceiving the nature and properties of 'Things in themselves.' He distinguishes in the human intellect two faculties, which, in the technical language common to him with the Germans, he calls Understanding and Reason. The former faculty judges of phenomena, or the appearances of things, and forms generalizations from these; to the latter it belongs, by direct intuition, to perceive things, and recognize truths, not cognizable by our senses. The perceptions are not indeed innate, nor could ever have been awakened in us without experience; but they are not copies of it; experience is not their prototype, it is only the occasion by which they are irresistibly suggested. The experiences in nature excite in us, by an inherent law, ideas of those invisible things which are the causes of the visible appearances, and on whose laws those appearances depend: and we then perceive that these things must have pre-existed to render the appearances possible; just as (to use a frequent illustration of Coleridge's) we see before we know that we have eyes; but when once this is known to us, we perceive that eyes must have pre-existed to enable us to see. Among the truths which are thus known *a priori*, by occasion of experience, but not themselves the subjects of experience, Coleridge includes the fundamental doctrines of religion and morals, the principles of mathematics, and the ultimate laws even of physical nature; which he contends cannot be proved by experience, though they must necessarily be consistent with it, and would, if we knew them perfectly, enable us to account for all observed facts, and to predict all those which are as yet unobserved" (vol. i. pp. 403–405).

Our author's verdict on this question is given in these words:

"We here content ourselves with a bare statement of our opinion. It is that the truth, on this much-debated question, lies with the school of Locke and of Bentham. The nature and laws of things in themselves, and the hidden causes of the phenomena which are the objects of experience, appear to us radically inaccessible to the human faculties. We see no ground for believing that any thing can be the object of our knowledge except our experience, and what can be inferred from our experience by the analogies of experience itself; nor that there is any idea, feeling, or power in the human mind, which in order to account for it requires that its origin should be referred to any other source. We are therefore at issue with Coleridge on the central idea of his philosophy" (vol. i. p. 409).

Were it to our purpose to discuss this problem with Mr. Mill, instead of simply tracing its bearings upon his scheme of thought, we should require a much more precise statement of it than we find in the foregoing passage, in which the association (however qualified) of Locke and Aristotle, as giving the same suffrage in reply to the same question, — the classification of Kant with the ontologists, and the indiscriminate reference of more recent "German philosophers" to the same side, — indicate, under the form of historical error, no less loose a conception of the opposite theses than of the advocacy arrayed on either hand. Aristotle was just as much a realist as Plato, though he made the realities accessible to us by a different path. Kant was the great iconoclast who discredited all objective entities as idols of the mind; and till the re-action under Schelling, there was no claim of any knowledge of "Things in themselves." In order to present the matter in a clearer form, we must disengage from each other two aspects of this problem, the ancient, and the modern; the identification of which by English writers is the source of endless confusion. Among the Greek schools, the rivalry between the real and the phenomenal, between "Things as they absolutely are," and Things as they relatively appear, was fought out, not on the field of our cognitive faculties, but in the open Kosmos. It was a question, not of knowledge, but of being; not *logical*, referring to the limits of thought, but *metaphysical*, concerning the constitution of existence. Instead of shaping itself into the form, "Can *we get to know* any entities, or must we be content with phenomena?" it asked, "*Are there any entities to be known*, or only regiments of phenomena?" In the view of one party, time and space comprised nothing but an eternal genesis of appearance out of appearance, — wave upon wave, with no abiding deep below. In the view of the other, the succession of phenomena was but the superficial expression, the momentary and relative activity of substantive objects and permanent potencies behind, which formed the constancies of the universe, and organically belonged to its unity. By neither party was man set over against the universe to look at it across an interval, as subject facing object. By both he was regarded as himself a part and product of the Kosmos, involved in the same problem, included in the same fate. Its constitution, whatever it were, spread into him and re-appeared there in miniature, and with no modification except that of cropping-up into consciousness and emerging from simple *being* into *being known*. Phenomena, entering us, turned up in the shape of sensations; entities, if there were any, in the shape of rational thought, of ideas remotest from sense, — of the true, the beautiful, the good. If in the makrokosm around there was more than phenomena, the personal mikrokosm could not but repeat the tale and show these *ὄντα* in our intellectual history. If, on the other hand, phenomena were all, then in us also there could be only sensations and their metamorphoses. It thus lay in the very genius of the ancient philosophy that the problem of *knowledge* should be subordinate to the problem of *being*, — the mere shadow or reverberation of it in our little grotto of consciousness; and that it should be judged downward, from the great circle to the little. That there could be any failure of concentric arrangement, — any misfit between existence and thought, — that if there were the real as well as the seeming, it could remain incognizable, — never occurred to the earliest representatives of this controversy. None were sceptics of realistic knowledge, except in virtue of a prior scepticism of real being.

Aristotle certainly had no such scepticism; and his controversy with Plato never touched the question *whether* we had ontological knowledge, but only the question *how* we had it. Plato explained it by identifying the objective *ideals* embodied in natural kinds with our subjective *general ideas* of the intellectual constitution of the universe: its hierarchy of essential types came up into conscious forms on the responding theatre of our reason; so that we could read its entities straight off, in virtue of our sympathetic share in the thoughts incarnated within it. For this doctrine of *immediate* fellowship of reason with its realities, Aristotle substituted a path of *gradual* approach to them: declaring that, while Nature developed itself deductively, thinking itself out into actuality from the general to the particular, and thence to the individual, we must trace the same line regressively, beginning with the sensible which is next to us, and ascending to the universals which are furthest. But this difference from Plato as to the method of knowledge, involved no difference as to the things known. The goal of reason was the same for both — the apprehension of real and ultimate entities. The thing known by the consciousness within us, itself lay in the world without us. This example shows that the denial of "*a-priori* ideas" carries with it no denial of ontological knowledge.

In modern times, from causes which we cannot stop to trace, this problem has been taken in the inverse order. The battle between the real and the phenomenal has been removed from the Kosmical to the Human theatre, and fought out on the enclosure of our faculties. Without prejudging the contents of existence, it has been asked, — "How far do our cognitive powers go? Are they fitted up in adaptation to phenomena alone? or does their competency reach to substantive being as well?" It has been supposed easier to stop at home and measure the knowing subject, than to pass out and determine the known object; and accordingly a Logical critique of Man has taken the place of a Metaphysical estimate of Nature. Such a critique (supposing that we have resources for conducting it), in giving us the measure of ourselves, gives us the measure of *our* world. Either our faculties will prove equal to the problem on both its sides; and then we shall stand where Plato and Aristotle left us: or will turn out blind to all except the phenomenal sphere; and then whatever else may lurk behind will be to us as though it were not, and the negation of knowledge will demand the non-affirmation of being. The alternative can be decided only by psychological self-scrutiny. Is the verdict given in favor of our ontological capacity? it can only be on the ground that, besides our mere sensations and their associated vestiges, we find in us an independent order of ideas, carrying with them intuitive beliefs affirmative of existence other than phenomenal, and no less entitled to confidence than the susceptibilities of sense. Is the verdict, on the other hand, a negative one? It may rest upon either of two pleas. The independent testimony of the Ideas of Reason may be denied, by resolving them back into elaborated traces of sensation. Or, again, their originality and intuitive character being allowed, they may be referred to the mere mould or configuration of our mental constitution, inevitable for us, but not on that account declaring itself necessary in nature; with authority, therefore, merely subjective, and destitute of all objective validity. It is on the former of these two pleas that Mr. Mill, in common with the whole school of Locke, takes his stand; while the latter is the ground assumed by Kant and his disciples. The same sceptical conclusion belongs to both: and the difference as to the analysis of the knowing powers involves no difference as to the things known, or rather, not known. This example shows that the affirmation of "*a-priori* ideas" carries with it no affirmation of ontological knowledge.

A problem imperfectly conceived cannot be effectively argued; and no "Coleridgian," it is probable, ever felt himself hit by our author's occasional reasonings against him. The keen aim and the steady hand are of no avail where there is an optical displacement of the thing aimed at. Be his polemic, however, against the opposite doctrine what it may, our present purpose is to track through his philosophy the vestiges of his own. Is our knowledge limited to phenomena? Then we must part with our mathematical entities, — Space, the *a-priori* ground of geometry, — Time, of successive counting, or number, — with the necessary Infinitude of both. We know them only in the limited samples of experience, as attributes of body and emptiness, of events and feelings, over an indefinite field. And the pure geometric figures, with the properties they involve, instead of being truer than Nature, are false copies of physical forms, yielding only approximate inferences, whose boasted "necessity" is nothing but dependence on inaccurate hypothesis. We must part also with our Metaphysical entities, — Substance, as the ground of

Attributes, be it Matter, for the properties of nature without us, or Mind, for the phenomena of consciousness within us; Kind, as the real unity of essence looking through a plurality of individuals; Cause, as a principle of dynamic origination, or more than the aggregate of phenomenal conditions. We must part with our Religious and Moral entities, — God, whether as transcendent cause of the universe, or Mind throughout it, or living Light of human Conscience; and all the ideal meanings in nature and life, whether owned as final causes by Science, or caught as the inner expressiveness of things by the intuition of Art. This copious surrender of natural beliefs is the inevitable consequence of the primary assumption; it is shared with our author by the Nominalist Divines of Oxford; and is no further special to him, than in the unwavering consistency and absence of self-deception with which he carries it out. Hence his contempt, — the more unsparing from its professing to spare, — for the recognition of *purpose* in nature; expressed in sentences like this: "Upon this peg he" (*i.e.* Professor Sedgwick) "appends a dissertation on the evidences of design in the universe; a subject on which much originality was not to be hoped for, and the nature of which may be allowed to protect feebleness from any severity of comment" (vol. i. p. 105). And similar is his impatience of any expression of *wonder:* "And here he" (Professor Sedgwick again) "begins by wondering. It is a common propensity of writers on natural theology to erect every thing into a wonder. They cannot consider the greatness and wisdom of God, once for all, as proved, but think themselves bound to be finding fresh arguments for it in every chip or stone: and they think nothing a proof of greatness unless they can wonder at it; and, to most minds, a wonder explained is a wonder no longer" (vol. i. p. 105). It is curious to compare these scornful words with the maxim of Bacon,* — "*Admiratio est semen sapientiæ;*" with the statement of Aristotle,† that Wonder is the primitive philosophical impulse; with the graceful saying of Plato, ‡ — "It is a happy genealogy which makes *Iris* the daughter of *Thaumas*," — *i. e.* which treats the messenger of the Gods, — the winged thought that passes to and fro between heaven and earth, and brings them into communion, — as the child of Wonder: "for this," he says, "is the special sentiment of the philosopher, nor has his pursuit any other source." The truth is, Mr. Mill expresses here, as in all else, the characteristics of the strictly *scientific* mind, whose work is done and whose contentment is attained when the order of phenomena is fully determined, and no premonition of the future remains to be gathered from the scheme of the past. Were this the end of Philosophy, as it *is* the end of Science, his view would be complete.

But not only, in our author's opinion, is our knowledge limited to phenomena. Among phenomena we can know only the internal — our own sensations, thoughts, emotions. The whole objective world vanishes under his analysis: first, its substantive pretensions; then, even its attributive. What do we know of matter? — nothing but its properties. What do we know of its properties? — nothing but the sensations they give us.

* De Augmentis Scient. lib. i., Montagu, vol. viii. p. 8.
† Metaph. i. 2. ‡ Theæt. 155.

An object is no more than an associated group of qualities, the enumeration of which exhausts what we have to say of it. A quality is no more than an assumed and unknown source of some affection of sense: so that not only does the hot, round, bright sun evade us; its heat, its form, its light evade us too; and we are aware only of a co-existent warmth and visual dazzle of the circular kind. The third chapter of the *System of Logic* (book i.) expounds this doctrine with great clearness and amplitude. In substitution for the ten categories of Aristotle,* Mr. Mill distributes all "nameable things"—all possible objects of thought and speech—into four classes, viz.:

* We are surprised that Mr. Mill should treat Aristotle's list as an attempt to classify "*Nameable things*," and drive them up into their *summa genera*. A mere glance at the list corrects this common misconception. "Nameable things" are the possible *objects of thought;* and consequently the "Names" themselves, the possible *subjects of propositions:* and were *these* the matter divided, we should have in the Categories a classification of possible *Subjects*, and in the Predicables, of possible *Predicates*, of propositions;—a very instructive pair of logical results, but certainly not what Aristotle contemplated. Without going through the list, it is evident at once that several of its terms (*e.g.* πρός τι, ποῦ, πότε) do not represent any possible subjects of propositions. The assortment is in fact an enumeration, not of things signified by *Names*, but, as Aristotle himself distinctly explains, of all possible meanings of *single Words*,—including Adverbs, Prepositions, and other *relational* words which are not *Names* at all. Regarded in this light, the catalogue is not indeed unexceptionable; but does not yield the utter absurdities which Mr. Mill naturally sees in it as a list of the most extensive classes into which things could be distributed. We are quite aware that Mr. Mill's "Nameable Things" are not limited to *Subjects*, but include also what is "capable of being *predicated* of other Things." Even this extension, however, does not cover the ground of Aristotle's Categories, (inasmuch as the relational words cannot be predicates any more than subjects,) while it disadvantageously trenches on the ground of the Predicables. In classifying *the significant atoms of language*, all mention of the two parts of the predicative relation is as yet intrusive, and is accordingly avoided by Aristotle. When we advance from the Accidence to the Syntax of Logic, we then want two new classifications: 1st, of Nameable things or possible Subjects; 2dly, of Predicable

"1st. Feelings or States of Consciousness.

2d. The Minds which experience those feelings.

3d. The Bodies, or external objects, which excite certain of those feelings, together with the powers or properties whereby they excite them.

4th. The Successions and Co-existences, the Likenesses and Unlikenesses, between feelings or states of consciousness. Those relations," it is added, "when considered as subsisting between other things, *exist in reality only between the states of consciousness* which those things, if bodies, excite; if minds, either excite or experience" (*Logic*, vol. i. p. 83).

Though the usages of language forbid our author to carry his reduction further, he gives us notice that the second and third terms are but sham categories, really resolvable into the first. Of "Mind" we know only the "feelings or states of consciousness;" of "Body," and its "properties," only the resulting "feelings or states of consciousness" again. The existence of myself, except as "a series of feelings,"—the existence of any thing other than myself, except as the feigned and unknown cause of sensations,—I have no title to affirm. Though the structure of human speech assumes them, it has no right to do so: and were it amenable to the true laws of our intelligence, it would leave us with only the first and fourth of the foregoing heads. We are thus shut up absolutely in Egoistic phenomena, without cognizance of any objective world beyond our own circumference, or subjective axis at our own centre.

things, or possible Predicates. From his running together of all these,—from his imperfect use of the distinction between the extension and the comprehension of a term,—and from his removal of the *adjective* out of ῥῆμα into ὄνομα, our author's account of the "Import of Propositions" seems to us less luminous and satisfactory than any other part of his "System of Logic."

This is unqualified Idealism: the more so, because Mr. Mill does not stop with the assertion that, apart from their properties, we are ignorant of the *nature* of Matter and of Mind; but pronounces us ignorant of their *existence*. The phenomena to which we are limited are regarded by other philosophers as at least phenomena of *something;* by him, as phenomena of *nothing*. Berkeley himself did not remove the objective world and swallow it up in the subjective: he merely changed it from material into Divine, and left the Personal entities, of Man and God, undisturbed and alone with each other. And even Fichte, the most thorough-going of all Idealists, while taking every thing into the subject, still did not break the vessel of personality, and spill and scatter its living water into phenomenal spray. Our author goes further, and says: we know of nothing without; we know of only change within; and our whole cognitive life consists in the conscious comparison and orderly notice of our feelings and ideas.

There is no part of Mr. Mill's scheme of thought in which this idealistic theory of cognition does not make itself felt. It induces him, as a psychologist, to cancel the word *Perception*, and to deny that in the process it denotes there is any thing more than associated Sensations. When we seem to be carried out of ourselves and referred to a world beyond, we are in reality only referred from one of our own sensations to others, — from a single member of a cluster to the rest, — from what we actually feel in one sense to what, in suitable positions, we might simultaneously feel in another. When we attribute *whiteness* to *snow*, we say that a particular sensation of color belongs to a group, the remainder of which, — a coldness, a softness, a sparkle, &c. — are expressed by the word "*snow*." It is co-existence of sensations, and nothing else, that we predicate. The extreme test of this doctrine is found in our apprehension of distance, form, and magnitude. If these can be stripped of their externality and resolved into modifications of self, — if they can be turned from synchronous relations in the space without us into successive feelings along the line of consciousness within us, — the Idealist has solved his hardest riddle. Our author has attempted this in reply to Mr. Samuel Bailey's attack on Berkeley's "Theory of Vision:" and, in spite of our good opinion of his cause, we are not surprised that his arguments have failed to convince the Sheffield philosopher. The question is, How do we see things to be external to ourselves? and what is our belief in their 'outness'? Mr. Bailey answers: It is an immediate intuition or revelation of the visual sense, requiring no other condition. Mr. Mill first answers: It is a mental judgment, consisting in the suggestion of tactual and muscular sensations by visual which have become associated with them in experience. But then, unfortunately, the tactual and muscular sensations are *not* external, whilst our quæsitum *is:* so that the thing said to be "suggested" does not fit the case. To escape from this difficulty, Mr. Mill next remarks, — "What we regard as external is not the sensation, but the cause of the sensation, — the thing which by its presence *is supposed* to give rise to the sensation: the colored object, or the quality residing in that object which we term its color" (vol. ii. p. 93). The "outness" then attaches to the "object," in distinction from the "sensation;" to the object therefore not as seen, or as felt, but as "supposed." What then is this "supposition"? Does the visual impression suffice to occasion it? If so, nothing else than vision is wanted for the belief of "outness," and Mr. Bailey is right. Or, must the supposition of an object wait for the sensations of Touch? Then upon *these*, though not upon visual feeling, a belief in "outness" must attend, — an objective apprehension upon a subjective experience: and Touch differs from Vision, in carrying with it *more than sensation*. This psychological addition to sensation, in which Mr. Mill after all has to seek his "outness," is what is commonly called *Perception* by those who trust it. With him it is part and parcel of an unauthorized "supposition" respecting an objective source of our feelings; and is not owned under any name which assigns its valid authority. But though he describes it in disparaging terms, he cannot dispense with it, and really take us out of ourselves by any manipulation of inward sensations: and the only difference between him and Mr. Bailey's disciples is this — that while they step into externality on the *terra firma* of reliable Perception, he is carried thither at a leap upon the back of a chimera. The advantage, so far, appears to us entirely on Mr. Bailey's side. Only, we cannot think him right in attaching the indispensable *perceptive* function to the simple visual susceptibility. It is to the eyes as *movable* organs that it belongs; and were it not for association thus established with the muscular system, we believe with Berkeley that sight would no more give us externality than smell. Not, however, that there is any magic in the "muscular *sensations*," giving them an exceptional power to do this great thing for us. Were the muscles insensible as ropes, they would retain, we believe, their distinction, so long as they differ from all our mere *senses*, in obeying the prior signals of our will, and introducing our inner causality into collision with outward obstruction. In that experience, we believe, lies the birth-point of our objective perceptions and our subjective self-consciousness; including both the Mathematical antithesis of *here* and *there*, and the Dynamical antithesis of *our own Power* and Power *other than our own.* With Mr. Mill we deem vision by itself incompetent to give this report. With Mr. Bailey, we accept the report as a revelation when we get it; and regard it as altogether beyond the resources of sensation, and needing description as a cognitive Perception.*

To follow the vestiges of our author's idealism through certain characteristics of his logic would involve too many technicalities, and too deep a plunge into the recesses of the Nominalist controversy. He naturally dislikes the language of classification, invented in a very different school; and, refusing to use it in defining the business of a predication, treats every proposition as

* How difficult it is, on Mr. Mill's principles, to deal with our objective belief, is evident on examining his account of the notions "Substance" and "Quality." In order to step on to these notions, he avails himself of the idea of *Cause.* "Quality"—hidden *Cause* of Sensation: "Substance"—hidden *Cause* of qualities. It is therefore in obedience to the exigencies of the Causal idea, that we are carried in thought *behind phenomena*, and set down on the ontological field. Yet, when Mr. Mill comes to expound this idea, he denies to it any but a phenomenal meaning: "When, in the course of this inquiry, I speak of the *cause* of any phenomenon, I do not mean a cause which is not itself a phenomenon" (*Logic*, i. p. 358). To work this same idea both ways,—now to get up our entities, and then to knock them down.—is surely making either too much or too little of it.

declaring simply a co-existence of attributes; thus interpreting both subject and predicate in their intension rather than their extension, and giving the counter-development to the quantitative methods of Mr. De Morgan and Dr. Boole. If we are at liberty to sacrifice psychological truth to the exigencies of a calculus of deduction, either principle is adequate to its end, though the advantage practically lies with the mathematicians. But on both sides the unfortunate copula seems to us to be put upon the rack and made to say what it does not mean; and the simple fact to be overlooked, that we naturally construe the subject of a proposition in its extension, and the predicate (which therefore may be an adjective) in its intension: so that neither co-existence of attributes nor equation of groups correspond with the living processes of thought and language. But on this special field we must not enter.

It is the instinct of idealism, whithersoever it turns, to translate objective terms and conceptions into subjective, and to draw all reality and meaning into the inward life. To this we attribute the characteristic prominence given, in Mr. Mill's Moral doctrine, to *self-formation and individuality.* The frequency with which he recurs to this topic, and the earnestness with which he speaks of it, show how high it ranks in his estimate. It is, indeed, the great province of Ethics which he would recover from the neglect of previous utilitarians. Paley, he admits, looks too exclusively "to the objective consequences of actions, and omits the subjective; attends to the effects on our outward condition and that of other people too much, to those on our internal sources of happiness or unhappiness too little" (vol. i. p. 151). And of Bentham's theory it is still more strongly said that

"It will do nothing for the conduct of the individual, beyond prescribing some of the more obvious dictates of worldly prudence, and outward probity and beneficence. There is no need to expatiate on the deficiencies of a system of ethics which does not pretend to aid individuals in the formation of their own character; which recognizes no such wish as that of self-culture, we may even say no such power, as existing in human nature; and if it did recognize, could furnish little assistance to that great duty, because it overlooks the existence of about half of the whole number of mental feelings which human beings are capable of, including all those of which the direct objects are states of their own mind.

"Morality consists of two parts. One of these is self-education; the training, by the human being himself, of his affections and will. That department is a blank in Bentham's system. The other and co-equal part, the regulation of his outward actions, must be altogether halting and imperfect without the first: for how can we judge in what manner many an action will affect even the worldly interests of ourselves and others, unless we take in, as part of the question, its influence on the regulation of our, or their, affections and desires?" (vol. i. p. 363.)

This is well and wisely said: and it greatly narrows the ground of difference between the opposite schools of ethics.. Only secure at the outset a perfect programme of human nature; take into account all its aims and affections, including its aspirations after "ideal ends;" accept these, ranged on their own scale of intensity and self-estimation, as given facts; let the whole picture, once drawn by thorough psychological survey, stand as true for humanity and unimpeachable by the defects of individuals;—and, under such conditions, Butler himself will consent to your computing your code on "the Greatest-Happiness principle." For, evidently, the "greatest happiness" of a nature which has moral affections to begin with, aims at perfection and ideas of it which it feels to be authoritative,—will be very different from that of a nature simply sentient, and having as yet to determine itself hither or thither by the relish of its pleasures and the repulsion of its pains. Each propensity, separately, brings us satisfaction when it gains its end: but if we are so constituted that, taken out of a certain order and proportion among the rest, that satisfaction is again spoiled; if the same is true of all in turn, so that for the whole series there is an ideal law, the dislocation of which is the wreck of our inward peace; if, further, there is inherent in this misery the special consciousness that it is what we have no right to incur,—then you can settle the due order of life by the rule of "happiness," should it so please you; for this rule is itself but the expression of a prior scale of natural excellence and authority. All inward rightness involving satisfaction, the satisfaction may be used as its sign. Only, unfortunately, the sign cannot well be made apparent, except to those who already know the thing signified.

Notwithstanding, however, the great part which this "Self-perfecting" by an inward ideal plays in our author's ethics, and its value as a formula for completing,—we should rather say, relinquishing,—the utilitarian theory, we find a difficulty in so combining his expositions of it as to settle it on any philosophical basis. In the passage just cited, it is described as covering one half of the whole ground of morality. Morality is, however, in all cases but a means to an end (*Logic*, p. 385), and that end is declared to be happiness. Mr. Mill accordingly points out, as will have been observed, that, without studying the effects of our conduct on our own characters, we cannot compute even its external influence on the affairs of ourselves and others. Here the self-training is vindicated on the general utilitarian ground that, without it, there will be an omitted class of consequences. We must take care of our affections and will, as being important to the interests of ourselves and others: and this particular position, as not an end in themselves, but an instrument of something ulterior, is essential to make the care of them a moral act. Yet elsewhere our author lifts this self-formation out of all subsidiary relations, and complains of Bentham that

"Man is never recognized by him as a being capable of pursuing spiritual perfection *as an end;* of desiring, *for its own sake,* the conformity of his own character to his standard of excellence, without hope of good or fear of evil from other source than his own inward consciousness" (vol. i. p. 359).

"What is that to me?" Bentham would reply: "did you not say that all morality is directed to an end beyond it? If this pursuit of yours is good on its own account, it does not belong to morality; and it is no imputation on me, as a moralist, that I say nothing about it. A man may make it his end to conform to his own standard of excellence: so much the worse for him if the standard is a bad one, talk as he may of spiritual perfection." And in truth Mr. Mill himself elsewhere expressly treats as *un*-moral and purely æsthetical this realization of inward harmony, this conformity with ideal laws; and pronounces it sentimental "to set this aspect of actions above the moral," which looks to their consequences:

"Every human action," he observes, "has three aspects: its *moral* aspect, or that of its *right* and *wrong;* its *æsthetic* aspect, or that of its *beauty;* its *sympathetic* aspect, or that of its *lovableness.* The first addresses itself to our reason and conscience; the second to our imagination; the third to our human fellow-feeling. According to the first, we approve or disapprove; according to the second, we admire or despise; according to the third, we love, pity, or dislike. The morality of an action depends on its foreseeable consequences; its beauty, and its lovableness, or the reverse, depend on the qualities which it is evidence of. Thus a lie is *wrong*, because its effect is to mislead, and because it tends to destroy the confidence of man in man; it is also mean, because it is cowardly — because it proceeds from not daring to face the consequences of telling the truth — or at best is evidence of want of that *power* to compass our ends by straightforward means, which is conceived as properly belonging to every person not deficient in energy or in understanding. The action of Brutus in sentencing his son was *right*, because it was executing a law essential to the freedom of his country, against persons of whose guilt there was no doubt: it was *admirable*, because it evinced a rare degree of patriotism, courage, and self-control: but there was nothing lovable; it affords either no presumption in regard to lovable qualities, or a presumption of their deficiency. If one of the sons had engaged in the conspiracy from affection for the other, his action would have been lovable, though neither moral nor admirable. It is not possible for any sophistry to confound these three modes of viewing an action; but it is very possible to adhere to one of them exclusively, and lose sight of the rest. Sentimentality consists in setting the last two of the three above the first; the error of moralists in general, and of Bentham, is to sink the two latter entirely" (vol. vi. p. 387).

If this distinction is good in our criticism of others, it will apply no less to our own case. And surely if there be any form of our personal energy which belongs to the second head, and takes shape from the "imagination" of ethical "beauty," it is the self-approximation to an ideal standard "on its own account." In proportion as the aim *to be* gains upon the intent *to do*, does "sentimentality," as above defined, take place of "morals." With what consistency, then, can Bentham's disregard of this aim be treated as a curtailment of morality by full half its whole amount? It seems to us that, in our author's scheme, this aspiration after an inward perfection floats about without settling in its proper place. It is as if he felt it more than utilitarian, and so let it have an ideal end of its own; yet also more than æsthetic, and so charged it with the half of human morals. It is the old problem of the *καλόν* and the *ἄγαθον*, — difficult to Plato, impossible to Bentham.*

In truth, there is nothing in the utilitarian theory,

* Mr. Mill's distinctions are usually taken with so much precision, that we hardly venture to confess our imperfect satisfaction with his account of the *Moral* as *Causative* of "foreseeable *consequences;*" and of the *Æsthetic* and *Lovable* as *Expressive* of inner "*qualities.*" All three, we should say, are equally *Expressive;* and the essence of their effect upon us lies in what they severally express. The Moral expresses *preference among springs of voluntary conduct:* the Æsthetic, *inward harmony or force, involuntary as well as voluntary:* the Lovable, *paramount affectionateness, moral or not.* It seems to us quite arbitrary to say that our *Approbation* is characterized by looking away from the principle and down to the consequences of action. We should say, its sympathy goes right up to the spiritual source within the character, just as much as in the cases of *Admiration* and *Affection.*

however enlarged, for this self-formation to rest upon, beyond the exigencies of our obligations to our fellow-men. *Why* should a man mould himself under the pressure of "a vague feeling and inexplicable internal conviction"? (p. 385.) Is it to escape the uneasiness of disappointed aspiration? This can be done by perseveringly neglecting the aspiration far more effectually than by realizing it, and so advancing it to an ulterior stage. Besides, if this were all, what else would the pursuit be but the indulgence of a spiritual luxury, — the highest refinement of egoism? Imprisoned within the circle of myself, conscious indeed of differences among my affections, but not warranted in treating them as significant of any thing, I am constituted of mere subjective emotions: I can but spin around my own centre, and whether on this axis of preference or on that, I equally fulfil my law of being. Plant me alone amid a desert of negation, with susceptibilities that are the index of nothing, and powers in communion with nothing; and whatever ferment of elements there may be within me, — storms of broken equilibrium and harmonies of returning calm, — they can but constitute some form of taste and prudence, and can never make a duty: there is no rule of higher and lower that could be pronounced valid for any second nature that should enter on the vacant field. One half of self, — if it be only self, — cannot claim the worship of the other, — any more than a ventriloquist can learn any thing from his two-voiced dialogue, or a single actor can play out a real drama by change of dress. For obligation we must have an authority, — for admiration, a beauty, — for reverence, a goodness, — beyond self and higher than self: and unless we may accept our subjective apprehensions of spiritual excellence as significant of objective realities, and look upon our "ideal ends" as the openings on us of a purer Will and the communion of a supreme Perfection, we do not see how they can ever be more than the phantasms of a vision or lend us any wing effectual against our own weight. Mr. Mill himself remarks, in concurrence with Mr. Grote, the fact that, in its primitive form, the sense of obligation is exclusively of the *personal kind.* "Personal feelings either towards the gods, the King, or some near and known individual, fill the whole of a man's bosom; out of them arise all the motives to beneficence, and all the internal restraints upon violence, antipathy, and rapacity: and special communion, as well as special solemnities, are essential to their existence" (vol. ii. p. 321). Is this so certainly a mere puerility of early society, doomed to be advantageously replaced by "the Impersonal authority of the Laws"? or is it only the most elementary expression of an ineffaceable feature in our nature? and do "the Laws" themselves perhaps prevail not as "impersonal" and abstract, but as representing the higher personality of the Nation, represented through the living voice of assembled dikasts? and does conscience itself speak in more solemn tone in proportion as it seems to reveal a Will greater than opinion and auguster than our own? And is it not then possible that we may yet return, with glorified interpretation, to that early stage, and by re-translating duties into personal relations between the Human and the Divine, restore to them the living power of affection and fidelity?

The subjective principle of our author's philosophy pervades his literary code; and very characteristically appears in an attempt, highly ingenious and suggestive, to answer the untiring question, "What is poetry?" He replies, It is the spontaneous expression of feeling; and all thoughts and words which pour out feeling, not for influence on others, but as in soliloquy, are in their essence poetry: and the poetic minds are those whose thoughts are linked by feelings, and determined into existence by the laws of emotion. Mr. Mill's poet must be all loneliness and intensity, — a kind of spiritual firework going off of itself in infinite night. So isolating a definition would in no case apply to other than lyric poetry; and our author has the courageous consistency to adopt the limitation, and to consider the drama and the epic redeemed from prose only by the intermixture of lyrical elements. Did we even accept this startling restriction, the theory, we think, makes far too much of mere quantity of sensibility; which is often strongly marked in minds eminently unpoetical. But above all it is any thing rather than solitary, self-evolved feeling that constitutes the poet. He more than any goes forth out of himself, and mingles his very being with the nature and humanity around him; entering into their essence by humbling his own, and directing on them the idealizing glance which looks in at their eyes and reads their heart. He lives, not to express himself, but to interpret the world, and become the vocal organ of the silent universe and the dumb souls of men.

The excessive appreciation of "individuality" which was noticed in a recent review of our author's treatise on "Liberty," belongs to the same general tendency. His sympathies,—unless in the form of pity,—scarcely seem to touch the common level of human life, or to acknowledge any vital connection with the general faith and conscience. His fears, his despondencies, his precautions, all look towards the social sentiment, in whose conservative moral elements he sees little else than the joint-stock opinions of mediocrity and vulgarity; and his hopes somewhat languidly and scantily fly to eminent and exceptional personalities who can see over the heads of the crowd. The old Pagan trust in "wisdom," with pathetic or supercilious gaze on all below, reappears in him: and "*thinkers*,"—"*great thinkers*,"—step forth so often upon his page, and conduct their mission with so much pomp, that the mother-wit of modest readers grows quite ashamed and blushes to the eyes. When, for instance, the announcement is made that it "is becoming more and more the grand effort of all minds of any power, which embark in literature,"—"to have something to say" (vol. i. p. 240), homely people, who never made "the grand effort," know at once that they have not "minds of any power," and naturally shrink before the knitted brows of such self-elaboration.

Many of our readers, we doubt not, will have felt a certain surprise and incredulity at finding Mr. Mill classed with "Idealists." The term seems to contradict some of his best-marked tendencies, and not at all to hit the kind of influence which his writings have exercised. Had we classed him with "Materialists,"* we

* The word "Materialism," it should be observed, stands, with a different range of meaning, in two distinct antitheses. As opposed to *Immaterial-*

should probably have been thought nearer the mark. And the truth is (for we must qualify a strong assertion by a yet stronger), he is *both*, and presents, in different parts of his doctrine, two opposite sides, which often practically co-exist, whether or not they are philosophically coherent. On the one hand, we have found him resolving all our knowledge, "both materials and sources," into *Self*-knowledge; denying any cognitive access to either qualities or bodies external to us; and shutting us up with our own sensations, ideas, and emotions. But on the other hand, though we *know* nothing but the phenomena of ourselves, we *are* nothing but phenomena of the world: the boast is vain of any thing original in the mind: the sensations from which all within us begins are the results of "outward experience:" the pretended *a-priori* ideas turn out *a-posteriori* residues: the volitions that set up as spontaneities are necessary effects of antecedents earlier than we: the truths we seem to win by pure deductive intelligence are but interpretations of physical induction: and the characters we think our own are but subservient copies of the influences around us. Our author's whole picture of man exhibits him as a natural product, shaped by the scene on which he is cast; and he rejects every theory without exception which has been set up,

ism, it is concerned with the question of the Mind's ultimate substance, and denotes the opinion that the Mental Phenomena are referable to the same substance which manifests the Physical; not to a different one, as the Immaterialist contends. As opposed to *Idealism*, the word is concerned with another question, viz. the equal or unequal originality and trustworthiness of our Subjective and Objective knowledge. To hold the balance even between them is *Dualism:* to resolve the latter into the former is *Idealism:* to resolve the former into the latter is *Materialism*. It is in this last sense alone that we have to do with the word.

in psychology, in logic, in morals, to vindicate the autonomy of human reason and conscience. And thus we are landed in this singular result: our only sphere of cognizable reality is subjective: and *that* is generated from an objective world which we have no reason to believe exists. In our author's theory of *cognition*, the *non-ego* disappears in the ego; in his theory of *being*, the ego lapses back into the *non-ego*. Idealist in the former, he is Materialist in the latter.

This subjection of man to physical nature exhibits itself in a Sensational psychology; which, while condemning Condillac's simplification of Locke as mere verbal generalization, does but stretch the same materials upon a different loom, and weave the whole web of our mental life out of the data of sense. The nearer we are to sensation, the less room is there for error and uncertainty: as we recede from it into abstractions of the understanding and ideas of reason, the tenure of our truths is more precarious: and consciousness, however entitled to be believed about tactual and ocular impressions, is to be distrusted in all reports which decline to go back thither for authentication. In spite of Mr. Mill's denying us all legitimate access to an external world, no one allows so little that is original to the mind itself, or places so little reliance on what there is. That a belief should be provided for in the mind's own constitution, and be inseparable from the very action of its faculties, is an idea which he resents like an affront; if it be so, it is a sheer tyranny of nature: there may be no help for it; he may be compelled to believe; but he will do it under protest, and declare that he has no ground for it, and would escape if he could.

"I am aware," he says, "that to ask for evidence of a proposition which we are supposed to believe instinctively, is to expose oneself to the charge of rejecting the authority of the human faculties; which of course no one can consistently do, since the human faculties are all which any one has to judge by; and inasmuch as the meaning of the word 'evidence' is supposed to be, something which when laid before the mind induces it to believe, to demand evidence when the belief is ensured by the mind's own laws is supposed to be appealing to the intellect against the intellect. But this, I apprehend, is a misunderstanding of the nature of evidence. By evidence is not meant any thing and every thing which produces belief. There are many things which generate belief besides evidence. A mere strong association of ideas often causes a belief so intense as to be unshakable by experience or argument. Evidence is not that which the mind does or must yield to, but that which it ought to yield to, namely, that, by yielding to which, its belief is kept conformable to fact. There is no appeal from the human faculties generally, but there is an appeal from one faculty to another; from the judging faculty, to those which take cognizance of fact, the faculties of sense and consciousness. To say that belief suffices for its own justification, is making opinion the test of opinion; it is denying the existence of any outward standard, the conformity of an opinion to which constitutes its truth. We call one mode of forming opinions right, and another wrong, because the one does, and the other does not, tend to make the opinion agree with fact — to make people believe what really is, and expect what really will be. Now a mere disposition to believe, even if supposed instinctive, is no guarantee for the truth of the thing believed. If, indeed, the belief ever amounted to an irresistible necessity, there would then be no *use* in appealing from it, because there would be no possibility of altering it. But even then the truth of the belief would not follow; it would only follow that mankind were under a permanent necessity of believing what might possibly not be true; just as they were under a temporary necessity (quite as irresistible while it lasts) of believing that the heavens moved and the earth stood still" (*Logic*, vol. ii. p. 94).

The case of supposed intuitive belief which is here in the author's contemplation is the so-called "principle of Causality," — the maxim that "every phenomenon must have a cause." Were we discussing this particular axiom, we should present it under another form, — "every phenomenon is a manifestation of power," in order to save it from being confounded with a very different, and by no means self-evident, proposition, — "every phenomenon has the same constant phenomenal antecedent:" and should protest against identifying the empirical expectation of "uniformity among natural successions" with the necessary belief in "Universal Causation." The first, involving a question of mere order among perceptible events, Mr. Mill is entitled to call "a fact in external nature," and to regard as waiting upon "evidence:" it is for the latter alone that axiomatic authority can justly be claimed. We have quoted the passage, however, with no view to this special instance, but solely to illustrate our author's treatment of "intuitive and necessary beliefs." We can thoroughly understand his reluctance to concede their *existence*, his precautions against installing mere prejudice and mental limitation into the honors of first principles, his scepticism of a pretension which has certainly been grossly abused. But when he says outright, that *a-priori* beliefs, really inherent in the mind, are totally unworthy of trust, however imperiously they may compel submission; and when he casts about for some appeal against them, — either from thought to "fact," or from faculty to faculty, — he seems to us to lose all his logical bearings, and forget the base which he had measured with so much care. What security can there be for *any* truth, — of "*fact*" or of thought, — *a posteriori* or *a priori*, — if the positive and primary affirmations of our mental nature may be suspected of making fools of us? The assumption of unveracity, once made, cannot arbitrarily stop with the province which Mr. Mill wishes to discredit. He himself also must, somewhere or other, come to an end of his "evidence" and "proof," and be landed on principles *not* derivative, but primary: and then he must either accept their coercion "because there is no *use* in appealing from it," or unconditionally rely on them as the report of truthful faculties; and in either case is on the same footing with his *a-priori* neighbor. Be the "proof" what it may which authenticates the belief, it is the faculty which, in the last resort, authenticates the proof. And whither, in the supposed cases of intuitive belief, does Mr. Mill contemplate carrying the appeal? He expresses this in two ways: (1) objectively; he would bring the belief to an "outward standard," to the test of "fact," "experience," "external nature:" (2) subjectively; he would remove the trial from one faculty to another, from the "judging" faculty to "sense and consciousness." But, as to the first, have we not been already taught that we know nothing external to ourselves? and even were it otherwise, the knowledge would have no other voucher than the instinctive apprehensions on which we are discouraged from relying. And as to the second statement, we have to ask, how are we to settle *which*, of a plurality of faculties, sits in the higher court? and by what title especially sense and consciousness are set in the chief seat, yet both of them debarred from "judging" any thing, and restricted to the reporting of our sensations and ideas as inward "facts"? If not qualified to "judge," how can they revise "judgments"? And if they are qualified, then their testimony must be accepted, with all that it carries in it, — the counter-realities of object and subject, and the very principle of causality inseparable from their discovery. By denying Perception as distinguished from Sensation, Mr. Mill himself incapacitates "sense" for bearing witness to any thing but the sensations within us: how then can he appeal to it for a verdict on a maxim claiming to be valid for the universe? He treats every thing external, — all body and all qualities, — as mentally feigned to serve as "unknown causes" of our sensations: but if the objective world is just an hypothesis invented to satisfy "the principle of causality," how can he appeal to it to pronounce sentence on that principle itself? He either disbelieves or believes this objective world. Does he disbelieve it, on the ground that all our knowledge is subjective? then his "outward standard" for testing the causal principle is non-existent. Does he believe it? then he does so on the strength of this causal principle itself, and, in accepting the hypothesis, grants the paramount necessity of "unknown causes" for known phenomena.

The dominance of Sensation in Psychology is naturally followed by the dominance of Induction in Logic.

Accordingly, our author's whole treatment of this subject carries out his crusade against "the a-priorities," and his thorough-going determination to hunt down all general propositions into elementary concrete facts. All his characteristic opinions respecting the process of reasoning are of the same type and tendency: that we draw inferences from particulars to particulars without passing through any generalization; that the deductive procedure has no cogency of proof, but is simply an interpretation of our notes of prior inductions; that the syllogism involves a *petitio principii;* that geometrical demonstration is only a carrying out of false physical measurements. These doctrines, though deriving fresh strength from Mr. Mill's powerful advocacy, are not new; and they are among the standing marks of what is called "the empirical philosophy." They depend for the most part on a peculiar view of abstraction, generalization, and naming, which would require us, were we to discuss it, to drag our readers into the innermost recesses of psychology. One remark only will we make in regard to our alleged inference from particulars to particulars, without use of any intermediate generalization. All advance to new truth implies the co-operation of two conditions: viz. certain objective data or facts, as material for the mental action; and a certain subjective mode of dealing with these data, — a law of the mind's action upon them. To the first we necessarily attend, and we consciously realize them, thinking distinctly both of the known thing from which we start, and of the previously unknown on which we are landed. But the other, being the mere form of our own life for the moment, takes effect of itself without asking leave of our self-consciousness: it is not reflected on, because it is itself our reflective act. All, therefore, that we need explicitly state to ourselves, and set forth as the "evidence," — or external inducement, — of a particular conclusion, is the particular datum which moved us to draw it: and for your belief that you are mortal you adduce sufficient reason when you say, — the people I have known and heard of have been mortal. But this would not act upon you as a reason at all, were it not a law of your mind to proceed, on sufficient hint from particular cases, to the idea of a *kind*, — in the present instance, *human kind*, — in which the same attribute inheres all through. It is only because you are an individual "*of a certain description*" (as Mr. Mill has it), — an example of the kind, — that you know yourself to be mortal. If, therefore, the latent condition of the process is to be laid bare, if the implicit principle of the reasoning is to be made explicit (and without this there is no psychological analysis at all), it is indispensable to state the general mental law in virtue of which particular data conduct us to a particular conclusion. That we do not make the universal proposition an object of thought and visible step to our inference (*e. g.* "all men are mortal," as proving that "we are mortal") is no justification of its expulsion from the logical analysis; the very object of which is, not to state the "evidence," but to go behind the evidence, in reasoning, — not to be content with the objective conditions of the process, but explicitly to give the subjective too. From a similar limitation of his view to the objective side of reasoning, and an oversight of Aristotle's distinction between what the mind has ἐν δυνάμει and what it has ἐν ἐνεργείᾳ, Mr. Mill has laid, as we think, an unreasonable stress on the charge of *petitio principii* against the syllogism. The Aristotelians at all events have an easy retort. If there is no deduction without *petitio principii*, there is no induction without concluding *a particulari ad universale:* and all our reasoning, of either kind, is in violation of logical rules. There is nothing in this paradox that will frighten us, when once we apprehend the true nature and limits of logical rules. It is evident that we could never make a step in reasoning, if we *only* reasoned; if we neither add any thing to our premises *ab extra*, nor draw any thing *ab intra*, that was not comprised in them before, no new thing ever can appear. So long as the mind itself is allowed to contribute nothing, out of its own modes of activity, to the enlargement or the evolution of the data, these data of themselves, objectively measured, will lie still for ever and yield nothing: and it is the mutual play of comprehension and extension, the metaphysical postulate of causation, and the idea of the unity of kinds, that put the dead materials in motion, and elicit a living advance.

If, in his aim to supplement Bentham, our author yielded to an idealistic impulse, he remained true, in what he retained from the great utilitarian, to the materialistic tendencies of the school. The inward side of ethics is made, in every aspect, dependent on the outward. Do we ask what determines the moral quality of actions? we are referred, not to their spring, but to their consequences. Do we inquire how we come by our moral sentiments? by contagion, we are told, of other people's approbation and disapprobation, not by any self-reflective judgments of our own. Do we seek for the adequate sources of a man's guilt or goodness? we are presented with an enumeration of the external conditions which made his character, like his health, just what it is. Instead of the self-formation, — the evolution from within towards an unrealized type of perfection, — we have man treated as a natural product, moulded by surrounding pressures on his sentient susceptibilities. There can be no doubt about the decisive preponderance of this latter view in our author's writings. Though he is willing for a moment to borrow a light from the subjective doctrine, and find something genial in its glow, he resolves it in the end into an illusory brilliancy, — the mirage of a mental atmosphere charged with earthly vapors and disturbed with accidental refractions. Though he recognizes the *fact* expressed by the words "Conscience," "Moral Rectitude," "Principle," and insists on its importance in human nature, he allows it only actual force (such as any superstition might win), not ethical authority; and, with James Mill, psychologically deduces it, with the aid of Hartley's law of transference, from the original datum of self-love. These apparent concessions constitute but the semblance of approximation between the two doctrines: it has never been about the *fact* of a moral consciousness that they differ, but about its *value;* and distrust of it is equally produced by its denial and by its disparagement. If it is nothing but a compendium of borrowed prejudices and interested preferences, all starting from egoistic pleasures, but by chemical combination wrought into a passion that forgets its birth, and now lords it over others with its "ipse-dixitism," it is idle to make a merit of acknowledging such a "spring of action" as this, and to imagine that, by doing so, human nature is presented in a more respectable light. Mr. Mill repeatedly protests against the common identification of the utilitarian scheme with the "selfish theory;" on the ground that the former, in determining the morality of actions, takes into account the consequent pleasures and pains to other people as well as to the agent. It certainly does so actually in Bentham's hands; and might do so legitimately under any philosophy which established an obligation other than prudential to consult for the happiness of others. This, however, is precisely what Bentham does not do: and for want of it, the unselfish superstructure of his system is simply imposed, without any logical cohesion, upon a completely selfish base. By speaking of pain and pleasure as if they were objective and impersonal quantities, carrying values irrespective of their individual appropriation, he slips into the delusive facility of treating the agent's happiness and that of others as interchangeable and homogeneous magnitudes in every problem. But in proving his first principle, — the exclusive governance of human life by pain and pleasure, — he rests entirely on the paramount value to each man of *his own* pleasures, and the impossibility that, without this element, life could be desirable to him at all. Nor was Bentham at all inclined, in his doctrine of human nature, at any time to think that the question of *meum* and *tuum* made no difference in the value of a pleasure. "Think not," he said, "that a man will so much as lift up his little finger on your behalf, unless he sees his advantage in it!" From his premises as they stand no rule of life can be consistently deduced, but the selfish one that the agent must be determined by a regard to his own happiness; including, of course, the portion of it that may be wrapped up with the happiness of other people. Bentham's own benevolence of disposition easily carried him over from this narrow rule to that of the greatest happiness of all persons concerned. But even his disciples have felt it to be one of the greatest *lacunæ* of his system, that no scientific proof identified the "happiness of all concerned," which was his rule, with the "happiness of the agent," which was his principle. It was only in so far as he was inconsequential that he emerged from the limits of the selfish system. The defect which he left has been carefully supplied in more recent developments of the doctrine, — especially by James Mill and Mr. Austin. The principle, however, resorted to for the purpose, involves and allows no departure from the selfish basis. It simply avails itself of association and interdependence, to extend the sphere of our personal happiness so as to include among its conditions the happiness of others. It justifies benevolence on the ground of self-love, — disinterestedness, as the ultimate fruit of interest. We are far from denying the importance of establishing the real harmony between the prudential and the social principles in our nature, or from doubting that a real advance towards this end is made good by the method so skilfully applied. But, after all, it leaves the "pleasure to one's self" as the actual spring, and the legitimating ground of every volition; it makes the claims of others' good contingent on its identification with our own; it recommends self-denial on the plea of self-indulgence: and thus never really crosses the boundary which separates interests from obligations, but simply pushing forward the lines of prudence till they enclose the whole ethical field, adopts the symbols and landmarks of duty, with an altered significance. We must honestly say, that this sort of recognition of others' happiness, as "cause of pleasure to ourselves," seems to us still to lie within the limits of the "selfish system:" by which we understand, the doctrine that the idea of pleasure to oneself is the mainspring that cannot, and need not, be absent from any act of the human will. And though this "theory of motives" appears in literature and life much more extensively than any systematic notions on morals, it has undeniably co-existed with the utilitarian doctrine in all the great representatives of the school. In the pages of Bentham and James Mill, the two theories advance, hand in hand, to the assault on "the ordinary morality." Why, then, if Professors Sedgwick and Whewell choose to attempt a joint repulse of them, should this be rebuked as either stupid or dishonorable championship?

There seems to be something irresistibly irritating to the utilitarian mind in the bare mention of an internal principle, known to us by self-consciousness, from which a moral theory may be developed. Paley cannot resist a quiet sneer at "the Moral Sense man." Bentham degrades him from the text into a foot-note; — will not have him in the same room, but puts the conceited fellow in the closet — and, baiting him there with a troop of jeers, makes even that too hot to hold him. James Mill considers him only less contemptible than Sir James Macintosh. And our author, impatient, it would seem, at having to spend pains on such a fool, scarcely listens to him enough to catch his thought and answer what he means. He more than once asserts, for instance, that "the contest between the morality which appeals to an external standard, and that which grounds itself on internal conviction, is the contest of progressive morality against stationary, — of reason and argument against the deification of mere opinion and habit" (vol. ii. p. 472). Why so? Why should the appeal to a common Conscience in mankind be more egoistic and anti-progressive than the appeal to a common Reason? Does an author, who has so distinguished himself in Logical psychology, and whose writings mark an era in its "progress," doubt that there is also a Moral psychology, equally exempt from a stationary doom? What matters it to the possibilities of development, whether the data for our ethical judgments are found within or without, — in a comparison of the springs, or a comparison of the results, of action? Take which system you will, you have, in fact, to carry your scrutiny into *both* spheres. Are you Utilitarian? in spite of your "external standard," you have to estimate "intention," "temptation," and other inward elements. Are you a Moral Consciousness man? the only thing settled for you within, is the relative authority of the several Springs of Action; and to get at the right act, out of several possible to the same spring, you must go out and look at its consequences, like a Benthamite. Of course, if there *are* no laws of Moral consciousness within us, and what we take for such are only picked-up opinions without common ground in our humanity, a morality appealing to them cannot make scientific advance: not, however, because they are internal, but because they are illusory. To explode error, on whichever side it lies, is certainly to secure progress. But Mr. Mill's proposition we understand to be, that on the *truth* of the one or the other of the two schemes it depends, whether morals are stationary or progressive. Such an assertion cannot appear just except to those who fancy the Moral Faculty to be, in the creed of its believers, a sort of oracular Pythoness seated in the mind, to pronounce categorically on every problem brought up for solution.

In spite, then, of the opposite tendencies co-existing in Mr. Mill's mind, his sympathy with the Subjective methods is not strong enough to secure a judicial insight into their real bearings. He is in the end so completely carried off by the objective school, that we doubt whether, if Comte's influence could have preceded that of the elder Mill, any introspective side, any psychological faith (at best rather shaky after its first enthusiasm is over), would have appeared at all. Had the two tendencies found their perfect balance and adjustment in himself, his occasional descriptions of them, as manifested in the history of philosophy, would have been unimpeachably correct. Yet, notwithstanding such outward resemblance to the truth as intellectual conscientiousness and adequate reading can secure, our author's historical illustrations, — when taken from ancient or from modern continental philosophy, — almost always affect us like a portrait in which the measurements and the features seem faithfully laid down, while the essential expression is missed. The friendly intimacy, the living communion of thought, is wanting between the artist and his subject, ere the picture can speak to you as true.. We can illustrate our meaning by only one example, selected simply because it broadly generalizes the relations between the metaphysical and empirical schools, and so enables us to dispense with much critical reference to the particular philosophers named.

"It has always been indistinctly felt that the doctrine of *a-priori* principles is one and the same doctrine, whether applied to the ὂν or the δέον — to the knowledge of truth or to that of duty; that it belongs to the same general tendency of thought, to extract from the mind itself, without any outward standard, principles and rules of morality, and to deem it possible to discover, by mere introspection into our minds, the laws of external nature. Both forms of this mode of thought attained a brilliant development in Descartes, the real founder of the modern anti-inductive school of philosophy. The Cartesian tradition was never lost, being kept alive by direct descent through Spinoza, Leibnitz, and Kant, to Schelling and Hegel; but the speculations of Bacon and Locke, and the progress of the experimental sciences, gave a long period of predominance to the philosophy of experience; and though many followed out that philosophy into its natural alliances, and acknowledged not only observation and experiment as rulers of the speculative world, but utility of the practical, others thought that it was scientifically possible to separate the two opinions, and professed themselves Baconians in the physical department, remaining Cartesians in the moral. It will probably be thought by posterity, to be the principal merit of the German metaphysicians of the last and present age, that they have proved the impossibility of resting on this middle ground of compromise; and have convinced all thinkers of any force, that if they adhere to the doctrine of *a-priori* principles of morals, they must follow Descartes and Hegel in ascribing the same character to the principles of physics" (vol. ii. p. 457).

Now we fully accept the statement here made, that, in all consistency, the metaphysical method either goes into both worlds, — what *is*, and what *ought to be*, — or keeps out of both. We further agree, that Descartes found a function for it in both, Locke in neither. But who the nameless philosophers are that, excluding it from the one, kept it in the other, we are quite unable to conjecture: and till we are better informed, we remain sceptical of their existence. Further, we cannot acknowledge that the metaphysicians in either field ever proposed "to discover the laws of nature" "by mere introspection into our own minds;" if by this is meant that they wished to dispense with "observation and experiment," and to set up as an "anti-inductive school." They always, and without exception, so far as we know, found room, within each of the two provinces, for *both* methods, — the *a-priori* and the *a-posteriori;* the one being deemed proper for the detection of entities, the other for the ascertainment of phenomena and their laws. When the phenomena were mental, the result was Empirical Psychology; when external, Empirical Physics. The two modes of procedure actually sit side by side, and receive some of their most characteristic developments in the "Ethica" of Spinoza; the psychological parts of which are as completely empirical as the researches of Hobbes, and full of direct and striking anticipations of the Mill doctrines themselves. We are not aware that any metaphysician, be he ever so "Coleridgian," can be named, who has supposed that the proper work of induction could be achieved by intuition. It was not until the "Baconians" came upon the stage and acquired ascendancy, that one of the procedures endeavored totally to expel the other, and unconditionally claim the whole field. The *a-priori* people never dreamt, in regard to their *a-posteriori* neighbors, of trying the writ of ejectment with which they now find themselves served. The only dispute between them was a *boundary* dispute, — *where* exactly, on the ascending slope, the perceptible laws of phenomena merged in the logical evolution of necessary being (such as space), on the descending. Haunted by the analogy of Geometry, in which sequences of pure thought seemed to open out relations and connections of real existence, the Cartesians undoubtedly pushed the *a-priori* claim beyond its just limits, and attempted conquests with it which it cannot make. And it is not unnatural that, in the exultation of victory over them, their opponents should meditate dispossessing them of every thing. As to the result, — if there be nothing but phenomena, these opponents will succeed: otherwise, we suppose, not. But that the result, whatever it be, will be sweeping, can be doubted by none. The "middle ground of compromise," by surrender of the natural and reservation of the moral field, is, we think, quite imaginary: and, with sincere deference to Mr. Mill's great authority, we doubt whether the position, Teutonically proved untenable to "all thinkers of any force," has ever been taken up by a single English writer, or attacked by a single German. Reid, Stewart, Hamilton, Whewell, all put limits on the resources of the *a-posteriori* method: and all carry the same rule of restriction into the natural as into the moral sphere; for the most part, amid mutual differences, leaving the same fundamental ideas in the field of exemption,—Space, Time, Substance, Cause, on the one hand; Personality, Moral Obligation, Preferential Freedom, on the other.

The characteristics on which we have ventured to dwell are more discernable in the occasional writings before us than in the author's systematic works. Nowhere, however, are they so conspicuous as broadly to challenge the eye: like all foundations, they hold what is above them in the light, but lie hid themselves. They have more to do, we believe, with Mr. Mill's marked influence upon his age, with both the fear and the admiration so strongly directed towards him, than his direct contributions to Logic and Political Economy. No writer, it is probable, was ever more read between the lines: his authoritative force of intellect, his perfect mastery of his materials, his singular neatness of exposition, marked him as a great power in the speculative world: but, as usual, the real interest felt was not less scientific than moral,—as to the direction in which that power would work. A certain air of suppression occasionally assumed by Mr. Mill himself, with hints for a revision of the existing narrow-minded morals, has increased this tendency. This suppressive air is the greatest fault we find in him; it is his only illegitimate instrument of power, for it weighs chiefly on the weak: and the shade which it passes across his face is sometimes so strong as almost to darken the philosopher into the mystagogue. Is the blame of this demeanor thrown on the tyranny of society? If that be all, tyranny is better broken in a land like ours by conscientious defiance than by ambiguous submission and argumentative complaint. It seems hardly becoming in an author who has attained the highest rank of influence in the intellectual councils of his time, to write as if there were something behind which, as a veracious thinker on human life and morals, he would like to say, but which, under the pitiable bigotry of society, must be reserved for an age that does not persecute its benefactors. Such a demeanor appears to us the counterpart, among speculative men, of dogmatic self-assurance among religious professors: and Pharisaism hurts the humanities and the humilities as much in the "*Wiser* than thou," as in the "*Holier* than thou." Nor is the effect of this manner better than its principle. Weak minds, as Mr. Mill observes of the theologians, are apt to begin wondering: and a manner so provocative of curiosity sets them thinking what these terrible secrets can be. Such questions are sure to find answerers; and among the busy-bodies and hangers-on of a school a certain cant of initiation arises which fosters every vice of the sectarian life. We have not Mr. Mill's positive faith in Discussion as an instrument for the determination of moral controversies. But still less have we faith in Reserve and supercilious avoidance.

In taking leave of our author, we repeat our grateful acknowledgment for most important light and aid from him over the whole middle ground of science which he has chiefly made his own. Thousands of students, beyond the circle of which he is the centre, are indebted to him for the power to think more closely and clearly, and the resolve to reach the ultimate ground of beliefs too lightly held. His writings are far more than the culminating expression of a particular school of thought: they are a permanent contribution to the intellectual training of the English mind. Could the haunting problems of Being be silenced, whilst we only listened to the flow and caught the rhythm of Phenomena; could we be content to hear it said that they are inaccessible to the human faculties, and not think in reply that nevertheless the human faculties may be not inaccessible to them, — no more effectual guidance need be demanded. But so long as the laws of "co-existence and succession" afford no refuge from the sense and need of a deeper beauty, right, and good, the most searching and exhaustive of scientific intellects will not persuade men to forego the hope of some higher philosophic genius to answer instead of dash their aspirations.

NATURE AND GOD.*

THE two brothers Humboldt, it is well known, applying each a fine genius to different pursuits, diverged in their convictions with regard to the supreme objects of thought and faith. William, in sympathy with the life of humanity, studious of its expression in language, in literature, in law, and in all the vicissitudes of civilization, never lost the traces of a Divine Government over the world, and even in the superstitions of mankind saw only a barbarous jargon attempting an eternal truth. Alexander, at home in the great Kosmos, fa-

* The present Relations of Science to Religion: a Sermon preached on Act Sunday, July 1, 1860, before the University of Oxford, during the Meeting of the British Association. By Rev. Frederick Temple, D.D., Head-Master of Rugby School. Oxford and London, 1860.

The Correlation of Physical Forces. By W. R. Grove, M.A., F.R.S. Second Edition. London, 1850.

The Mutual Relations of the Vital and Physical Forces. By Dr. Carpenter (Philosophical Transactions, 1850).

Principles of Human Physiology. By Dr. Carpenter. Fifth Edition, 1855.

The Order of Nature, considered in reference to the Claims of Revelation. By Rev. Baden Powell, M.A., F.R.S., &c. London, 1859.

The Intellectual Development of Europe, considered with reference to the Views of Mr. Darwin and others, that the Progression of Organisms is determined by Law. By Prof. Draper, M.D., of New York. Communicated to the Zoölogical Section of the British Association (Athenæum, July 14, 1860).

Glimpses of the Heaven that lies about us. By T. E. Poynting. London, 1860.

National Review, October, 1860.

miliar with the ways of Nature from her rude Titanic workshops to her finest harmonies of life, significantly declared himself to be of "the religion of all men of science." That his implication of "all men of science" in his own negative doctrine is far too sweeping, — not less so, indeed, than the Bishop of Oxford's counterpart assertion that "no men great in science favor Mr. Darwin's hypothesis," — is evident not only from the older examples of Newton, Boyle, Cuvier, and Davy, but from many of the newest representative names, Oersted, Herschel, Owen, Faraday. Still, there is ample evidence of a certain general tendency in Natural Science to foster habits of thought embarrassing to religious conviction. On a first view it certainly appears strange that the men most conversant with the Order of the visible universe should soonest suspect it empty of directing Mind; that they should lose their first faith on the very field where natural theology gleans its choicest instances of design: and on the other hand, that humanistic, moral, and historical studies, — which first open the terrible problems of suffering and guilt and contain all the reputed provocatives of denial and despair, — should confirm and enlarge, rather than disturb, the prepossessions of natural piety. The result, however, ceases to be paradoxical, on closer inspection of the relation between physical and moral knowledge.

The jealousy between natural science and religion is of very long standing. From the time of Anaxagoras onward, every attempt to explain by secondary causes phenomena previously unreduced has been regarded as an audacious wresting of some province from the gods.

And, on the other hand, as early at least as Epicurus, the investigators of nature began to tolerate the reference to Divine agency merely as a provisional necessity, to be superseded in each field as it was explored, and serving only as a decent disguise for our residuary ignorance. The dialogue of the *De Naturâ Deorum* exhibits, in the persons of Balbus and Velleius, the same rivalry between Theology and Physics which often animates the Section-rooms of the British Association. The antiquity of the controversy attests its deep-seated origin, in causes beyond the range of the Biblical records and the peculiarities of the Christian doctrine. The Scriptures, in the presence of the Baconian logic, have merely encountered the inevitable fate of any inflexible *litera scripta* existing side by side with ever-widening inductions. A consecrated theory of the phenomenal universe, embodying the perishable imaginations of one age or people, necessarily blends with every religion, however charged with essential and inspired truth; and, as necessarily, comes to be discredited as discovery extends, till it has to be discharged from its spiritual receptacle. The series of questions on which the conflict has been renewed in modern times between the closed "Word" and the opening Works of God is as long as the chain of inductive sciences themselves; and the result has been invariable, — the patience of nature overcoming the authoritative plea of miracle. Copernicus, in spite of the hierarchy, has cried with more effect than Joshua, "Sun, stand thou still!" Ships are daily chartered to those Antipodes which Lactantius declared to be impossible, and Augustine unscriptural, and Boniface of Metz, beyond the latitude of salvation. Witchcraft, so long preserved by the Mosaic Law among our list of crimes, has disappeared from every European code; and demoniacal possession in mania and epilepsy, though in the Gospels giving form to the miracles and evidence to the Messiahship of Christ, has been unable to hold its ground against the exorcism of the College of Physicians. The common parentage of the human race, already rendered distasteful by Prichard's suggested probability of a black Adam and Eve, has become an open question with the advance of ethnology, notwithstanding the absolute dependence upon it of the whole scheme of ecclesiastic theology. The tower of Babel faded into a myth, as the affinity of languages was better understood. Egypt, so long measured by the patriarchal chronology, and cowed by the song of Moses and Miriam, has at last taken a strange revenge upon her fugitives, by discrediting their traditions, and exposing the proofs of her dynasties and arts beyond the verge of their Flood, nay, prior to their Eden. The terrestrial cosmogony of Genesis, in spite of all the clamps and holdfasts of a perverted exegesis, has long been knocked to pieces by the geologic hammer. And now it would seem doubtful whether, even with regard to the specific types of organized beings, the idea of sudden creation may not have to be altogether relinquished in favor of a principle of gradual modification.

One by one, these questions may be determined and pass away. And if this were all, a mere glance at the past results, without appealing to the supreme security of truth, ought to tranquillize all religious alarms: for who that has in him any intelligent image of our modern Kosmos would think it "for the glory of God" to have back again the little three-storied, or seven-storied structure, in which the Hebrew and early Christian imagination found room and time for every thing, earthly, devilish, and Divine? Every thing has turned out grander in the reality than in the preconception: the heavens that open to the eye of a Herschel, the geologic time whose measures direct the calculations of a Lyell, the chain of living existence whose links are in the mind of a Hooker, Agassiz, or Darwin, infinitely transcend the universe of Psalmist's song and Apocalyptic vision. However obstinate the battle may seem to be on each of these particular points, as it arises, the combatants again and again fight out a peace at last: — why, indeed, should the theologian object to find the scene of Divine Agency larger, older, more teeming with life, than he had thought? But all these collisions have a significance far deeper than the special topic of each occasion. They are signs of a more fundamental conflict, whose essence remains when they are set at rest; — of a real, ultimate, irreducible *difference*, easily mistaken for *contradiction*, between the whole scientific and the whole religious mode of approaching and viewing the external world.

Christianity, engaged in establishing immediate relations between Man and God, takes little notice of Nature; which might in fact be absent altogether without material injury to a scheme pervadingly *super*natural; and which was actually to vanish in order to the final realization of the Divine purpose for Humanity. The defining lines of the religion run, so to speak, overhead of Nature, and pass direct from spirit to Spirit: Given, the human consciousness of sinful need and the sigh for holy life; given also, the Divine response of forgiveness, rescue, and communion; and the essential idea is constituted. The circle of thought and feeling which it collects around it has only a negative relation to the outward Kosmos, and finds Nature rather in its way. Still, when compelled to look the visible world in the face and recognize it as the depository of some permanent meaning, Christianity, like all pure and spiritual Theism, can only regard the universe as the manifestation and abode of a Free Mind, like our own; embodying His personal thought in its adjustments, realizing His own ideal in its phenomena, just as we express our inner faculty and character through the natural language of an external life. In this view, we interpret Nature by Humanity; we find the key to her aspects in such purposes and affections as our own consciousness enables us to conceive; we look everywhere for physical signals of an ever-living Will; and decipher the universe as the autobiography of an Infinite Spirit, repeating itself in miniature within our Finite Spirit. The grandest natural agencies are thus but servitors of a grander than themselves: "the winds are His messengers; and flaming fire, His minister." Using Nature as his organ, He transcends it: the act in which he does so is the exercise of his own Free Volition, rendering determinate what was indeterminate before: it is thus the characteristic of such act to be *supernatural:* and Man, so far as he shares a like prerogative, occupies a like position; standing to that extent outside and above the realm of necessary law, and endowing with existence either side of an alternative possibility. At both ends therefore of the scheme of Kosmical order, are beings that go beyond it: all that is natural lies enclosed within the supernatural, and is the medium through which the Divine mind descends into expression and the Human ascends into interpreting recognition. The effect of this faith upon the study of objects and phenomena is obvious enough. They will be interesting, not on their own account, but as signs of the Thought which issues them: in quest of this, conjecture will turn inwards; and, taking counsel from the higher moral consciousness, will come back to them and see meanings and motives they do not contain. The observer will be in danger of converting the universe into the mere reflection of his own conscience and emotions; of overlooking its calm neutralities; of reading some special smile in its sunshine and judgment in its storms; or, when experience and culture have rendered these simple interpretations no longer possible, of following some more elaborate, but still premature, clue of design, and losing himself in a labyrinth of misconstrued relations. The disposition of the human soul to seek for its own prototype and start at its own shadow in the outward universe, is a solemn and significant fact. But it can no more do the work of natural knowledge, than the inspection of a foreign people's expressive looks and gestures can supersede the patient study of their language, — a language formed by the working of the same feelings and ideas, yet not intelligible through mere sympathy with these. At a moment when our thirteen inches of summer rain are episcopally explained, in diocese after diocese, as a punishment of some unspecified sin, and are about to be stopped by deprecation, we can scarcely wonder at the well-known contempt with which both Bacon and Spinoza have visited the applied doctrine of Final causes.

Science, on the other hand, brings to the scrutiny of Nature quite a different order of faculty and feeling. It lays aside, as intrusive, the inner moral consciousness with its postulates and beliefs; and enters the field under pure guidance of the Perceptive and Comparing powers. It might accomplish the whole of its avowed aim, with less embarrassed speed, if the mind could actually be reduced to an unmoral, impersonal mechanism of intellectual elaboration; transfusing nothing of itself into the universe, but logically working up, in crystalline arrangements of resemblance, co-existence and succession, the phenomena given from without. This *a priori* limitation of its instruments involves a corresponding limitation of its field; precluding it from the whole area of free causality, and enclosing it within the range of phenomena now determinate. For the same reason, the order of its advance through this field must be ever one and the same, — from sensible particulars to related groups, from minor to major laws, from classifications with a single base to others that take account of many. Beginning with the rudest raw materials of observation, — the πρότερον πρὸς ἡμᾶς, — it carries up the rules they yield into the next rank of things, taking on some refined addition to make the expression adequate to the case; and so on, till the formula which shaped itself at the bottom of nature finds its way upward to the top, and humanity itself, as a scientific object, seems to come out as a mere culminating development of the earliest and lowest term. The hierarchy of laws which Science constructs accomplishes the grand end, of enabling her to predict the course of nature. In part, they are direct rules of empirical and concrete succession, simply describing the order of bodies and their appearances, as in Plane Astronomy. In part, as in Physical Astronomy, they are rules combined out of the decomposed conditions of analyzed phenomena. In either case, the power of prediction is attained; and equally so, whether the rules present the *ipsissima vestigia* of nature, as we believe to be the case with Kepler's laws, or whether, by some device of reduction and substitution, they furnish mere equivalent elements, tantamount, in all their combinations, to the natural facts. The Ptolemaic foreknowledge of eclipses was manifestly due to artifices of this latter kind: and we incline, with Adam Smith, to refer even the Celestial Dynamics of Newton to the same head. Be this as it may, the mere ability to reason out future individual phenomena by strict deduction from some equation of abstract conditions impresses us with a sense of Fate: the logical cogency of the inferential steps is mistaken for a material nexus among the objective facts: and, when taken in conjunction with the uniformity revealed by inductive observation, fixes upon the scientific fancy that nightmare of Universal Necessity, beneath which every higher faith either is suppressed or cries out in agony. In a universe thus regarded there is no room for any thing but determinate phenomena: and the semblance of somewhat else in man is readily explained away, by simply throwing him in among natural objects, studying him exclusively from the outside, and disparaging the possibility or the validity of self-knowledge. Had he ever so free a causal power, *its* phenomena also, once summoned to exist, must be determinate, must vary with the scope and weight of his limiting conditions, must be no less open than any other facts to the statist's method of averages: so that you have only to shut the door on the inner consciousness, and restrict us to the gate where the facts come out, in order to lose witness of the supernatural in man, and draw him also within the meshes of inevitable Law.

The radical antithesis, then, between Religion and Science consists in this: — that the former, proceeding on the data of our Voluntary and Moral faculties, carries a supernatural interpretation through the universe, and sees in nature the expression of affections and will like our own; while the latter, proceeding on the data of our Perceptive and Generalizing faculties, discovers uniformities of phenomena, and accepts the conception of necessary law not only as the key to Nature, but as exhaustive and ultimate. Let the maxims which are self-evident to either of these sets of faculties be applied to the sphere of the other, and the effect can only be to discredit and dissipate the objects in that sphere. If every phenomenon is the momentary expression of free volition, — if the supernatural reigns everywhere and alone, then is nature an illusion, and the demarcation is erased between Primary causality and Secondary law. If, on the other hand, "we know nothing but phenomena," — if our cognitive endowments are exhausted upon "resemblances, co-existences, and successions, — then is the Order of nature our only reality, — its Causality, our dream; and of God, — who is not "a phenomenon," — we cannot rationally speak.

The most obvious way of escape from this dilemma is, to restrain the pretensions of each class of faculties within its own province, and protest against its ambition of universal empire. Let the moral and spiritual intimations, it is said, have their own authority and sustain their own beliefs; they need not be meddled with, so long as they stop at home and do not overrun the Kosmos with their theology. Let the observing and inductive tendency push on, — the mensurative and deductive calculus work out its results; — they can but give us new truth, so long as they deal only with finite things, and do not trespass upon the sphere of Personality and Infinitude. This is the tone prevailingly assumed both by liberal divines and by reverential or cautious men of science; and it suffices to establish an armistice between them which is at least an agreeable change upon open war. To this compromise Bacon habitually resorted: and quite in the sense of his philosophy it is found pervading the writings of the late lamented Baden Powell. To us, we confess, it is profoundly unsatisfactory: especially when the two separated provinces are treated, not as two independent and incommensurate kinds of knowledge or kinds of faith, but the one as knowledge, and the other as faith. Mr. Baden Powell intended, we are sure, to be not less loyal to his Christian Theism than he was to his Inductive philosophy. When, however, after volumes of proof that the universe discloses nothing but immutable law and material development, so orderly indeed as to bespeak Thought, but so inexorable as to be silent of Character, after treating the supernatural as intrinsically incognizable, and the moral and spiritual as entirely out of relation to the rational faculty, he briefly relegates us to "faith" for our grounds of religious conviction, we certainly feel that the door is rather rudely slammed in the face of our inquiry, and that we are turned out of the select society of the philosophers who know, to take our place with the plebs who believe. It is utterly destructive of the equipoise of authority between the two spheres, to characterize the one as "knowledge," which involves objective certainty, the other as "faith," which goes no further than subjective assurance. This it was which exposed Bacon to the false, but not unnatural, suspicion of Atheism: and the painful negative impression of unsolved problems, so generally left on Mr. Baden Powell's readers, is mainly due to the same crudeness of distinction. The truth is, he had effectually thought out the one side of the question which was congenial with his intellectual habits and pursuits, without gaining any corresponding command of the other: and his imagination, left alone with the astounding revelations of modern science, was not simply possessed but overpowered by the conception of all-comprehending and necessary laws. A more balanced reflection would at once have shown the futility of the distinction he wished to establish. If by "*faith*" he meant reliance on a principle as self-evident, *i.e.* recommended only by its psychological necessity; — if by "*knowledge*," distinguished from faith, he meant an acquired apprehension of truth on evidence other than its own; * then there is just as much "faith" concerned in Science as in Religion; and just as much "knowledge" in Religion as in Science. Not a step could Geometry, Arithmetic, Physics, advance without assumptions respecting Space, Time, external Substance, which are no less pure and absolute gifts of our pyschological constitution than the moral assurance of our responsibility. And in Ethics, the propositions — that it is wrong to punish an unconscious act, that extreme temptation mitigates guilt; — in Religion, that the hypocrite's prayer is unavailing, that to the pure in heart God is best revealed, — are *known* not less certainly than in Science the place of the North from the pointing of the needle, or the recent birth of an animal from the mother's milk.

Even apart from the inexact and unequal balance maintained by Mr. Baden Powell between the rival claims, a mere compromise founded on a division of territory is intrinsically impracticable. The *savant* cannot help advancing his lines of thought into human and moral relations and esteeming them amenable to him. The theologian cannot help applying his faith to the universe, for the supernatural is conceivable only in relation to the natural, and the transcendency of God involves the subordination of the world. And if a man be at once *savant* and theologian, how is he to manage the partition of his creed? One side of him denying all knowledge but of necessity and nature, the other

* We do not propose these as satisfactory definitions of "faith" and "knowledge:" but the terms, if treated as mutually-exclusive opposites, appear to admit of no others. And this is the case with which we have to deal.

believing only freedom and God, is he to take turn and turn about with the "Yes" and "No," and care nothing about their discord or their harmony? Whether as a logical invention or as a work of art, we cannot admire this composite figure, half *philosophe*, half saint; on the left of the mid-line, a Diderot, on the right, a Fenelon. No earnest mind can endure a life of double consciousness, or excuse it on the pedantic plea of different faculties. Many or few, their testimony must all converge on the unity of truth, and is falsely construed till it does so. If the report of "the moral and spiritual powers" be trustworthy, — if there lives an Eternal Will immanent in the universe and communing with ourselves, it is impossible to avoid the inquiry, in what relation this Primary and Voluntary Cause subsists to those Secondary Laws of phenomena which it is the business of Science to define. How are the seemingly contrary beliefs forced on us by our outward and by our inward apprehension to adjust themselves in reconciled co-existence?

Is there any middle term which can aid the mutual understanding between the Religious and the Scientific view of nature? — any fundamental thought common to both, or passing as an essential from the one to the other? We think there is, viz. the idea of *Force*. That this really is an intermediate conception, more than physical, less than theological, will probably be conceded on both sides. It is less than theological: for, in league with the epithet "material," it can quit the Theist, and take service with the Atheist. It is more than physical: for the term certainly goes beyond the meaning of the word "Law;" it expresses neither any observable phenomenon, nor any mere order of co-existence or succession among phenomena. To our objective Perception and Comparison nothing is given but movements or changes; to our Inductive Generalization, nothing but the sifting and grouping of these in space and time. Such mental aggregates or series of phenomena complete what we mean by a Law; but are only suggestive *signs* of a Force in itself imperceptible. As defined by Mr. Grove, the word denotes "that active principle inseparable from matter which induces its various changes" (p. 14). So well aware, indeed, are the more rigorous Inductive logicians (as Comte and Mill) of the hyperphysical character of this notion, that they would expel it as a trespasser on the Baconian domain; or, if it stays, strip it of its native significance, in order to reduce it to their service. Let any one, however, only imagine the sort of jargon into which, agreeably to this advice, our language of Dynamics would have to be translated; let him try to express the several intensities in terms of Time-succession, and he will need no other proof of the utter helplessness of physics without this hyperphysical idea. Mr. Grove most justly remarks: "The word 'Force,' and the idea it aims at expressing, might indeed be objected to by the purely physical philosopher as representing a subtle mental conception, and not a sensuous perception or phenomenon. To avoid its use, however, if open to no other objection, would be so far a departure from recognized views as to render language scarcely intelligible" (p. 12).

It is admitted, then, that we have here a physical postulate indispensable to the interpretation of nature, yet not physically known. Its objective reality is guaranteed, the suspicion of its being a "mental figment" is excluded, by the same security on which we hold the infinitude of Space and the impossible co-existence of different Times, viz. its subjective necessity as a condition for conceiving objects and phenomena at all:— a necessity, we must add, evident in the habitual language, not only of those who consciously acknowledge it, but equally of those who, like the Positivists, affect to believe in a *γένεσις* of things without a *δύναμις*. Being thus, at the same time, real in its existence, and ideal in its cognition, Force admits of being investigated both physically and metaphysically: and take it up in which aspect you will, the results are remarkable and concurrent.

The tendency of natural science in its earlier stages is to establish a plurality of "Forces." Each separate family of phenomena throws back its distinctive characteristics on the dynamic source to which they are referred: and Nature is conceived to have on stock as many powers as she has kinds of product to display. Thus it is that we fill out our list of mechanical, chemical, vital, mental forces. The only differences actually observed lie among the phenomena: but these are taken as exponents of corresponding differences in the causes behind. The very distinction and organization of the Sciences themselves proceed upon this principle: each science taking up from among the properties of matter some one type, and chasing it, as it were, through the universe, and writing out the history of its achievements. Latterly, however, especially since the application of a more refined research to the so-called "imponderable agents," the old lines of classification have been losing their mechanical straightness and sharpness, and the coloring of the several provinces has faded into softer contrast, tending to something more than harmony. The first effect of the prism, in the hands of Newton, was to destroy the simplicity of light, and to disengage it in idea from heat: the last effect, in the hands of Bunsen, has been, in the very act of giving extension and precision to the analysis, to twine together, in a web of wonderful relations, the luminiferous, the calorific, and the chemical rays. By the undulatory theory, the same calculus embraces the measurement of sound and of light. Galvanism, manipulated by Davy, became the most powerful of chemical agencies. And, by both direct and converse proofs, Oersted and Faraday have compelled electricity and magnetism to exchange effects. The several modifications of motion produced by all these agents carry in them mechanical momentum, and avail to overcome cohesion and gravitation. By combining such facts as these, Mr. Grove has shown, in his ingenious and striking Essay cited at the head of this Article, that all the forces comprised under the term "Physical" are so "correlated" as to be no sooner expended in one form than they re-appear in another, — in fact, to be convertible *inter se;* and therefore to be not many, but one, — a dynamic self-identity masked by transmigration. Not content with a dead pause at Mr. Grove's resting-place, Dr. Carpenter, in his communication to the Royal Society, has carried the argument to a higher point, and shown that the law extends to the Vital forces: and, in his *Human Physiology*, he conducts it to its climax in the Mental forces. The energy of volition communicates itself to the motory nerves; these again hand over the stimulus to the muscular fibre; by whose contraction, finally, some mechanical movement is produced: each step of the process being marked by a waste or consumption of the transmitting medium, but an undiminished propagation of the transmitted force. It is not within the scope of our present design critically to estimate this subtle speculation; but simply to record it as the last result of dynamic generalization. The conclusion is, that the plurality of forces is an illusion; that in reality, and behind the variegated veil of heterogeneous phenomena, there is but one force, the solitary fountain of the whole infinitude of change.

This position, however, immediately opens a further question. If we are to reduce our numerical variety of forces to one, *which* member of the series is to remain with us as the type of all? Where is the initial point of these migrations? How are we to know the *propria persona* of the power from its disguises? Shall we more rightly presume that the lowest term, — the mechanical, — passes upwards and re-appears in the form of mind? — or that the highest rather descends, divesting itself of prerogative qualities at each step, and appearing at last with quantitative identity alone? For answer to these questions we must turn from the physical to the metaphysical scrutiny of the main conception. We have seen that it is a hyperphysical idea, a postulate of Reason, applied to nature: and to find its essence and true type, we must disengage ourselves from its applications and detect its pure form in our intellectual constitution. Cast your eye, then, along the series enumerated by Grove and Carpenter, and ask yourself in which of these forms the dynamic idea originally necessitates itself. Is it that you have to supply it on seeing an external body change its place? or, on witnessing some chemical phenomenon, as an acid stain of red on a blue cloth? or, on noticing the needle quiver to the North? It will be admitted that, if we ourselves were purely passive, all these changes might cross our visual field with only the effect of a time-succession, — first, one movement or condition, then another: while, conversely, if, without any of these phenomena exhibiting themselves before us, we ourselves were in the active exercise of Volition more or less difficult, the idea of Force would be provided for. It follows that *Will* is the true type of the conception, identical with it as a primitive intuition; and that its lower forms are but an attenuated transcript of this, stripped, by artificial abstraction, of all that is superfluous for the exigencies of scientific classification. The habitual resort of philosophers to this, when they want an illustration of the dynamic idea, might convince them that it is *more than* an illustration, — that it is the sole and exhaustive case, of which the rest are but mutilated conceptual repetitions, and without which there would be no others. Dr. Carpenter, with his usual clearness in penetrating to the essential point, seizes at once on the "sense of effort" as the ground of all our causal thought, — as the "form of Force *which may be taken as the type of all the rest;*" declares that "our consciousness of force is really as direct as is that of our own mental states;" and admits that, "in this particular case, Force must be regarded as the direct expression or manifestation of that Mental state which we call Will." But he stops short, as it seems to us, of the true breadth and simplicity of his reduction, when he adds, — "In the phenomenon of voluntary movement, we can scarcely avoid seeing that Mind is *one* of the dynamical agencies which is capable of acting-on Matter; and that, like other such agencies, the mode of its manifestation is affected by the nature of the material *substratum* through which its influence is exerted." * If Force is known to us from within, if it is the name we give to self-conscious exercise of power, then that is just the whole of it known to us at all; — not "*one* particular case," leaving "other such agencies" to be learned in some different way; but the absolute dynamical conception itself, co-extensive with every actual and possible instance. Take away the "consciousness of force" in ourselves, and with the keenest vision we should see it nowhere in nature. Endow us with it; and we have still no more ability than before to *perceive* it as an object in the external world, observation giving us access only to phenomena as distributed in space and time. Nor, from knowing it within, do we acquire any logical right to *infer* it without, except in virtue of an axiom of Reason inseparably present in it, — that "all phenomena are the expression of Power," — the counterpart of that power which issues our own. This it is which constrains us to think causation behind nature, and under causation to think of Volition. "Other force" we have no sort of ground for believing, — or, except by artifices of abstraction, even power of conceiving. The dynamic

* Human Physiology, § 585.

idea is either this, or nothing: and the logical alternative assuredly is, that Nature is either a mere Time-march of phenomena, or an expression of Mind.

The physical and the metaphysical scrutiny of this indispensable scientific conception converge, then, upon one conclusion; — that all Force is of one type; and that type is Mind.

This resolution of all external causation into Divine Will at once deprives the several theories of kosmical creation or development of all religious significance. Not one of them has any resources to work-with that are other than Divine: you may try what you can do with this kind of force or with that: but you cannot escape beyond the closed cycle where each is convertible with Volition. To you it may not appear under its full aspect: for "Force" is precisely Will from which *we omit* all reference to the living thought: but its objective character is unaffected by this subjective default. We lament to see the question between a sudden and a gradual genesis of organic types discussed on both sides, — not indeed by the principals in the dispute but by secondary advocates, — too much as if it were a question between God and no-God. In not a few of the progressionists the weak illusion is unmistakable, that, with time enough, you may get every thing out of next-to-nothing. Grant us, — they seem to say, — any tiniest granule of power, so close upon zero that it is not worth begrudging; allow it some trifling tendency to infinitesimal increment; and we will show you how this little stock became the Kosmos, without ever taking a step worth thinking of, much less constituting a case for design. The argument is a mere appeal to an incompetency in the human imagination; in virtue of which magnitudes evading conception are treated as out of existence; and an aggregate of inappreciable increments is simultaneously equated, — in its cause to *nothing*, in its effect to *the whole of things*. You manifestly want the same Causality, whether concentrated on a moment, or distributed through incalculable ages: only, in drawing upon it, a logical theft is more easily committed piecemeal than wholesale. Surely it is a mean device for a philosopher, thus to crib causation by hairs-breadths, to put it out at compound interest through all time, and then disown the debt. And it is vain after all: — for dilute the intensity, and change the form, as you will, of the Power that has issued the Universe, it remains, except to your subjective illusion, nothing less than Infinite and nothing lower than Divine. And hence it is an equal error in the Theist to implicate his faith in resistance to the doctrine of progressive development, — be it in the formation of the solar system, in the consolidation of the earth's crust, or the origination of organic species. That doctrine would be atheistic only if the first germ on the one hand, and the evolution on the other, were root and branch undivine, — some blind material force that could set itself up in rivalry to God's. Inasmuch, however, as all forces are convertible, and that, too, not by culmination into Volition but by reduction from Volition, they are but His mask and can never be His competitors: and if ever they seem less than Will, it is only by a self-abnegation which is itself one of the highest acts of Will. Why, but for the fallacious suspicion to which we refer, should you object to recognize a law of progression in nature any more than in human history? You think it Providential that *Man* should be conducted from low beginnings, through the struggles of a various experience, to a civilized existence beyond the dreams of an early world. You follow, not without a solemn piety, the steps of a Lessing or a Bunsen tracing the Education of our race. From the painful impression left upon you by the long and wide spectacle of savage life, by the meanness of a thousand superstitions, by the cruelties and flagitiousness which darken even the most brilliant and sacred eras, you fly for relief to the thought, that these are but transitory stages on the way to better things; — that they do not in themselves give the true idea of the world; — that they must be viewed in connection with the ulterior destination on which all the lines of the past converge. You even argue that, were there nothing of this movement in advance, — were every thing human stationary as Chinese society or periodic as the Stoic's universe, — all would look too much like Fate: it is not in a perpetual noon, but only in a brightening dawn, that Divine hope rises in the heart. Why, then, if it be reverential to think thus of man, should it be atheistic to think the same of nature? What is kosmical development but the counterpart of human progression? Without an ever-living movement of idea, how can we conceive of an Eternal Mind at all? And if there be a Divine plan through all, how is its law to be read off and its drift deciphered, but, as every infinite series is found, by legibly exposing some adequate segment of its terms, and spreading its steps along the ages? We pronounce at present no opinion on the scientific question to which Mr. Darwin's book has recently imparted a fresh interest. Looking at the speculation with rather a logician's than a naturalist's eye, we confess that our prevailing impression, at a little distance from the fascinations of the author's skill, is of the extreme exility of the evidence compared with the immensity of the conclusion. Should, however, the doctrine of Natural Selection become as well-established as that of successive geologic deposition, we venture to predict that works on Natural Theology will not only survive this new shock to the idea of creative paroxysms, but will turn it to account as a fertile source of theistic evidence and illustration. It is matter for regret and surprise that Mr. Darwin himself should have set forth his hypothesis as excluding the action of a higher intelligence:

> "Nothing" (he says) "at first can appear more difficult to believe than that the more complex organs and instincts should have been perfected, *not* by means superior to, though analogous with, human reason, *but* by the accumulation of innumerable slight variations, each good for the individual possessor" (p. 459).

Surely the antithesis could not be more false, were we to speak of some patterned damask as made, *not* by the weaver, *but* by the loom; or of any methodized product as arising *not* from its primary *but* from its secondary source. All the determining conditions of species, — viz. (1) the possible range of variation, (2) its hereditary preservation, (3) the extrusion of inferior rivals, — must be conceived as already contained in the constituted laws of organic life; in and through which, just as well as by unmediated starts, "Reason superior to the human" may evolve the ultimate results. In a perfectly analogous case the products of human industry distribute themselves over the earth according to the laws of Political Economy, all springing from the spontaneous pressure of human desires: yet who would think it a just antithesis to say, that the ebb and flow of wealth and arts are due, *not* to any Providence of God, *but* to the hunger of mankind?

At the same time, though Primary and Secondary causation do not exclude each other, we own the difficulty of clearly adjusting their relation in our thought: nor can we pretend that it is abated by resolving all power into Will. In the supernatural sphere, indeed, — the communion of Spirit with Spirit, — the Divine with the Human, — this Personal conception of power meets every exigency; because here the relation all depends on the free play of affection and character. But the governance of *Nature* by Personal Volition is less easy to conceive, the more we are impressed by the inflexibility, the neutrality, the universal sweep of her great laws. For mere manageable clearness, if that were all, some credit might be given to the old Deistical representation, of God as once contriving the universe, and then stocking it with properties and powers which dispensed with his further agency. Unfortunately, these properties and powers once installed in the kosmical executive, are too apt, like mayors of the palace, to set up for themselves: and the more all definite idea of a creative epoch, marked by sudden birth of the heavens and the earth, breaks up and distributes itself, the less has this theory to hold it together, and the more urgent becomes the cry for an immanent and living God. The religion of the present age, in all its newer and more vigorous manifestations, represents this cry. Re-acting against the usurpations of secondary causation, wearied of its distance from the Fountain-head, it flings itself back with pathetic repentance into the arms of the Primary Infinitude, and tries to feel even the iron clasp of nature as the immediate embrace of God. It is a pure and high impulse: yet, when tranquil enough to go in search of its philosophical ground, it must become conscious of dangers and self-variance on this side too. It is impossible to resolve all natural causation into direct Will without raising questions (we say it plainly, but with reverence) of the Divine psychology. You say, He personally issues all the changes in the universe. Is there, then, a volition for each phenomenon? and if so, what constitutes a single phenomenon? — each drop of rain, for instance, or, the whole shower? or, the wider atmospheric tide which includes the other term of the broken equilibrium? or, the system of aerial currents that enwrap the earth, and of which this is as much an element as the rain-drop of the shower? or, the tissue of conditions, without which such currents would not be what they are, — including, at a stroke, the constitution of water and of air, the laws of caloric, the distribution of land and sea, the terrestrial rotation, the inclined equator, the solar light and heat? Where, in this mighty web of relations, are we to fix, and how to insulate, the *unit of volition?* Driven, by the infinite multiplicity of phenomena, to recognize in some form the occurrence of *generic* volition, you encounter the ulterior question, what, then, constitutes *the principle* of grouping for each genus, whereby what is manifold towards us is *one* from Him? Are the objects of his determining Thought concrete things and integral beings, individuals or kinds, such as Natural History deals with in its classifications? Or, are they rather those functions or properties into which we analyze bodies, — which run together to constitute an individual, and separate to traverse a host; — so that he thinks in the order of Science, with a volition for each Law, — now gravitation and all that it carries, — then, Electricity throughout its sweep? Lay out the conception which way you will, the two divisions cross each other. In the contemplative religion of many a cultivated man, they doubtless come, the one or the other, as may turn uppermost, with no sense of inconsistency. But down in subtler depths the perplexing mystery has been felt, ever since Plato's εἴδη, after vainly grappling with it, left it to the consciousness of the world.

Mr. Poynting, in his *Glimpses of the Heaven that lies around us*, assumes the *Scientific* order of Divine volition; supposes the Kosmos to be thought-out, Law by Law, in the track of Newton's, Dalton's, Oken's, Faraday's generalizations; and feels every shadow gone in the simple recognition of God as personally executing the whole scheme. His book is not less picturesque in exposition and ingenious in combination than it is bright and joyous in tone; and to young readers, able to adapt themselves to its somewhat fantastic form, it gives a valuable *coup-d'œil* of the newer methods of scientific thought, though perhaps with too little discrimination of positive results from speculative interpretation. For our fastidious gravity, we must confess, the visionary and supernatural dress of the first part of the work, — in which the author, escaped from the body, has the world explained to him by a celestial lecturer, — is more a burden than a help. But doubtless we are heavy of wing: and in compassion to such infirmity, the author, in a second part of the volume, re-appears in the flesh, and takes his stand upon the level earth again, and gives a prose version of the "Divina Commedia" that precedes. From this part we gather the theory that God's supreme end is the revelation and spiritual reproduction of Himself in humanity; that history, Scripture, nature, are constituted throughout to serve as the school and discipline of our race; that the lower ranks of organized beings are sent forth as prefigurements, in advancing series, of man; that the several orders of force, — mechanical, chemical, vital, mental, — by which nature is built up, are developed modes of atomic attraction and repulsion; which again are resolvable, atoms and all, into a direct exercise of Divine power in lines converging on given points of space. An atom is a geometrical centre on which God directs force in all radii, thus constituting an attraction thither. Did the radii mutually impinge with perfect precision, they would give a statical resultant: but arriving with slight inaccuracy, they form an eddy round the centre, and so surround it with a zone of repulsion. Two atoms unite, when, through rotation in opposite directions, their osculating surfaces are moving in the same; while under reverse conditions they retreat. An atom quivering makes its lines of gravitating force quiver too; and hence the phenomena of light and sound, and whatever else is reducible to undulation. By changes, often ingeniously rung, upon these elementary assumptions, the atoms are made to climb into their place and build the world and its organisms; and the lines to vibrate in such mode and degree as to furnish law after law in every science from physics to physiology. The hypothesis, in its resolution of matter into force, bears an essential resemblance to Boscovich's; and, as might be expected, breaks down at the same point, — the attempt to step, with only quantitative help, to the qualitative phenomena of nature. All the optical history, for instance, of a sunbeam is elaborately deduced: and the physiological changes along the visual nerve are also set forth: and both series of propagated movements are regarded as wonderful provision for enabling us to see. But when the question is asked, how it is that one vibration of atoms gives the sensation of heat, another that of light, a third that of sound, the only answer is, such is the will of God, who, "as soon as the quivering beats on eye or spirit," "raises in the mind the idea of light," or of heat, &c., as it may be. Were it not, then, for this interposed special volition, the visual idea would not arise, and trains of vibratory processes would be as inoperative on the eye as they are upon the ear. There is thus no more fitness in one of the mechanisms than in another, or in any than in none at all, to produce its appended perception: for this flows from a Divine act which might just as well interchange the antecedents or dispense with them entirely. And when we further remember that all the prior movements are also described as God's own volitional force, we seem to lose ourselves in a gratuitous circuit, in which He devises and works his own complex machinery for providing his own occasions for interposing his own volitions. We are reminded irresistibly of Malebranche: who, in the chain of material causes and effects, saw a scheme of nature offered to the apprehension of Minds; and, in the constituted faculties of minds, beheld a provision for the cognition of Nature; yet sunk an impassable chasm between them, and made intercommunication impossible, except by miracles, *mero arbitrio,* that superseded both. With Malebranche, however, the direct Divine act was limited to the intermediation between Mind and Matter, each of which could operate in its own sphere though not cross over to the other. But Mr. Poynting's spinning machinery of atoms is the immediate activity of God: the whole mental life of man, and the ordinary exercise of his faculties, are so too; not less than the intercourse between the one and the other. When the objectivity of Nature, and the subjectivity of Man, and the whole scheme of relations uniting them, are all thrown into the Infinite together, all distinctions of being disappear, all problems vanish, and complex tissues of adaptation seem to lose all serious meaning and take the aspect of an empty play of thought, evoking conditions in order to meet them. For our own part, we confess to a very sceptical appreciation of the whole atomic doctrine, so unfortunately mixed up by Dalton with the law of definite proportions: and cannot help regarding the idea expressed by the word "atom" as a purely fictitious contrivance for escaping the contradictions of infinitude, an arbitrary stop in face of the perils of that wilderness, a logical thrust of the ostrich-head into the sand. And it may be due perhaps to this disrespectful estimate, that we find it painful to picture the Divine agency expending itself in rectilinear descents upon these centres, and in eddies round them, and quiverings from them, and a continuous evolution of nature from nothing else than such questionable rudiments. If such things really go on, we are not anxious to wrest them from the men of science and their "secondary laws," in order to claim them for the Primary.

But besides the questionable character of this atomic starting-point, and the incongruous mixture of necessary deduction and interpolated miracle, the exposition is open to the objection which attaches to every scheme of mere Divine self-evolution: it is, or in the mind of consequential thinkers it must become, Pantheistic. We use this word, not as a loose term of current reproach, — reproach often directed against precisely what is most pure and true in the religion of thoughtful men, — but rigorously, to mark the absence in a scheme of the universe of any thing or being properly objective to God: and this feature we cannot but regard as a fatal loss of philosophical equilibrium. Mr. Poynting anticipates this objection, and meets it thus:

"I have been told that some people will suspect the views of the universe here set forth of being Pantheistic. If there should be any such persons, let me beg them not to be frightened by their own spectral fancies. The views here given, instead of being Pantheistic, are the antidote for Pantheism.

Pantheism is the conception of the Universe as God. According to it, nature and human minds are all only parts of one Mysterious All, called God, but not thought of as a personal Being, as having thoughts and affections like the Christian God.

Now instead of saying that the Universe is God, I distinctly say that the Universe is only the *sign and effect* of God — his word, just as our words are signs and effects of our being. Instead of saying the mind of man is only a part of God, I distinctly say that the very explanation of our existence is, that God desires not to multiply *Himself*, but that He craves otherness — beings not Himself; but only like Himself, sympathizing with Him, — sons and heirs, not members of his own being.

The conception of God here presented is intensely unpantheistic, because it is intensely personal. God is thought of here as a being of love, goodness, thought; as, in fact, a Father. The whole doctrine of the book depends upon the soundness of our attributing to Him sympathies like those which we ourselves possess." (*Introduction*, p. xxi.)

This emphatic disclaimer is perfectly satisfactory, so far as the author's own faith, and the conscious aim of his teaching, are concerned. It is also true that, throughout his volume, the Personality of God, and his Transcendency beyond Nature, are never compromised; and that the ascription to Him of emotions and conceptions akin to ours is carried even to the verge on which reverence begins to tremble. But it is not enough that you save the Divine personality, if you sacrifice the Human; without relation to which lesser, as substantive moral object, the greater, left to shed affections only on its own phenomenal effects, cannot sustain itself alive. Our author's theory appears to us to make no adequate provision for the personality of Man, — to treat him merely as the highest natural product, the last organism prefigured by the imperfect approaches of other animals, and crowning the long line of homogeneous development. Mr. Poynting, indeed, himself believes, and *intends* to work out the belief, that God "craves *otherness*, beings not Himself:" and if this intention be successfully carried out, our scruple is groundless. How far the discrimination of man from God is adequately made, — how far it establishes them in real relations of Person to Person, — may be estimated by the following statements:

"How often had a poor doubting mind confessed to me, 'You say that God is in contact with us, and gives his Holy Spirit to those who ask Him. Yet I look back through all my life, and I am not aware of any inspiration, any revelation, any suggestion, that has not come, like all my thoughts and feelings, by my ordinary faculties and instincts. It seems to me that I have been left alone with my own mind, and God has not at all interfered in its workings.' *I now saw that what we call the ordinary working of the mind itself, the law of its faculties, the movement of its impulses, was the very flowing of the Holy Spirit*" (p. 75).

The same doubt is met with the same answer in the Second Part: where it is said:

"We have watched our minds, we have prayed and striven, but we have been able to detect no trace of any stirring in our spirits beyond the natural action of our faculties and instincts.

Let us, then, consider these ordinary impulses and faculties. When we feel the impulse of Benevolence, the love of the Beautiful, the love of Knowledge, when we feel the Sentiment of Conscience approving or disapproving, when we feel the Reason leading us on from step to step of truth we know not how, — whence do these impulses and movings come? what is their fountain? Do *we* invent these movements? Do *we* originate or direct them ourselves? No, the movements seem to come in upon us like streams of life from a source outside our Will. Now what is the *source* from which these streams or movements come? Is there an inexhaustible supply of such streams, powers, impulses, shut up in secret wells within us, and is there some mechanical contrivance for unlocking these wells at our need, and letting these streams flow in upon our consciousness? I reply, we know of no such wells; we cannot, indeed, imagine them. We have never had experience of any such contrivance. On the other hand, there is a Cause, a real known cause at hand all around us — God himself, the Eternal fountain of Life and Power — quite sufficient to account for the phenomena" (p. 365).

If every feeling which streams in upon me, and every facultative activity that goes out from me, is thus foreign to me and is the Personal agency of another Mind, what remains to be my own? Where am I? My subjective experience, my objective energies, all given away, the whole essence is gone, and I have no longer any pretension to rank as a Person. The only conceivable residue of humanity left, after the Holy Spirit has thus claimed its own, is an empty capacity for the reception and transmission of alien influences and emanations. Mr. Poynting accordingly speaks of the soul as "an organ, — God's great organ," — the music of which is from the breathing and inflowing of God's Holy Spirit (p. 310): — the very image employed, if we remember right, by Tertullian, in order to express the entire superseding of the human personality by Divine inspiration in the sacred writers. To say that we stand related to God, as the artfully-constructed instrument to the skilled hand that makes it speak, is to exclude the conditions of moral life, and make us His fabric rather than His sons. Perhaps our author would refer us to other passages, in which he seems to reserve *the Will* as man's peculium: as in this sentence:

"Every sensation, every thought, every feeling, every motion of every muscle, destroyed a fibril in the *voluntary, or man's part* of the frame; every motion of heart, every motion of the lungs, and each other organ connected with the preparation and circulation, destroyed a fibril in the *involuntary, or God's part* of the frame" (p. 158).

Will, however, cannot stand alone, to make *a person*, when every thing else has been alienated. It fails of the very conditions of its exercise, unless surrounded, within the same individuality, by the data, and aided by the light, of other faculties, forming with it the proper nature or constitution of the living *self*. To will, without affection to desire, and reason to compare, is impossible: the *style*, so to speak, of affection, and the style of reason, are just as personally characteristic, as the style of willing: and to banish the two former into the Divine Personality, while retaining only the third for the human, is at once to "confound the persons" and "divide the substance." In proof of the impersonal and alien nature of our Reason, Conscience, Benevolence, &c., our author appeals to their *involuntary* character, and asks whether "*we* originate and direct them." He may test the value of the argument by putting the same question respecting *God's* Reason, Benevolence, Holiness, &c. Are these products of His Will? Did He "originate" or "invent" them? And if not, are they foreign to Him? On the contrary, they are of His innermost essence; forming the spiritual background of pre-requisites to Volition; more than all else defining His real and ultimate Self, precisely because *not* effects of His Will, but beyond Him to create or to destroy. In short, if it is Will that goes to make personality, it must carry with it, not its products alone, but its indispensable conditions. And these are just the circle of impulses and faculties which our author forbids us to appropriate.

We think, then, that Mr. Poynting has not adequately guarded his doctrine on this side; and has left, in strictness, but one Person in the Universe. Let us add that, in this, he stands associated with a great and holy company, and with them yields only to the excess of a noble affection. It has ever been the tendency of intense and paramount devotion to take nothing to itself, and give every thing to God. Minds engaged in habitual contemplation of the Infinite seem to become conscious, not of littleness only, but of nothingness in the Finite: and the vain attempt to hold the two in co-existence ends in passionate casting of the Finite away. They pass by meditation into a certain speculative form of Christian self-abnegation; and feel, with Augustine, that, ethically, Humanity has no standing before God; with Malebranche, that, intellectually, it has no light but His; with Tauler, that, spiritually, its only strength is to pass, exposed and weak, into His hand; with Spinoza, that, substantively, it vanishes into a mode of His reality. Transiently, every religious man, it is probable, touches one or other of these dizzy verges of thought, where the spirit trembles between the supreme height and nothingness. And there are seasons in the history of every church and nation when, in re-action from a temper of false security and pragmatical self-assertion, it is well for the consciousness of a people to be snatched away, and planted for a while where it may look into the solemn space and feel the awful breath. But the permanent equilibrium of human thought is not there. The sense of Duty returns; the strife of Reason starts afresh; the toil of the Will resumes its tools; — and the latent assurance of personal faculty and of real freedom to use it, feeling its natural root, grows up into the light again; and pushes its green terrestrial margin ever further upon the overpowering expanse of Divine Necessity. Augustine converts the world: but Pelagius is its counsellor day by day. And we hold it indispensable to any tenable theory of Religion, that finite natures, and especially the human personality, should be secured in their real rights, and so interpreted as to remain, in some intelligible sense, objective to God.

This condition, it is evident, no theory can fulfil which represents God as evolving the universe "*out of Himself*." He is then both its substance and its phenomena; and it is in no way differenced from Him, except by His transcending it. A blunt way of avoiding this consequence was resorted to by the more Judaically-minded Fathers of the Church in their doctrine of "creation out of *Nothing;*" — a doctrine which, holding its ground so far as material or fabricated nature is concerned, yielded, at the higher stage of human and spiritual existence, to the Alexandrine notion of the extension of the Divine Logos: and thus made way for the distinction between a mere *creature* and a *son* of God. This blank "Nothing," — whatever philosophers may say against it, — was at least effectual for cutting off all obligations to antecedent material, whether within or without the Eternal substantive Being, and compelling the recognition of the world as something *other* than God. To this grand Hebrew distinction, a true instinct led the Church to cling through all the seductions of Gnosticism: and though the formula embodying it may give way, philosophical Theism cannot afford to surrender the distinction itself in any re-action towards Greek and German modes of thought. Our age professes itself weary of the old mechanical Deism, and cries out for the Immanent and Living God. It is well: but, even for Immanency itself, there must be something wherein to dwell; and for Life, something whereon to act. Mind, to think out its problems, — unless those problems are a dream, — cannot be monistic, — a mere subjective infinitude, — its tides and eddies all within. What resource, then, have we, when we seek for something objective to God? The first and simplest, in which accordingly philosophy has never failed to take refuge, is *Space*. Inconceivable by us except as coextensive and co-eternal with Him yet independent of Him, it lies ready, with all its contents of geometrical property, for the intuition of his Reason. And to Thought, which thus comes out of its eternity, and engages itself upon determinate relation, we cannot help ascribing the cognition of *Time*, with its attendant, *Number*. Thus, the circle of quantitative data is complete, and the ground of all mensurative and deductive intellect is there. Will this, then, suffice? Can we follow out the Kosmical problem to its end upon this track? The experiment has been too tempting for philosophers to resist; and again and again they have worked in this vein, and tried to exhibit the universe as a *deduction*, thought-out "*more geometrico*" from axioms of Eternal Reason; to dispense altogether with creative *volition*, as the source of order; and to connect even physical qualities and phenomena by a conceivable chain of logical necessity with the self-evidence at fountain-head. But though in these attempts the most has been made of quantitative methods and conceptions, — though, for instance, *Extension* has been set up as the essence of Body, in the same way as Thought is the essence of Mind, — it has proved impossible to avoid resort to other conceptions, — as Substance, Attribute, Cause. Still, with these purely metaphysical and *a-priori* ideas added to the mathematical, it was supposed possible for Reason to evolve the world by following out the steps of a demonstration. The Necessity of things was coincident with the Necessity of thought: the *nexus* of Nature's development was the nexus of logical sequence: cause and effect were identical with premiss and conclusion: creation of being was discovery of truth: and final causation was the attainment of a Q. E. D. To complete the organism of such a system has been the vain ambition of many a keen and spacious intellect: and in the Ethics of Spinoza and the Dialectic of Hegel the pretension has, in modern times, twice culminated and twice fallen. The principle of their failure is this:

they did not, — for, in truth, they could not, — keep their promise of borrowing nothing from experience and observation, and working every thing from ontological self-evidence. Physical postulates lurk in their metaphysical axioms: and however ready we may be to admit the *a-priori* necessity of such ideas as "Substance" and "Cause," and so far to let them stand on the same list of primary entities with "Space," — as Real yet not empirically Known, Ideal yet not mental fictions, — still there is this difference; — that they are intrinsically *relative* notions, each of them member of a pair, and that the other and correlative term — "Attribute" antithetive to Substance, "Effect" or "Phenomenon" to Cause — is simply physical and an indispensable condition of its companion. Under the cloak therefore of stately metaphysical axioms, as they march in plenipotentiary array, concealed entrance is given to material assumptions: and in the subsequent logical progress, it is just these inductive principles which cunningly slip out and lay the plank across many a chasm that were else impassable. Thus, the unsatisfactory results of these bold attempts, their inevitable slip out of their pure Monism, may well confirm our reasonable presumption, that nature cannot be treated as a geometrical or logical necessity; that, were God alone with the inner Laws of Thought and the outer data of Quantity, no universe need ever have been; and that to evolve the result intelligibly, we must go beyond the assumptions of the mathematics and metaphysics. In other words, there must be something else than Space objective to God.

Whether it is rationally conceivable that God should,

— so to speak, — *supply Himself* with objectivity, by a "creation out of nothing," — or whether, as Sir W. Hamilton contends, the conception is absurd and self-destructive, we need not pause to inquire. The idea is in any case discredited by modern science. It arose from an interpretation of the Mosaic cosmogony: it belongs to the doctrine of the six days and the sudden "beginning" of their work; and loses all support, even from the imagination, as soon as the creative process is deprived of starts and catastrophes, and construed into a slow perpetuity of change. An instantaneous summons of a Kosmos out of nothing seems to require as its product a world perfected at once, in simple answer to the call; as the idea is enounced, so must it be realized; and nothing could be more incongruous with the ecclesiastical notion of absolute origination than that, in response to the Creator's *fiat* there should appear, for instance, a red-hot earth, requiring millions of years before its human and historic purpose could even open. The measure of its ulterior progress inevitably becomes the measure of its earlier emergence. But if we must pronounce this conception superseded, there is only one resource left for completing the needful objectivity to God; viz. to admit, in some form, the coeval existence of matter, as the condition and medium of the Divine agency and manifestation. We freely allow that this is an assumption, resting on quite other grounds than those which support our belief respecting Space. But it is an hypothesis which neither religion nor philosophy, beyond the pantheistic circle, has been able to avoid; which, at one extreme, Hebraism admits in its Chaos;

and, at the other, Hellenism in the *ἄπειρον, ἀνάγκη, τὸ μὴ ὄν*, of Plato, and the *ὕλη* of Aristotle. Our mental constitution itself, indeed, seems to contain a provision for the belief: just as every phenomenon, necessitating the idea of Causation, carries us to God; so every attribute, necessitating the idea of Substance, refers us to Matter. And all the physical indications point unambiguously the same way. Stupendous as the chronometry is which the Geologist places at our command, its utmost stretch into the Past brings us apparently no nearer to a lonely God: nature is still there, with no signs of recency, but still in the midst of changes that have an immeasurable retrospect. May we not, then, fairly say that the burden of proof remains with those who affirm the absolute origination of matter at a certain or uncertain date? Failing the proof, we are left with the Divine Cause and the material Condition of all nature in eternal copresence and relation, as Supreme subject and rudimentary object.

This position, however, needs some obvious limitations. We do not mean, of course, to claim perpetual existence in the past for the particular material objects we see around us: or, for any of the kinds of beings now extant: or, even for all the *properties* which matter now exhibits: for, prior to the appearance of organization, for instance, the physiological qualities and actions were not assumed. Stripping off, as we retire backward, the more refined, as being the more recent, modes, and endeavoring to reach the simplest skeleton of the constitution of matter, we meet with a familiar distinction which may prevent us, in taking what logical necessity requires, from taking more than it requires. We refer to the distinction which the attacks of a purely sensational philosophy and the neglect of a purely deductive only tend to confirm between the Primary and the Secondary qualities of Body. The former are those which are inseparable from the very idea of Body, and may be evolved *a priori* from the consideration of it as solid Extension or Extended solidity. The latter are those which we could not thus evolve by reflection, but which, having no necessary implication with the definition of body, must be learned, like all contingent things, from experience. To the former class, for instance, belong Triple Dimension, Divisibility, Incompressibility; to the latter, Gravity, Softness or Hardness, Smell, Color, &c. As the former cannot absent themselves from Body, they have a reality coeval with it, and belong eternally to the material datum objective to God: and his mode of activity with regard to them must be similar to that which alone we can think of his directing upon the relations of Space, viz. not Volitional, to cause them, but Intellectual, to think them out. The Secondary qualities, on the other hand, having no logical tie to the Primary, but being appended to them as contingent facts, cannot be referred to any deductive thought, but remain over as products of pure Inventive Reason and Determining Will. This sphere of cognition, *a posteriori* to us, — where we cannot move a step alone but have submissively to wait upon experience, is precisely the realm of Divine originality: and we are most sequacious where He is most free. While on this Secondary field His Mind and ours are thus contrasted, they meet in resemblance again upon the Primary: for the evolutions of deductive Reason there is but one track possible to all intelligences; no *merum arbitrium* can interchange the false and true, or make more than one geometry, one scheme of pure Physics, for all worlds: and the Omnipotent Architect Himself, in realizing the Kosmical conception, in shaping the orbits out of immensity and determining seasons out of eternity, could but follow the laws of curvature, measure, and proportion. And so, in the region of the demonstrative sciences, to us the highest that mere intellect attains, where most we feel our thought triumphant and seem to look down on dominated nature, there is His Mind the least unconditioned, and there alone comes into experience of necessity.

There is, then, on the one side and the other of this boundary-line, a ground in Nature for the action of a purely Intellectual Divine power, evolving consequences by necessary laws of thought; and for the action of a purely Voluntary power, weaving in what is absolutely original, and executing the free suggestions of design. And there is a justification for both forms of religious philosophy; — that which attempts the "*a-priori* road," which detects Divine vestiges in the mysterious significance of Space and Eternity and Substance, or in the diagrams which suit alike the terrestrial and celestial mechanics, — which feels it a solemn thing that One and the same Reason pervades the universal Kosmos; — and that which, on the track of experience, recognizes marvellous combinations, and delights in the surprises of beauty and design. The only fault of either method lies in its self-exaggeration and intolerance of the other. When, however, we come close to the question, in what way the Volition of God applies itself to the objective material on which it works, the difficulty still recurs: does it move in the lines of nature's general laws and forces, so that each one of these has as it were a volition of itself: or, does it alight upon the concrete and living results in individualized, especially in conscious, and supremely in moral, beings? If we take the first side of the alternative, we throw the aims of God into the order of the Inductive analysis of nature, and seem to withdraw all realized things and persons from his contemplation: we engage him in weaving worlds and creatures to which, except as compounds of a thousand lines of skill, he is indifferent. If we take the second side, we relieve indeed this moral anxiety, but, in rendering each integral being the object of a distinct and unitary purpose, we throw out of intelligible gear the several laws which science shows to be confluent in that one nature, and seem, in claiming them also for the Will of God, to send the volitions in cross directions.

We do not deny that these conflicting modes of thought are hard to reduce into complete harmony; or into harmony at all without selecting one of them as of superior authority and entitled to exercise a regulative influence over the other. Were we never to look beyond physico-theology, we believe the controversy between the two would be perpetual; the naturalist, and every sympathizing observer of individual objects and kinds, being so prevailingly impressed with adaptations of organism and life as to see the final causes there; the student of the physical sciences, on the other hand, being so possessed with the conception of grand imperial laws that override all single integers of being, as to deem all concrete design subordinate or doubtful, and engage the Divine interest chiefly upon the method and tissue of the universal order. The indications of purpose which Paley finds in the fitness of the eye for its special use, Baden Powell rather sees in the symmetry and uniformity of the great optical laws, which still speak of Mind, though they sweep over tracts of time and space where vision cannot be. The scale must be turned and the verdict gained by appeal to the *Moral* sources of religion within us. Volition, in its very nature, is at the disposal of *Character:* and the character of God, — the order of affections in Him, — the ends that are highest in regard, — we learn, not from the tides, the strata, or the stars, but from the intimations of Conscience, and the distribution of authority in the hierarchy of our impulses. The perfection which is our ideal is but His real; the image of Him thrown upon the sensitive retina of the soul by his own essential light. The moment we refer to this interpreter, we know that if intellectual tastes are good, personal affections are better, and reverence for goodness the best of all: we can no longer dream that the sense of symmetry, the delight in beauty of thought or things, can have paramount disposal of the Divine Volition: we must recognize as supreme with Him the Love towards personal beings capable of sympathy with his nature, of trust in his direction and free aspiring to his likeness. If the moral order of the universe be the τελειότατον τέλος, the physical must stand to it in the relation of an instrument: general laws are for the sake of particular beings: and the order of nature, whatever other ends it may embrace, has primary reference to the personal agents on its scene, who, in the endowment of freedom, occupy a position above nature. Does this reduction of the scientific laws to a secondary place withdraw them from God and convert them into his deputies? Not in the least: they are secondary, not in nearness to his Person, but in rank within his Thought: and there is in this nothing to interfere with his execution of his own design, and letting his Will be the only Force. The volitional character of the several modes of natural power does not require that they be willed upon their own account, so that they carry in their aspect the features and movements of the Divine character. As the methods of his activity they variously traverse, in their classification, the grouping of his purposes. He is immanent in Nature: but his real life is known only beyond Nature. To believe the first alone of these clauses is Pagan, to believe the second alone is evangelical; Christian philosophy must blend them both.

There is, however, a limit beyond which we find it difficult to carry out, with satisfactory clearness of conception, the doctrine of God's *immediate* agency in nature. The secondary qualities of matter, the "physical forces" of the world, may readily be regarded as mere disguises or mere signs of Himself. But *living* beings can hardly be conceived as simply the *nidus* of power not their own, — the organism theirs, the function, not. We cannot follow Descartes in treating them as mere automata. Their whole distinctive significance lies in their being separate centres of at least incipient individuality; and to represent them as only media of a Divine incarnation is offensive alike to science and to religion. Here, then, it seems impossible to dispense with the idea of *delegated* power, detached by one remove from the universal source, and lent out for a term of life to work the conditions of a distinct existence. The instincts and spontaneities of animals constitute a true Divine guidance, adjusted as they are in accurate relation to their external position, and restrained within definite limits of possibility: but this very method and preconception imply an abstinence for the time being of direct and momentary volition, and a consignment of the whole phenomena, in group or system, to a determinate "nature" or "constitution." The difference is perhaps, after all, incident only to our point of view, and would disappear could we contemplate the world "under the form of eternity." We live down from moment to moment; we deliver forth our volitions one by one in linear detail; we have experience enabling us to interpret generic acts of Will inclusive of complexity of relations and a persistence in time: and cannot present to ourselves the Divine power running into fixed types, or trace the deep-rooted unity of these seeming islands in the sea of things with the continuous continent of the Infinite Will. Be it remembered too, that there are two kinds of union with God, — dynamic and moral; and that moral union requires dynamic separation; which accordingly widens as we ascend in the scale of being, till a true Self, — a free Personality, — appears, sufficiently beyond the verge of Nature to give an answering look to the very face of the Most High. At this culminating extreme we have a real trust of independence, — subjectivity perfected, — causality realized. At the other and initial extreme where the material datum lies, we have passive potentiality, — mere objectivity, causality not yet begun. Between this infranatural commencement and supernatural end, the Creative agency moves, to build and animate the mighty whole which we call Nature; at each advance receding from the bare receptivity of matter, and approaching, through the spontaneous vital energies, the actual individuality of personal existence. In this great cycle, Matter is the negative condition of Divine power; Force, its positive exercise; Life, its delegation under limits of necessity; Will, under concession of freedom. And if we may venture to speak of a yet higher stage which evades the reach of words, — that saintly posture of the soul which Scripture designates by the term Spirit, may we not say, it is the conscious return, by free identification, of every delegated power into harmony with its Source? And so, the dynamic removal finds its end in moral unity.

But these questions deepen and widen under our hand; and we must close them. We have endeavored to throw a line or two across the gulf which unhappily divides the *savans* from the theologians of our day. Whether any communication will pass along them we do not presume to say. But of this we are sure; — that the alienation they seek to remedy can be but transitory, having no foundation in the nature of things, arising only in the crossing lights and illusory darkness of human fancy. Inasmuch as Deductive Science represents the Order of God's intellect, Inductive Science the methods of his agency, Moral Science the purpose of his Will, the blending of their voices in one glorious hymn is as certain as the Oneness of his nature and the symmetry of his Universe: and it must be a very poor Science and a very poor Religion that delay by discord the approach of that great harmony.

SCIENCE, NESCIENCE, AND FAITH.*

If we intended to review either of these books, we should not name them both. Each of them has a scope too vast for the span of our critical measurement. The Reviewer's steps are short and few, and would soon be lost in Mr. Maurice's five centuries of Metaphysics; still more in following Mr. Spencer's genesis of the universe from chaos to the Crimean war. In the historical work, suffice it to say, the student will find a faithful guide to the deeper literature and life of modern Europe; copious in knowledge, catholic in judgment, genial in spirit; betrayed, perhaps, here and there into some waywardness and disproportion by an impatience of psychology, and a distrust of all "human notions" that have become systematic and exact; but essentially true to the genius of great representative writers even in the most opposite times. In the speculative book of *First Principles*, we have

* First Principles. By Herbert Spencer, Author of "Social Statics," "The Principles of Psychology," &c. London: Williams and Norgate. 1862.

Modern Philosophy; or, a Treatise on Moral and Metaphysical Philosophy from the Fourteenth Century to the French Revolution; with a Glimpse in to the Nineteenth Century. By the Rev. Frederick Denison Maurice, M.A. London: Griffin, Bohn, and Co. 1862.

National Review, Oct., 1862.

a kind of prose Lucretius; an attempt to show, both by inductive generalization from admitted laws, and by *a-priori* inference from the ideas of Matter and Force, how the Kosmos, natural and human, has evolved itself, and, on the assumption of a homogeneous nebular stuff to begin with, must have become what we find it to be. To those who are versed in scientific literature, the mere statement of the thesis will characterize the work. Enterprises of so bold a sweep recommend themselves only to minds that have unbounded confidence in logical architecture, and can venture, with a few well-shaped abstractions at the base, to build and arch to any height. They are uncongenial with the cautious temper of the practised observer: and differ in their vastness and vagueness from those special vaticinations in which, more by glance than by experiment, a Newton, an Oken, or a Goethe may decipher the style of nature. They are neither the perceptive readings of a genius intimate with the world, nor a *bonâ fide* generalization taking up into itself without fear or favor all the threads of ascertained order; but a framework of hypothesis, constructed from the metaphysical terms in which science is obliged to speak, and filled-in *ad libitum* with such picked phenomena from every field as may symmetrically fit. In such a scheme, the masses of fact presented, though occupying the main area, are of subordinate moment to the lines of thought: and Mr. Spencer himself, we are convinced, would have attained no trust in his Kosmogony, had he not, in the true spirit of a logical enthusiast, felt his footing sure on his *a-priori* ground. But for this, the enormous disproportion (oppressive enough even on Mr. Darwin's limited field — the mere "Origin of Species") between the weight of the conclusion and the tenuity of the induction must have overpowered him; and he must have doubted the use of dressing-up a few score of plausible appearances with a whole universe of phenomena out of the reckoning altogether. For our own part, we must confess that this new book of Genesis appears to us no more credible than the old. While its doctrine is too big for physical proof, it is of the wrong kind for metaphysical. We should as soon think of giving an *a-priori* receipt for a pudding, as for a solar system or a jelly-fish. If mere intellectual force could conquer an intrinsically unmanageable task, it would yield to the prowess of our author. With the resources of a scientific culture he unites a severe logical habit, an originality of combination, and a precision of expository method, to which no reader can be insensible; and which want nothing but a securer set of first principles to justify the somewhat positive tone of self-reliance characteristic of him, as of most system-building intellects.

Passing by, however, the substantive matter of both Mr. Maurice's history and Mr. Spencer's Kosmogony, we fix attention on a single fundamental problem, which has a pervading influence on both works, and receives from them contradictory answers. What is the highest legitimate object of Reason in man? Is he precluded from passing beyond the finite order of "co-existences and successions," which Science scrutinizes and defines? or, is he capable of apprehending the Infinite Cause behind, of which Religion speaks?

Mr. Maurice not only believes that knowledge of Divine Reality is possible, and is given, but looks upon the whole course of human history and thought as its witness and illustration. Mr. Spencer not only rejects as failures all attempts hitherto to cross the confines of phenomena, but undertakes to prove that the human mind has no organ for cognizance of the Supreme Cause: so that Religion resolves itself into the acknowledgment of an inscrutable background, in front of which all the luminous shapes of knowledge have their play. While the one writer sees in the working of devout wonder and the sense of an eternal living thought the mainspring of all intellectual search, the other deplores the darkening influence of sacred ideas upon the human understanding, and opposes Science to Religion as the known to the unknown — the perceptions of day-light to the dreams of night.

We have no doubt that Mr. Spencer represents, in this doctrine, the prevailing sentiment of living scientific men, and the tendency which for some time to come will gain force against all resistance. It is a necessary price which we must pay in re-establishing the distinction and just relation between the sphere of phenomena and that out of which phenomena come; between also the faculties in us which apprehend the one, and those which are organs for the other. We have not yet escaped a period, co-extensive with the history of Christianity, during which, from blindness to this distinction, religion has identified itself with interpretations of nature now known to be false; and it must suffer the re-action against a discredited prophet unable to make good his word. Compare the picture of the universe in the imagination of a Herschel, a Lyell, a Darwin, with the same scene as disposed in the thought of Isaiah, of Paul, of Chrysostom: look at the celestial architecture of the Apocalypse, and then at what the telescope reveals: think what is implied in the mere conception of a "Solar system," and the changed classification from "Heaven and Earth" to "Suns and Planets:" remember that with the disappearance of the supernal halls from the sky, and of the abyss with its infernal chains from the subterraneous strata, a host of inhabitants are dislodged, and fallen angels and imprisoned spirits and tormenting fiends lose themselves in the cold void: and can you wonder that, on the one hand, Augustine would hear nothing of antipodes, or Rome of the Copernican idea, or the Dean of York of the geological; or, on the other, that those who had dissolved the fictitious palace of the Most High should suppose they had discovered a mere darkness or a blank within? The modern redistribution of the kosmical bodies in space undeniably involves a total break-up of conceptions previously guaranteed by sacred authority. So, too, with regard to the origin of the universe in time. What has become of the date which many of us learned at school: "B.C. 4004, Creation of the world"? Limit the term "world" as you will, suppose it to say nothing but of this planet; still, with what amazement must we now look back on the practice of entering its birth in the annual register, like the battles and budgets and debates that make up a *Times* New-Year's Day retrospect! Into what magnitude has that "chief event of a year" opened before us! Walking through a geological museum, and estimating its intervals by what unit of time we please, we not only discover the "Creation of the world,"—like a Chancery suit,—to be "rather a process than an event," but are constrained to give it an asymptote for its measure, arriving at our own position from out of an indeterminate immensity. Instead of being the flash of a moment, or a week, from which the great periods of national vicissitude on the world may be sharply reckoned, it breaks into indefinite duration, and they shrink into a point. Yet they, too, have rebelled against the limits we had allowed them; and human history, while dwarfed by physical, asks, with every new discovery, for larger room and more numerous centuries in our imagination. After every allowance for uncertainty in the earliest vestiges of humanity, the concurrent evidence of Egyptian archæology, of the laws and affinities of language, of comparative religion, and of the stone implements, if not more positive remains of man, found in not the most recent deposits, must be held to imply an indefinitely more remote beginning and more gradual development of our race upon the earth than we had been taught to believe.

The alteration thus introduced into our modes of conception is the same throughout. Larger space, longer time, slower movement, finer gradation, than we had dreamed of, have everywhere to be admitted. Among objects, nothing isolated; in events, nothing sudden; a web of infinitely extended relations, in which *this* is part of the same mesh with *that;* a history of infinitely divisible changes, in which to-day is born of yesterday, and the shifting shadows glide and never leap; — these are the new aspects under which modern knowledge presents the system of the world. And though it still leaves vast *lacunæ* where, if you insist on it, you may find room for things unique and lonely, and starts of existence *per saltum;* yet, as these gaps are being steadily filled in, and look just like older chasms where similar fancies lie in ruin and now visibly grassed over, there arises an increasing presumption against exceptional crises of surprise. Hence, on the whole, we are passing over to the idea of evolution, rather than creation; of a creeping upwards, little by little, in place of a leap out of nothing; of the lower type of phenomenon preceding the higher, and the better coming out of the worse. Nor can any well-informed man seriously doubt that in this idea the order of genesis is more truly represented, than in that which it replaces.

What is the meaning, what especially the religious bearing, of this change? It is essentially an assertion of neglected rights on the part of *Nature;* — that sphere of unconscious *growth*, which has always been recognized as copresent with Man and God, the beings of conscious thought and power; but has not always received the attention due to an immeasurable empire and an everlasting law. Christianity in particular was, from its very essence, so absorbed with the immediate relation between Man and God, as to look upon the universe as the mere theatre of their alienation and re-union, — the visible *stage* of a moral drama, — the scene built up, above, below, for the solemn tragedy of human probation and Divine Justice, and reflecting in its lights and glooms the changing phases of the plot. It was but the tabernacle raised for the abode of spiritual beings, — the heavens "a tent" for the Eternal "to dwell in," — the earth a hospice for the Mortal to lodge in; sprung from the fiat of yesterday, dissolved by that of to-morrow, and meanwhile pliant alike to the steady purpose or the sudden occasions of the Almighty Will. However true and needful was this claim of transcendent reality for Moral relations and living Minds, it doubtless made too little of the kosmical system, usurped its rights and misconceived its ways; and scarcely left any adequate interest attaching to the patient scrutiny of its facts and laws. For such tranquil pursuits we need an absence of passionate problems and the presence of a durable world: and we cannot imagine in a Tertullian the researches of an Aristotle, or transfer to a Carlstadt the reasonings of a Galileo. At last, however, in re-action from the exclusive ascendancy of the Christian idea, Nature resumes her place — it may be, more than her place; shows her uniformities spreading everywhere through space and time; pushes her claims far up into the being of man himself; and requires us to think again what it is that irremovably belongs to God.

The answer to this question appears to us simple: Science discloses the Method of the world, but not its cause; Religion, its Cause, but not its method: and there is no conflict between them, except when either forgets its ignorance of what the other alone can know.

When, for instance, the old book of Genesis announces God as the Cause of all, it speaks the language of pure Religion, which cannot be traversed or met, except behind the field of mere phenomena. When it relates that it took six days to make the universe, and recounts what was done on each; how, first, Day and Night, then Heaven and Earth, then Land and Sea, were parted from each other; how, between the creation of vegetable and animal life, the greater and lesser lights were set aloft; how the water and the air were peopled before the solid ground, and man came last of all to rule the other tribes and live upon the fruits of the field; — in all this, it essays the language of Science, and is open to correction from every fresh reading of the order and method of the world. And so, when the modern book of Genesis wants years by the million for every day of that Creation-week; when it deals with spaces in which ten thousand of those "firmaments" would be lost; when it alters all the elements and transposes all the order, and distributes to be done for ever what had been gathered up to be despatched at once; when it substitutes a perpetuity of birth and death in things for an outburst of creative labor succeeded by eternal rest; — in all this, it also speaks what Science has a right to say, though it compels all the prophets to retract and apostles to sit still and learn. But if, on the strength of this right, it goes on to say, "these ways of nature are all in all, and behind them there is nought for man to apprehend," it usurps a function not its own, and affirms that which lies not less beyond its competency than was the Newtonian astronomy beyond that of the Hebrew kosmogonist. No discoveries of method touch the question of causation. Whether the way of procedure be *this* or be *that*, be such as we now think, or such as once was fancied, or such other as may hereafter be conceived, is indifferent to the background of Reality, which throws the procedure forth. As religion has no voice about the order of phenomena, conversely, the order of phenomena has nothing to say about religion: they sit perfectly clear of each other: nor is any delusion more absolute than the notion that the one can ever contradict the other. Causality, with which alone religion in this relation has to do, is not amenable to the same faculties that take cognizance of method,— those by which we perceive, compare, arrange: it cannot be heard, smelt, or seen: no lens can fetch it into view; no generalization reach further than its effects; no classification grasp more than its outward expressions. It is no object of sense; or of inference from any combination of the data of sense: and a merely observing, sifting, discriminating mind, however keen its perceptions, however delicate its feeling of resemblance and difference, could never come across it. It may—nay must—be thought: it may be named: but it is added on by the intellect to the experiences of perception; not drawn by the intellect out of them. It is by an inner necessity of Reason that we refer all phenomena, single or grouped, disposed into this picture or into that, scattered in negligence, or reduced by induction, to an originating Power: and precisely at this point it is, where Science has already come to an end, that Religion begins, and undertakes to speak of that which remains when the account of phenomena is closed.

Seeing, then, that the two spheres have no contact, or contact only at a point, it is not less futile to imagine atheistical encroachment from physical knowledge than to be afraid lest the tangent should cut a slice out of the circle. The more we discover, the more phenomena will there be crying out for their Cause. Is their field widened every way? so much the more august must his universal presence be. Is their succession immeasurably older? so much the sublimer what we conceive of his duration. Is their symmetry more exact and their cycle more determinable? so much the surer the order of his thought. Is the method of their issue, not by paroxysms of omnipotence, but by perpetual flow of power stealing to the roots of things? then does the Genesis cease to be historical, and we are at it ourselves; and may read it no longer in the preterite, but in the progressive tense; saying not that once he *did create*, but that now and always he *is creating* the heavens and the earth. If the Theist was ever right, according to the measure of his day, assuredly nothing has been found out to put him in the wrong. If the poor little universe that overarched the tents of Abram, and had been there only for a few generations, made its claim felt to be of origin Divine, it certainly has not forfeited that claim by prefixing to its age the reaches of geologic time, deepening around it the heaven of Newton, and suspending itself in the balances of Clairaut.

'But was the Theist ever right?' it may be asked. Granting that science makes his case no worse, and can never acquire a title to contradict him, still we may inquire what, intrinsically, *is* his case? What can we say, and on what warrant, respecting that invisible sphere of Power behind phenomena?

That *something* may be truly said about the Cause of things has been rarely questioned, since the New Academy ceased to parade its doctrine of universal nescience. Men have spoken in terms different enough: but, far from saying "we cannot tell," have variously affirmed, (1) Nature has a Divine Author; (2) Nature has no Divine Author; (3) Nature is Divine, and its own Author: and these several doctrines have been discussed upon common principles and on objective grounds, in perfect assurance that somehow or other the controversy was rationally terminable, and truth attainable. If there was any thing on which, in this matter, Theist, Atheist, Pantheist demonstrably agreed, it was surely this, — that the problem on which they all engaged was amenable to thought, and might be solved. Else, why plunge into it, and pronounce upon it? Without the assumption that knowledge is possible, the very attitude of quest is impossible. Yet Mr. Spencer, analyzing the doctrines of these three men, and discharging all their mutual discordances, finds them all concur in this, — that the object of their search is hopelessly out of reach, in a darkness beyond the limits of thought itself. It is a bold feat of eclecticism to sift out any common "soul of truth" at all from the two contradictory propositions of Theist and Atheist: but to make it consist in precisely what each, by its very existence, excludes, — to draw a declaration of nescience from two positive professions of knowledge, implies an almost Hegelian dexterity of logical cross-examination. We must say it seems to us a burlesque application of the questionable maxim, — every human belief has a "soul of truth," — to take up not only inconsistent opinions, but positions of which one must be true and the other false, and by pretending to dissolve their variances, precipitate the residuary "soul." The process cannot be soundly carried through. Between "Yes" and "No" there is nothing common. If you discharge their differences, one of them disappears. If you save any thing from both, the falsehood and contrariety are uneliminated still. You may choose, but cannot compromise, between them: and if there be a delusive show of some joint element, it can only be gained through sophistical manipulation of the propositions, inserting by implication what is required to be got out again by explication. We could allow something to our author's argument, if he turned it round and rested it on the real dissidence, instead of the pretended concord, of ontological beliefs; if, with Bossuet in his *Variations of Protestants*, he said, 'the truth is in none of you; for truth is one; and you are all at sixes and sevens, and have not a shred of unity to show.' But to bring into court three differing men, each sure that he knows, and tell them, 'the truth is in all of you; for you all mean to say, that you are quite in the dark,' is a strange combination of paradox and reproach.

The position which is thus curiously gathered from the critique of opposite opinions, — viz. that the Supreme Cause is incognizable, — is not left, however, without support from more direct and positive reasoning. On this we must say a few words. The hardy old-fashioned Atheist used to say outright, 'There is no God,' and forthwith to set his faculties and yours at work upon the problem, to get to the bottom of it.

Of late, — thanks to Sir W. Hamilton, — we have fallen upon a more refined and idealized form of the same doctrine, a purely subjective atheism, which leaves with the Divine Reality permission *to be*, but withdraws from us the power *to know;* and says, — 'Apprehensible by us there is no God.' The trial of the case is thus removed from the outer court of existence, where we seek the limits of real being, to the inner tribunal of psychology and logic, where we investigate the limits of human reason. There is certainly a modest look in thus apparently contracting the problem within a narrower circle and bringing it home to the familiar seat of our self-knowledge: and it has a sound of meekness to say, 'We pretend not to make our line the measure of things as they are; beyond its end there is the unfathomable still: only we find that it stops short of God; and if he be, it is in the abyss we cannot reach.' Yet we greatly doubt whether the seeming simplification is not sophistical, and the humility a self-deception. The limits of thought are not in effect easier to determine than the limits of being: and the battles once fought on the field of Metaphysics are renewed, one by one, and fought over again on the field of Logic: nor have Locke and Kant, with their critique of faculty, closed a single question previously opened by the contemplation of existence. The haunting old realities, Space, Substance, Essence, Cause, are not got rid of by stopping in our own chamber and refusing to go forth among them: they re-appear in their shadows on the floor and their reflections on the wall; and in the dress of *a-priori* thoughts awaken the same faith or scepticism which they had provoked on the field of necessary being. Suppose it, however, to be otherwise: suppose the cognitive limits accurately defined: suppose the line separating the possible light from the irremovable darkness incontrovertibly drawn. What then? in order to fall on the right side of the line, an object must comply with certain conditions: and conversely, before you exclude it, you must be able to deny those conditions. But how can you do this of an object quite unknown? by what right do you prejudge a hidden reality, and so give or refuse it predicates as to assign its place? Is it not plain that, in declaring it absolutely inscrutable, you assume it to be partially known? and that, like children in some blindfold game, you have taken a peep at it before letting it go into the dark and professing that you cannot see it at all? It is but the semblance of intellectual humility, which must thus presume a knowledge in order to disclaim it.

The doctrine of religious nescience has been rendered so familiar by Mr. Mansel, as to belong to the common stock of contemporary thought, and to make any full exposition of its grounds unnecessary. It assumes that God, if acknowledged at all, must be entitled to the epithets "Absolute" and "Infinite" on the one hand, and "Cause" on the other. Supposing this to be admitted, several contradictions arise between the parts of the admission; and some positions to which thought is incompetent altogether. To be "Absolute," for instance, means, to be out of all relations: to be "Cause" means, to stand related to an effect: and the same object cannot be both. Again, "Infinite" Being is unexclusive being, to which nothing can be added and no new predicate attached: "Causal" Being is transitive and productive, passing to conditions not occupied before, and adding to the stock of existence, or functions of existence, chargeable upon it. The epithets are therefore incompatible. Moreover, the very nature of Thought itself imprisons us within the circle of relative things: for it carries in it a necessary duality, and consists in marking off and distinguishing, — object from subject, body from space, attribute from substance, prior from posterior, and individuals, classes, and qualities *inter se*. Apart from a field or term of comparison, *any*-thing proposed for thought becomes *no*-thing, and only a vacancy remains: nor is the vacancy itself appreciable but by standing over against the self that looks into it. If then to think is, on the one hand, to note the confines of things, it can never pass beyond the finite: and if it is, on the other, to discriminate their contents and properties, it can never pass beyond the relative. The Absolute and Infinite cannot therefore present itself to the intellect at all.

So the warrant for the doctrine of religious nescience is simply this: that God is "absolute;" and we can know nothing but the relative.

Of one point, however, Mr. Spencer declares, we may be sure; and *that*, upon the highest guarantee, — the same *a-priori* necessity of thought which enforces the nescience itself, — viz. *that the Absolute exists* in reality, though denied to apprehension. For, were it otherwise, there could be no relative; relativity itself being in its term cognizable only by contrast with the non-relative, and forming a duality with it. Take away its antithetic term, and the relative, thrown into isolation, is set up as absolute, and disappears from thought. It is indispensable therefore to uphold the Absolute in existence, as condition of the relative sphere which constitutes our whole intellectual domain. Be it so: but, when saved on this plea, — to preserve the balance and interdependence of two *co*-relatives, — the "Absolute" is absolute no more; it is reduced to a term of relation: it loses therefore its exile from thought: its disqualification is cancelled: and the alleged nescience is discharged.

So, the same law of thought which warrants the existence, dissolves the inscrutableness, of the Absolute.

What, after all, then is the amount of this terrible nescience, victoriously established by such a flourish of double-edged abstractions? Let not the dazzled observer be alarmed: with all their swift dexterities, these metaphysical whifflers draw no blood: if they do more than beat the air, they cleave only ghostly foes that need no healing and are immortal. It all comes to this; that we cannot know God out of all relation, apart from his character, apart from his universe, apart from ourselves, — vacuum within, vacuum without, and no difference between them, but everywhere a sublime equivalence of being and of blank. Privation of this knowledge we suffer, not in our capacity of *ignorant* creatures, but in our capacity of *intellectual* beings; intelligence itself consisting in *not having* cognition of such sort: so that, if we had it, we should cease to understand, and pass out of the category of thinking natures altogether. If any one chooses to imagine that this would be a promotion, and to feel himself aggrieved by his exclusion from it, far be it from us to disturb so transcendent a grief: but from the common human level his dream of privilege is indistinguishable from the reality of loss, and his ambition of apotheosis seems tantamount to a longing for death. God other than "Absolute," God as *related* to nature, to humanity, — as embracing and quickening the finite world, as the Source of all order, beauty, good, — in every aspect which distinguishes the Living from the Existing God, — we are not by the hypothesis debarred from knowing. This is enough: and every step beyond this would be a step out of knowledge into ignorance, a lapse over the brink of reason into unreason. We protest against these relative apprehensions being left to us with an apology, and disparaged as "regulative knowledge," — a kind of pious frauds put upon our nature, — falsehoods which it is wholesome for us to believe. Their relativity is a ground of trust, and not of distrust; presenting precisely that union of the Real and the Phenomenal, Being and Genesis, the One and the Many, the divorce of which, in the interest of either, has falsified almost every philosophy. True, God so regarded, will not, in the rigorous metaphysical sense, be absolutely infinite. But we know no reason why he should be; and must leave it to the schoolmen who worship such abstractions to go into mourning at the discovery.

The doctrine of nescience is further defended by appeal to Spinoza's principle, that to predicate is to limit, — "Omnis determinatio est negatio." Whatever you affirm of any subject introduces a boundary into its nature, and shuts the door on a possibility previously open. How then, it is asked, can the Infinite be the object of thought? To think is mentally to predicate: to predicate is to limit: so that, under the process, the Infinite becomes finite: and to know it is to destroy it. If so, however, the Infinite can have no predicates, — none of the marks, that is, or characters of existence, and will be indistinguishable from non-being. To deny it to Thought, yet save it to existence, — as Mr. Spencer proposes, — is thus impossible. If it is an incognizable, it is also a nonentity. What is intrinsically out of thought is necessarily out of being.

Or will you look at the Infinite from the affirmative rather than the negative side; and instead of guarding it from what it must *not* be, consider what it must comprise and be? Then we shall give just the opposite account of it: ceasing to say that it can have *no* predicates, because no limits, we shall demand for it *all* predicates, because all phases and possibilities of being. To the Infinite, as unexclusive, every thing affirmative belongs; not only to be, therefore, but to be known; — to subsist within the sphere of intellect as well as in every other sphere. To claim it for Being, yet withdraw it from Thought, is thus again impossible. If it is an entity, it is not an incognizable. The Infinite which is real in existence is possible in cognition.

We cannot see, therefore, the slightest logical advantage in the new subjective atheism over its broader objective counterpart. The denial, for all minds, of any possible knowledge of God, is tantamount to the denial, for him, of real being. Not only do the two negations appear to us morally equivalent, with only a tinge perhaps of more reluctant dreariness in that which is at present in vogue; but they are inseparable without metaphysical contradiction. Mr. Spencer must, it strikes us, concede either more to ontology or less; either fall back on the maxim, "All we know is phenomena;" or go forward from his assurance *that* the Infinite Cause is to admit some possible apprehension of *what* it is. The law of thought which is his warrant for the simple *existence* does not stop there, but has something to say of the *nature* too: it is either good for nothing, or good for more than he accepts. Reserving this point for the present, we may exhibit the doctrine in still another light, before taking leave of its metaphysical aspects.

Every relative disability may be read two ways. A disqualification in the nature of thought for knowing x is, from the other side, a disqualification in the nature of x for being known. To say then that the First Cause is wholly removed from our apprehension is not simply a disclaimer of faculty on our part: it is a charge of inability against the First Cause too. The dictum about it is this: "It is a Being that may exist out of knowledge, but that is precluded from entering within the sphere of knowledge." We are told in one breath that this Being must be in every sense "perfect, complete, total—including in itself all power, and transcending all law" (p. 38); and in another that this perfect and omnipotent One is totally incapable of revealing any one of an infinite store of attributes. Need we point out the contradictions which this position involves? If you abide by it, you deny the Absolute and Infinite in the very act of affirming it; for, in debarring the First Cause from self-revelation, you impose a limit on its nature. And in the very act of declaring the First Cause incognizable, you do not permit it to remain unknown. For that only is unknown, of which you can neither affirm nor deny any predicate: here you deny the power of self-disclosure to the "Absolute:" of which therefore something is known; — viz. that nothing can be known!

It is matter indeed of natural wonder that men who, in standing before the First Cause, professedly feel themselves in face of the impenetrable abyss of *all* possibilities, should take on themselves to expel that *one* possibility, that the Supreme Reality should be capable of self-revelation. Among the indeterminate cases comprised in their inscrutable abyss they cannot help including this, — that the Mysterious Being *may* be Conscious Mind. Let them deny this, and their profession of impartial darkness becomes an empty affectation: they so far exchange their attitude of suspense for one of dogmatism. Let them admit it: and how, with the possibility of God, can they combine an impossibility of revelation? May it be that perchance all minds live in presence of the Supreme Mind, source of their own nature and of the nature that surrounds them, yet that he cannot communicate with them, and let them know the affinities between the human and the Divine? Is there a possibility of kindred, yet a necessity of nescience? Who is this Uncreated that can come forth into the field of existence and fill it all, yet by no crevice can find entrance into the field of thought? that can fling the universal order and beauty into light and space, yet not tell his idea to a single soul?—that can bid the universe into being, yet not say, "Lo! it is I"? So little credible do we find this combination, that, when we hear men insisting on the dumbness of the Everlasting Cause, we cannot imagine but that the religious interpretation of the world has already ceased to be open to them; and that, however they may assume, with Mr. Spencer, a neutral attitude towards the spiritual and the material conceptions of the Ultimate Reality, the controversy has in effect, though perhaps unconsciously, died out for them by prejudgment.

To assure me that some familiar conception is totally impossible, and goes dead against the "first law of thought," is the polite metaphysical way of saying "you are a fool;" and the frequency and *gusto* with which your men of formulas resort to this euphemism are highly amusing; and with the timid and self-distrustful win doubtless a temporary success. Nobody knew, till Hamilton and Mansel told him, that whenever he talked of things beginning or ending, of time, of space, of power, all his terms were "inconceivable," and all his propositions "contradictions." This was discouraging: and now Mr. Spencer steps in with a new opprobrium. He has discovered a set of *pseudo-ideas*, a species of mental impostors, that do somehow turn up in the mind, but have no proper business there, and must be cast out into limbo, or wherever else their settlement may be. They include, as might be anticipated, all the elements of ontological belief, usually referred to an *a-priori* source. They are charged with falsehood, for no other reason that we can discover than that, being symbolical transcripts of sensation, according to the exigencies of our author's psychology, they refuse to acknowledge their parentage, and put on quite independent airs. And they are distinguished from true ideas, — as generally the "inconceivable" from the "conceivable," in this, that they do not, like the latter, come before the *imaginative or representative faculty*. After assuming this test of "true and false," of "clear and obscure," of "thinkable and unthinkable," — and it is the test which Hobbes has bequeathed to his followers, — it is all plain-sailing out of the *a-priori* seas. If, among our mental stores, phenomenal perception, and what grows out of it, may alone be held valid as knowledge, the ideas of reason, with regard to real and ulterior being, are condemned without a hearing as ignorance. Repudiating these one-sided assumptions, we maintain the equal validity of our phenomenal and our ontological apprehensions.

That all consciousness and thought are relative, is not only true, but a truism. That this law visits us with disability to transcend phenomena is so little true, that it operates as a revelation of what exists beyond. The finite body cut out before our visual perception, or embraced by the hands, lies as an island in the emptiness around, and without comparative reference to this cannot be represented: the same experience which gives us the definite object, gives us also the infinite space: and both terms, — the limited appearance and the unlimited ground, — are apprehended with equal certitude and clearness, and furnished with names equally susceptible of distinct use in predication and reasoning. The transient successions, — for instance, the strokes of a clock, — which we count, present themselves to us as dotted out upon the line of permanent duration; of which, without them, we should have had no apprehension; but which, as their condition, is unreservedly known. Time with its one dimension, Space with its three, we are compelled to regard as infinite; not in the mere subjective sense, that our thought of them suffers no arrest; but in the objective sense, that they in themselves can have no beginning or end. In these two instances of relation, between a phenomenon given in perception, and an entity as its logical condition, the correlates are on a perfect parity of intellectual validity. You may disparage the underlying ground as "negative:" and negative it is so long as your attention only uses it to pitch on the phenomenon it carries: but this order is reversible at will: and the moment you change the focus of your thought and bring the containing field into your view, your representation of space is not less positive than that of body. Plus and minus are themselves relatives, and change places according to the starting-point and direction of your measurement. "The darkness," says Malebranche somewhere, "strikes upon our perceptions as well as the light: it effaces, no doubt, the glare of colors; but produces in its turn effects of its own." You may decry the ideas of the "infinite" and the "eternal" as not "clear:" and clear they are not, if nothing but the mental picture of an outline can deserve that word. But if a thought is clear, when it sits apart without danger of being confounded with another, when it can exactly keep its own in speech and reasoning, without forfeiture and without encroachment, — if, in short, logical clearness consists, not in the idea of a limit, but in the limit of the idea, — then no sharpest image of any finite quantity, — say, of a circle or an hour, — is clearer than the thought of the infinite and the eternal. Or, finally, will you perhaps admit these to their proper honors as mere *thoughts*, — positive thoughts, clear thoughts, — but deny to them the character of *knowledge?* This course is open to you on one condition; that you restrict the word "knowledge" to the discrimination of phenomena from one another, and refuse it to the discrimination of them from their ground; and say, for instance, "I know the moon to be different from the sun; but I do not know it to be different from the space in which it floats:" or, "I know Cæsar's life and date to be other than Seneca's; but I do not know either from the eternity in which it appears." Can any thing, however, be more arbitrary than such a definition? more repugnant to common sense and common language? nay, more self-destructive? for only as differenced from their common ground can things ever be known as differenced from one another: erase the primary differentiation, and all others are for ever kept out of existence. We have no guarantee for any except in the assumed veracity of our perceptive and logical faculties: and that guarantee we have alike for all. We conclude then, on reviewing these examples of Space and Time, that ontological ideas, introducing us to certain fixed entities, belong no less to our knowledge than scientific ideas of phenomenal disposition and succession. The two types of cognition are different in this: that the one gives to our apprehension the unchangeable constancies of the universe, — whatever is, not what will appear, — and so supplies no after-sight, no foresight, but simply insight: while the other gives us the order and the lines of change; and so enables us to reproduce the past in thought and anticipate the future. Both kinds of discernment have the same warrant: both are alike indispensable to the harmony of Reason with itself and with the world: neither can affect independence of the other: and the attempt to glorify exclusively the characteristics of either is a mere professional limitation of mind, whether in the priest of Nature or the priest of God. The charge of nescience, advanced on the plea of the relativity of knowledge, is double-edged, and cuts both ways. True it is that the Infinite, discharged of all relation to the Finite, could never come into apprehension; as, without body, we should not know the truth of space: and that, in the attempt to deal with it absolutely, thought, overleaping its own conditions, is baffled and perplexed. But it is no less true that the Finite, discharged of all relation to the Infinite, is incognizable too; as, without the comprehending space, bodies could not mark out for us their determinate figures and positions: and that, in spite of every vow to ignore all except phenomena, Science is obliged to resume into itself certain metaphysical elements, were it only as the vehicle of description for its own work. On either hand, these are unfruitful propositions. What is the use of telling me that an "Absolute" which came into no relation would be inapprehensible? It is only saying that an unmanifested Infinite could never be found out; that an everlasting silence would be totally inaudible. Vapid words, in a universe full of visions and of voices!

What we have said with regard to Space and Time applies equally to the case of Causation. Here, too, the Finite offered to perception introduces to an Infinite supplied by thought. As a definite body reveals also the Space around, and an interrupted succession exhibits the uniform Time beneath, so does the passing phenomenon demand for itself a Power behind: the Space and Time and Power not being part of the thing perceived, but its condition; guaranteed to us, therefore, on the warrant, not of Sense, but of Intellect. They are all on the same footing: we think them all by the same necessity: we know them all with the same certainty. Mr. Spencer freely allows that we are obliged to regard every phenomenon as the manifestation of some Power; that "we are obliged to regard that Power as Omnipresent" (p. 99); that "we are no more able to form a circumscribed idea of Cause than of Space or Time, and we are consequently obliged to think of the Cause which transcends our thought as positive though indefinite" (p. 93); that we have a right to trust this demand for originating power; and that on this reposes our indestructible belief in an ultimate Omnipotent Reality. Here already are several predicates assigned which hardly consist with the proclamation that the Primary Existence is wholly unknown: that Being, it seems we may say, is One, Eternal, Ubiquitous, Omnipotent, manifested as Cause in all phenomena. Is there not more explicitness here than could be expected from an entity absolutely latent? But this is not all. Our author further identifies the

First Cause with what appears in Science under the name of "Force," and is tracked through the metamorphoses of physical, chemical, vital, and other phenomena. The dynamic principles that we carry into our interpretation of nature, that Force is persistent through all expenditures, and one under every disguise, — are in truth but the transformed expression of the axiom of ultimate Causation. The primary and secondary agencies being thus merged into one, and conjointly made objects of *a-priori* apprehension, the next question naturally is, — what in the last resort means this word "Cause"? Pursued backward to its native seat, as a form of the intellect itself, what type does the thought present? Mr. Spencer truly says, "the force by which we ourselves produce changes, and which serves to symbolize the cause of changes in general, is the final disclosure of analysis" (p. 235): he admits that we cannot match our own voluntary effort against an external force, and regard them as susceptible of a common measure, without assuming them to be like in kind (pp. 58, 254): and as "no force save that of which we are conscious during our own muscular efforts is immediately known to us," while "all other force is mediately known," it is clearly the inner volition that serves as prototype of all exterior power, and defines what the intellect intends by the word Cause. Now combine these several propositions. One power we immediately know. That power is Will. Others, if assumed by us, must be assimilated to this. But behind every phenomenon we must assume a power. And all such powers are modes of one and the same. And that one is identical with the First Cause and

Ultimate Reality of Being. The inference is irresistible, that by a fundamental necessity of thought we are constrained to own an ever-living Will, a Personal Agent, as Author and Administrator of the universe. This is precisely what the Theist maintains; and includes all that he can gather from the bare contemplation of physical nature, apart from the moral experiences and the spiritual history of humanity. Collected from so limited a ground, the ground too least rich in phenomena of the highest expression, it is but a meagre and imperfect form of faith. But still it dissipates the theory of nescience. It vindicates some distinct apprehensions of the "Supreme Reality." And drawn as it is directly from the statements of an author who controverts it, it is a matter of some curiosity to see how he evades the apparent cogency of his own premises.

He forsakes the line of proof by a very simple device. The likeness between our own force and that which operates around us, though a necessity, is also, he conceives, an illusion of thought: and so we must give up our first natural belief that the universe is at the disposal of a Mind, the Divine counterpart of ours. There is no other conception open to us in our apprehension of outward causality: and yet this conception fails, and betrays us into absurdity. How so? Because it implies that the weight which I lift with my muscles must, in order to pull against me, be furnished with muscles too: and whatever teaches me that the objects about me are not alive destroys the assumed resemblance between the inner and the outer world. The case is thus stated:

"On lifting a chair, the force exerted we regard as equal to that antagonistic force called the weight of the chair; and we cannot think of these as equal without thinking of them as like in kind; since equality is conceivable only between things that are connatural. The axiom that action and re-action are equal and in opposite directions, commonly exemplified by this very instance of muscular effort *versus* weight, cannot be mentally realized on any other condition. Yet, contrariwise, it is incredible that the force as existing in the chair really resembles the force as present to our minds. It scarcely needs to point out that the weight of the chair produces in us various feelings according as we support it by a single finger, or the whole hand, or the leg; and hence to argue that as it cannot be like all these sensations, there is no reason to believe it like any. It suffices to remark that since the force as known to us is an affection of consciousness, we cannot conceive the force existing in the chair under the same form with endowing the chair with consciousness. So that it is absurd to think of Force as in itself like our sensation of it, and yet necessary so to think of it if we realize it in consciousness at all" (p. 58).

There would be something in this reasoning, if the muscles were the Personal Agent disposing of the chair, and their sensations the power he put forth. The causality, however, does not lie in them, but behind them; they are themselves obedient to a mandate from within; and their sensations, which occur only in the execution of the act, do not even begin till that mandate has given the signal. Were the muscles altogether insensible, the power at head-quarters would not on that account be disqualified for action, or be unconscious of itself. We may entirely discharge out of the account the whole of this merely ministerial apparatus, with all its supposable varieties. It is not this which even the simplest individual, — be it that small "child" so much dandled by the psychologists, or the everlasting "peasant" preferred by bachelor philosophers, or the "fetish-worshipper" in favor with Mr. Mill, — attributes to the external objects acting upon him: and his discovery that they do not possess it disabuses him of no previous idea. What he plants in idea behind the phenomena that strike him is similar, not to his muscles which obey, but to his Will which bids: and of *this* idea, though it has a history to go through in correspondence with his culture, no progress of reason, we feel assured, will ever disabuse him. At last, as at first, — because by a necessity of thought which runs through all experience, — he has to think of Causality as meaning Will, and to borrow all his dynamic language, — "attraction," "repulsion," "tension," "percussion," "active," "passive," "weak," "strong," "overcome," "resist," — from familiar instances and conditions of Will. If not, there must be some point and some process for unlearning his original postulate, and substituting some other idea of power. Yet this can never be. For, confessedly, it is beyond the competency of experience, however refined, to disclose any thing but *laws:* the mystery of *force* evades the penetration of the observer, and therefore has no presence among the materials of inductive generalization: Science did not give it, and Science cannot take it away: it lies on another field, where the correction or corroboration of phenomenal knowledge can never meet it. Born as a pure intellectual datum, it remains among our intellectual reserves, withdrawn not only from every actual, but from every possible contradiction: — an indestructible and unalterable postulate, inherent in the very organism of Reason itself. Does this require us then, as our author insists, to "endow the chair with consciousness," and, with Kepler, to set a separate spirit on each planet for its guidance? By no means. The theory of Living Causality involves no such puerilities; is no more negligent than Materialism itself of the lessons of scientific generalization: only it puts upon them a somewhat different interpretation. On the fundamental fact to be construed there is sufficient agreement. Undisciplined Man looks on all moving and impressive things as animate; starts at the spirits in the wind, the rushing water, and the forest gloom; and feels upon him a host of awful eyes in the watching lights of heaven. Civilized Man goes among these things, and tabulates them all; takes meteorological notes; draws up nautical almanacs; calculates when the timber will become available as coal; and in a few weeks reduces even a new comet to rules, and publishes its road, in the *Times* newspaper. Wherein consists the essence of this change? Will you say, "Nature which we supposed alive at the beginning, we have found at last to be dead"? We should rather reply, "Nature which in our childhood seemed charged with the caprices of a thousand spirits, has become, for our maturity, organ of the faithful thought of One." The widening circuit of law, the merging of anomalies, the ever-growing tissue of analogies, do not touch the inner nature of causality: they are but the spread of unity where plurality was before. So long as the provinces of the visible world, and the corresponding sets of phenomena, struck our perception one by one, they needed for their explanation a god a piece: when two were fused together, the separation of their causes lapsed as well: and when, by the apprehension of some universal law, the great kosmical conception, embracing heaven and earth in a common order, assumed consistency, the miscellaneous crowd of spirits necessarily disappeared, in favor of the One Mind that manifestly thought out the whole. By this change, the provincial departments of nature, formerly invested with independent life, fell into subordination; — became simply instrumental; — and, when taken apart for separate contemplation, could reveal *method* only, not *causality*, which had now retired into the unitary background. The notion of distinct *laws*, mechanical, chemical, vital, — mere *modes* of causal procedure, — succeeded to that of distinct personal agents, and furnished lines of demarcation, often entirely new, between field and field of nature: but as this notion does absolutely nothing either to supersede or to satisfy the axiom of causation, the personal agents expelled by it leave a function unfulfilled. That function, vacated by their many wills, is taken up and absorbed into One; the singleness of the world expressing the singleness of its Cause. The early identification then of Causality and Will can never be disproved, and is never lost: the spiritual element is not discharged by any discovery of Laws: dislodged from this or that detached seat, it simply ceases to be scattered and becomes concentrated: and as Science weaves phenomena into unity, Religion blends the Divine Powers into One. We are told it is "Fetishism" to look on the world as instinct with Living Mind. If so, it is at least that imperishable element which Fetishism has in common with the highest Theism. We are told, it is the effect of Philosophy to exorcise every spirit from the universe, and reduce it to an aggregate of unconscious laws. If so, it is at least that effect of Philosophy which it shares with mere stupefying Custom; — an infirmity of technical habit, — not any vision of what is special to its field, but an acquired blindness to what remains beyond. There is doubtless a different reading of the world present to the mind of the man of Science, and to the soul of the Poet and the Prophet; the one spelling out the order of its phenomena; the other, the meaning of its beauty, the mystery of its sorrow, the sanctity of its Cause. But seeing that it is the same world which faces both, and that the eyes are human into which it looks, we can never doubt that the two readings have their intrinsic harmonies, and that the articulate thought of the one will fall at last into rhythm with the solemn music of the other.

On full survey of the logical conditions of this great problem, it seems to us that Mr. Spencer has alighted on the least tenable of all the possible positions. We can understand the Positivist with whom laws are ultimate, and who turns causation out of doors into metaphysic night. We can understand the Theist, who says that, on whatever ground you know the First Cause to exist, on the same ground you know that Cause to be a free Mind. But we cannot understand the intermediate position, which allows a field to

Ontology, but condemns it to perpetual barrenness; which admits and demonstrates the ὅτι ἔστι, but meets the τί ἐστι with only negations and despair. To prepare the way for this paradox, both the Theistic and the Atheistic doctrines are charged with contradictions which they do not contain. The *self-existence*, for instance, which the latter ascribes to the universe, and the former to God, is declared to be "rigorously inconceivable," because "to conceive existence through infinite past-time, implies the conception of infinite past-time, which is an impossibility" (p. 31). We cannot answer for the consciousness of others: and in the face of this frequent assertion we hardly like to speak for ourselves. Yet after repeated reflection we cannot at all detect this alleged "impossibility." To form an *image* of any infinitude, — be it of time or space or number, — to go mentally through it by successive steps of representation, — is indeed impossible; not less so than to traverse it in our finite perception and experience. But to have the *thought* of it, as an idea of the Reason, not of the phantasy, and assign that thought a constituent place in valid beliefs and consistent reasoning, appears to us not only possible, but inevitable: and the large part it plays in mathematical science alone suffices to vindicate its worth for the intellect. So far as *this* difficulty goes, "self-existence" appears to us perfectly susceptible, and equally susceptible, of intelligible predication regarding the universe and regarding God. Not that the two assertions — the Atheist's and the Theist's — remain at all upon the same footing beyond the circle of this particular criticism, and are equally free from other difficulties attaching to the claim of self-existence.

Mr. Spencer treats the two cases as parallel throughout, and charges it on Theists as a gross inconsistency that they demand for their Ultimate Reality the very attribute which they forbid the Atheist to affirm of his. "Those who cannot conceive a self-existent universe; and who therefore assume a creator as the source of the universe; take for granted that they can conceive a self-existent creator" (p. 35). "If we admit that there can be something uncaused, there is no reason to assume a cause for any thing" (p. 37). Far from admitting this indiscriminating doctrine, that self-existence may go either everywhere or nowhere, we submit the distinction that while, by the laws of thought, phenomena demand causation, entities dispense with it: and it is, we presume, in obedience to this law, that our author himself plants his "Absolute Reality" behind the scenery and changes of the world. It is not existence, but entrance upon existence and exit thence, that must be referred to an originating power. And inasmuch as the universe resolves itself into a perpetual genesis, a vast aggregate and history of phenomena, the Theist is perfectly justified in treating it as disqualified for self-existence; and in passing behind it for the Supreme Entity that needs no Cause. This distinction is no invention of mere theology: it is recognized in other fields. No one asks a cause for the *Space* of the universe: and it depends on the theory we may form of its *Matter*, whether that too is excepted from the category of originated things. But everywhere the line is drawn upon the same principle; that entities may have self-existence; phenomena must have their Cause.

It is an old reproach against gross forms of religion,

that they teach worshippers to suppose God "*altogether* such a One as themselves." This reproach is now a favorite weapon, used by the nescient philosophy, against those who worship a Divine nature *in any respect* such a one as their own: — against all therefore who see above them any Divine object at all; for plainly, in the total absence of common attributes, no apprehension, no reverence, no sympathy, no suspicion of existence even, would be possible. Unless man is the monopolist of mind in the universe, and it culminates in him, higher intelligences, however they transcend him, must resemble him up to the extreme limits of his thought; and to take the rudimentary experiences of spiritual faculty in himself as his base of conception for the Universal Mind is no more presumptuous than from his paper diagrams and calculations to construe the geometry of the heavens, and lay down the orbits of the stars. It is singular that an author who both insists on the necessary belief of a First Cause, and declares that the only causation we know is our own, should also write as follows in derision of the theologians:

"If for a moment we made the grotesque supposition that the tickings and other movements of a watch constituted a kind of consciousness; and that a watch possessed of such a consciousness insisted on regarding the watchmaker's actions as determined, like its own, by springs and escapements; we should simply complete a parallel of which religious teachers think much. And were we to suppose that a watch not only formulated the cause of its existence in these mechanical terms, but held that watches were bound out of reverence so to formulate this cause, and even vituperated, as atheistic watches, any that did not venture so to formulate it; we should merely illustrate the presumption of theologians by carrying their own argument a step further" (p. 111).

Standing as it does for a "theologian," this is of course meant to be a great fool of a watch. Yet, till it gets excited and begins to "vituperate," its "first experiments in thinking" do not seem so much amiss. For do they not contrive to hit somehow upon the exact truth? Give the "springs and escapements" their "grotesque" change of meaning and function; let them cease to be "mechanical," and become vital and mental; let the watch, in virtue of them, be able to think and will, and raise questions of causality: and then, when it guesses its own origin from a being similarly gifted with rational and voluntary powers, does it not pitch upon the fact? Had it not a watchmaker? and was he not furnished with just the conscious faculties which had been newly awakened within itself? The endowments by which he made it, are they not like those by which it found him out? To us, we must confess, the "springs and escapements" of our author's satire seem a little out of order; and the logical "ticking" of the watch less at fault than the reasoning which makes fun of them.*

If of such type be the presumption of theologians, it is at least a happy presumption, in that it solves its

* The watch is so evidently in the right, that it is not easy to explain where the point of the illustration is supposed to lie. If the absurdity be meant to consist in this, that the watch attributes to its maker, not simply *faculties*, but in addition *organs* like its own, the "simile" breaks down in its application: for no theologian ascribes to God any thing analogous to the human organization, — of muscles, brain, nerves, &c.; or fails to guard expressly against any intrusion of "parts and passions" into the idea of him.

problem truly. To carry out the illustration a little further, suppose, as the first fruit of their much thinking, a dispute and jumble of cross-tickings among the watches; and that one, — attached to the "know-nothing" party, — faced full upon our first reasoner and said: 'Do not tell me about a watchmaker: such person is impossible, except in the dreams of your miserable egotism. *Some* Cause certainly you and I must have had: but if every creature is to set up a Maker like itself, where shall we be? You and I can do a little thinking, no doubt; but that is because we have wheels; it is a kind of ticking they have. We can also choose this way or that; but only because there is an elastic thread in us that goes tight and loose by turns. We fancy ourselves living, and seem to go of ourselves: but if you attend to the winding-up that happens to us, you will see it is only a mechanical force turning itself into vital. So, for us to be alive and knowing, there is no need for the Cause of us to be so. No, no: your watchmaker-theory is too mechanical for me: watch-evolution is better, as far as it goes. "I suppose we grew." But of the Real Cause the only thing I know is, that it cannot be a watchmaker: it cannot be in any respect like us: it cannot think: it cannot will: it cannot live: and to believe any thing of the sort is "transcendent audacity."' Is this nescient watch entitled, merely by its humor for negations, to the praise of eminent modesty, and also to the prerogative of high rebuke? To drop the illustration, does a profession of ignorance, does an immunity from theological belief, confer a right to stigmatize the faith of others as "impieties"?

Such censure, however, does the sensitive zeal of Mr. Spencer administer to us for irreverent speech in our pages* regarding the Supreme Cause; — speech so irreverent as to cast into the shade the presumptuous fellow who lamented that he had not been consulted at the making of the world. What is the sacrilegious violence, — the Titanic scaling of the heavens, — that calls down this lightning of reproof? Simply the utterance of these three thoughts: that, though Sense may vary, Reason must be uniform in all beings: that the uncreated nature conceded universally to space it was difficult to deny to matter in its Primary Qualities: and that, as Mind must be one, so must Righteousness be one, whether in Heaven or upon earth. As our author himself maintains that Matter can have no genesis and suffer no destruction, it cannot be the second of these positions that offends him. The first declares precisely what the most calm and cautious of modern savans, Oersted, wrote a treatise to establish, — the Unity of Reason throughout the universe; the ubiquity of space and time securing the relations of measure and number everywhere; and all other knowledge being entangled with this constant element. The third declares the corresponding Moral principle, — the Unity of Goodness, — the persistency of Right, — the identity of Real Excellence, from sphere to sphere of character. Is it "audacity," is it "irreverent," to apply these principles to the Highest of Spiritual Natures? Then it is "audacious" and "irreverent" to own him as Mind, or speak of any Divine Righteousness at all: for to do so is to assume a constant essence

* See the Essay on Nature and God, p. 121.

embodied in these words. Mr. Spencer's conditions of pious worship are hard to satisfy: there must be between the Divine and human no communion of thought, no relations of conscience, no approach of affection, no presence of Living God with living soul: to the jealous prophet of an empty "Absolute" these things are all "impieties." And the "true religion" which condemns them consists in "the consciousness that it is alike our highest wisdom and our highest duty to regard that through which all things exist as The Unknowable" (p. 113). When we ask against *whom*, what dear object of sacred loyalty, our grievous irreverence has been committed, the name of this blank abstraction is given in. Far be it from us to deal lightly with the sense of Mystery. It mingles largely with all devout apprehension, and is the great redeeming power that purifies the intellect of its egotism and the heart of its pride. But you cannot constitute a Religion out of mystery alone, any more than out of knowledge alone: nor can you measure the relation of doctrines to humility and piety by the mere amount of conscious darkness which they leave. All worship, being directed on what is *above* us and transcends our comprehension, stands in presence of a mystery. But not all that stands before a mystery is worship. The abyss must not be one of total gloom, — of neutral possibilities, — of hidden glories or hidden horrors, we know not which, — of perhaps the secure order of perfect Thought, or, equally perhaps, the seething forces of a universe fatefully and blindly born. Such a pit of indeterminate contingencies will bend no head, and melt no eye, that may turn to it.

Some rays of clear light must escape from it, some visions of solemn beauty gleam within it, ere the darkness itself can be "visible" enough to deliver its awfulness upon the soul. Without positive apprehensions of a better than our best, — of a Real that dwarfs our Ideal, — of a Life, a Thought, a Righteousness, a Love, — that are the Infinite to our Finite, — there is nothing to revere, nothing to decide between despair and trust. To fling us into bottomless negation is to drown us in mystery and leave us dead. True reverence can breathe and see only on condition of some mingling and alternation of light and darkness, of inner silence and a stir of upper air. Nor do we believe that any of the appropriate effects of "true Religion" can outlive the simple trust in a Personal Ruler of the universe and human life.

MANSEL'S LIMITS OF RELIGIOUS THOUGHT.*

THE Canon of Salisbury must have entertained a strange idea of the exigencies of the orthodox Christian faith, when he provided it, by bequest of his estates, with a fresh defence every year till the day of judgment. To the Aberdeen merchant whose munificence evoked Archbishop Sumner's *Records of Creation* and Mr. Thompson's *Christian Theism*, it seemed sufficient if a new buttress were added, or a new approach were opened, to the edifice every forty years. Even at this rate the pure gospel must become coated over, like the focus of a labyrinth, with excessive protection, or be accessible, like an Egyptian sanctuary, through an endless propylæum. But if Oxford is to widen its zone of "evidences" just forty times as fast, and annually drive back the lines of "heretics and schismatics," it is alarming to think how the little oratory of true worship will lie in the midst of a Russian empire of demonstration; with certain proof of one text at least, that scarcely will "the world itself contain

* The Limits of Religious Thought examined in Eight Lectures, preached before the University of Oxford, in the year 1858, on the Foundation of the late Rev. John Bampton, M.A., Canon of Salisbury. By Henry Longueville Mansel, B.D., Reader in Moral and Metaphysical Philosophy at Magdalen College; Tutor and late Fellow of St. John's College. London: Murray, 1858.

National Review, January, 1859.

the books that have been written." To judge, however, from the seventy years or so that have elapsed since the foundation, the Bampton Lectures are not unlikely to melt into oblivion at one end as fast as they come into existence at the other. In proportion to the number of eminent names that appear in the series, including Heber, Milman, Whately, Hampden, and Thompson, it is remarkable how few of the volumes can be regarded as permanent enrichments of our theological literature. The nomination to the lectureship seems to oppress the natural forces of even strong minds; to reduce genius and learning to commonplace, if it does not tempt them into heresy. In a few exceptional instances, — as Bishop Hampden's volume on the Scholastic Philosophy, — the series illustrates the painful cost at which reputations are won in theology; in many more it shows the facility with which they may be lost. Among the recent annual occupants of St. Mary's pulpit have been two accomplished logicians, Provost Thompson and Dr. Mansel; but the *Lectures on the Atonement* had no trace of intellectual identity with the lucid and comprehensive *Outline of the Laws of Thought;* and now the acute and well-read author of the *Prolegomena Logica* gives us, on the greatest of subjects, a book which, in spite of its careful elaboration and literary skill, will probably convince no one but himself, and be felt by many of his best readers to unsettle the very bases it was written to establish.

There are two ways in which you may conduct a process of religious persuasion. You may appeal directly to the sources of spiritual conviction in the human mind, and endeavor to awaken the mood and present the thoughts, from which belief in Divine things becomes conscious and distinct. Or you may think it needless thus to begin at the beginning, and, taking the matter up at a later stage, may seek to ward off and remove objections by which the springs of faith have lost their action. The former method is creative and sympathetic; the latter is corrective and antagonistic. The one develops what is latent; the other suppresses what is obtrusive. The one rests in affirmation; the other negatives denial. By the rules of logic these two methods ought to be equivalents in validity; and in the treatment of any subject purely intellectual they would actually be so. But religious faith, once broken by logical doubt, no logical refutation, it is probable, ever restored; so long as its inner ground remains unenlarged, so long as no new field of moral consciousness is opened, the mere dialectic discussion of data grown ineffectual must remain, we believe, without result. This, indeed, is only a consequence of the essential difference between a philosophy and a religion. In the apprehension of our Divine relations the logical faculty has but a secondary function, — to justify, to reconcile, to organize, to unfold certain given convictions; and is misapplied in the attempt to evoke or re-instate what is not there. Hence it is that, in many a mind, a mass of sceptic clouds, charged with thunders of denial, will cling steadfast to its cold heights against your keenest blasts of argument; and then, by some unnoticed change in the climate of the soul, will silently disperse. And hence also it is that men who have got rid of their own scepticism are so seldom able to shake other people's. To their old companions in doubt, they seem to have deserted their camp by a mere spring of caprice; and they are themselves disappointed, when they would account for their altered position, that they cannot trace the approach to it by a more intelligible path. They find themselves using — to the disgust of their associates — the very same evidences which used to affect them with *ennui* or contempt; and from the refutations which once appeared demonstrative some secret cause seems to have drawn all the pith away. The removal into a higher region of belief is seldom effected by retracing the logical staircase which brought us to a lower; but rather by flinging away some detaining weights, and passing with spontaneous ascent into congenial altitudes.

From insensibility to this fact, theologians greatly overrate the power of mere critical refutation directed against heretical doubt. They fancy that it must undo in the sceptic the process which it seems to render impossible to themselves; and when a book like Butler's *Analogy* appears, they regard the orthodox case as complete, and its triumph secure, except with the wilful or the stupid. The clerical pride in that ingenious work, the constancy with which its arguments are reproduced, the exultation with which its dilemma is presented to every opponent, curiously contrast with its utter inefficacy upon the minds it was intended to influence, and show how wide the chasm which separates the systematic divine from the troubled hearts he has to help out of their perplexities. Who ever heard of a Deist turned into Christian by reading the *Analogy?* or of a Christian brought by it into higher conceptions of his religion? Its whole force is expended in baffling simple Theism, or any Christianity that assumes it, and compelling you to take either more than this or less than this, — to go on to orthodoxy or fall back on atheism. Equally admired as a logical feat by sceptics who strain at a gnat and dogmatists who swallow a camel, it hurts and browbeats every intermediate feeling; and even where it carries the intellect, does so by perplexing the moral sense, and reducing reverence to lower terms. That this fatal tendency belongs to the very essence of the argument, will appear from the barest sketch of its structure.

It is altogether an *argumentum ad hominem*, addressed, on behalf of ecclesiastical Christianity, to the believer in simple Theism. He is taken up on his own ground; and nothing more is asked from him at the outset than he is accustomed to allow, — that the world and human life evidence the existence and exemplify the moral government of an Infinite and Holy God. Go with me this one mile, says Butler, and I will compel you to go twain; resting with me at last in the assurance that the scheme of Redemption, as orthodox men understand it, has the same Author as the scheme of Creation. For not a questionable feature can you name in my theology which has not its exact counterpart in yours. It is needless for me to deny or explain the difficulties; it is enough that I retort them, and show that you also are in the same case. Do you object to the *miraculous* origin of Revelation? — I remind you of the miraculous origin of Nature. Are you repelled by the mystery of the Incarnation? — It is no darker than any other union of the Infinite with the Finite, of spiritual freedom with physical necessity.

Are you shocked at the notion of hereditary corruption? — What say you, then, to the natural entail of disease and character? Is it incredible that the punishment of the guilty should be ransomed by anguish to the innocent? — I refer you to the whole history of human life, where all redemptions are vicarious, and the best men pay in sacrifice and sorrow for the deliverance of the worse. If, in the face of these difficulties, you can hold to your Natural Religion, why should they disturb your acceptance of a Revelation to which they still adhere? If the two schemes come from the same Author, what more likely than that they should exhibit the same features?

This argument, it is evident, far from relieving any perplexity, lets it lie in order to balance it by another. It duplicates the sense of painful embarrassment, by detecting the same repulsions in the sceptic's residuary belief which have already determined him to partial unbelief. So far as the reasoning succeeds, it is not by lightening objections in the ecclesiastical scale, but by weighting them more heavily in the theistical; and the only new feeling it can give to an opponent is this, that however ill he may think of other people's God, he has no reason to think better of his own. If he is driven to accept a scheme of doctrine on this ground, he surrenders his higher sentiment to a lower necessity, and betrays the devoutness of his faith from shame at a logical reproach.

The cogency of this reasoning appears to us not less questionable than its piety. Granting even that every ugly feature found in the received "scheme of redemption" may be refound in the "scheme of creation," we submit that it occupies a totally different place in the two, — constituting the very text and substance of the one, and only, as it were, a foot-note in an appendix of the other. In the constitution of the world, those parts and arrangements which perplex our sense of the Divine justice and goodness are insignificant exceptions in a grand and righteous whole; and the gloom they would occasion, did they stand alone, is lost in a "more exceeding glory." They do not speak the essence and spirit of the system; they are the silent enigmas that lie out of relation to it; and are superable by faith only from their relative unimportance. It is otherwise with the doctrines by which the creeds offend the moral sense and the natural pieties: — the hereditary curse of sin and ruin; — the eternal punishment of helpless incapacity; — the conveyance of an alien holiness by imputation, and the transfer of an infinite penalty from an offending race to a saving God; — these are no exceptional incidents in the orthodox scheme, but its organic members, its very plan and life, the only thing it has to offer in exemplification of the character of God. These are not the "difficulties" of its "revelation," but the whole of it; if these are not revealed, — its advocates will tell you, — nothing is revealed; and a theology that omits them wants "the essentials" of the Christian faith. Thus the darkness, the negations, the sorrows of Natural Religion are made, not simply to re-appear in this Christianity, but to constitute it and be the only soul it has; while the illuminated side of theism suffers eclipse and falls into shadow as a "non-essential." This inversion in the proportion of light to gloom on passing from the one system to the other appears to us utterly to vitiate the conclusion from their Analogy; indeed, in strictness, to destroy the Analogy itself.

Nor is this the only fallacy involved in Butler's reasoning. His fundamental maxim, that "Revelation and nature, having the same Author, may be expected to *exhibit the same features*," may be admitted, until he adds, "and *therefore to contain the same difficulties*." There is, we suppose, *some* limit to the resemblance which may be reasonably looked for between the two systems. No one's anticipations would be satisfied by their being perfectly alike, — each, in its disclosures, an exact *fac-simile* of the other. And if so, — if the presumption be irresistible in favor of some difference in the midst of the visible affinity, — where should we fitly seek for the lines of divergence? Surely the very antithesis, "*Natural*" — "*Revealed*," is an index to the true seat of contrast. Precisely what Nature hides, is Inspiration given to unveil; it is where the one is silent that the other has to speak; and only in so far as the first leaves us in the dimness of perplexity does the second vouchsafe its light. The "difficulties," therefore, of unaided Theism are exactly what we should *not* expect to find over again in a religion sent to our rescue; and just in proportion as we do so, does the gift forfeit its character as a "Revelation," and remain undifferenced from our prior darkness. To insist that the universe and the gospel come from the same Author, and to forget that they contemplate different ends, supplementary of each other, is to do violence to all laws of rational presumption.

We are far from saying that there is any thing inconceivable in a partial revelation, which shall leave many obscurities not cleared up: nor dare we prescribe, by any *a-priori* rule, how much must be given, and how much left. We only say that it is the essence of revelation to dissipate darkness; that whatever it does, be it little or be it much, must be of this kind; that, though it may let old perplexities lie unsolved, it contradicts its nature if it introduces new ones; and that as its very idea and aim is to give the key and method of the Divine administration to those who were in danger of missing its spirit amid conflicting details, the antecedent probability is extreme in favor of a luminous simplicity, and against its reproducing the identical riddles on which it takes compassion.

We well know that to question Butler's perfection is, in the eyes of churchmen, little short of the sin against the Holy Ghost. We can honestly say that it is not without trying hard to believe in him, and not without admiring recognition of his merits as an ethical thinker, that we find his theology, as expressed in his great work, oppressive to the religious feeling and unsound in its logical elaboration. This being the case, it is not surprising that Dr. Mansel's book gives us just the same experience: for it is essentially an adaptation of the same argument to the altered conditions of modern philosophy. The chief difference is the following. Butler concerned himself with the outward constitution of things in both the spheres which he compared, — with the actual laws and arrangements of the world on the one hand, the organic facts and system of redemption on the other. For every thing apparently objectionable in the latter he was ready with some corresponding ill look in the former; and having set the deformities in equilibrium, there he left them to cancel each other. How far they are real or not is indifferent to his reasoning, which dwells only on their parallelism, not on their intrinsic validity. He no further accounts for them than by referring to the small measure of our present faculty as applied to the immensity of the Divine scheme; and supposes that they would disappear, even from our view, were our horizon enlarged, and a wider survey obtained over the relations of things. Dr. Mansel, on the other hand, rests nothing on the objective analogy of natural and supernatural arrangements, and every thing on the subjective incapacity of the intellect for dealing with either: his plea is, not that God has set similar puzzles in the world as in the gospel, but that man brings the same logical disqualification to both. It matters not, therefore, in his argument, what the particular adjustments of nature or doctrines of Scripture may be: change them ever so much, on this side or on that, they would suit us no better. Our difficulties are not in the things, but in ourselves; — not matters of degree, brooding heavily here and vanishing there, and variable with our opportunities; but, being carried about with us in the very structure of our faculties, are constant for every possible system, and never short of irremediable contradiction. That the rationalistic critique of the orthodox faith is successful in finding insuperable inconsistencies, is not denied; but you have only, it is said, to apply the same logical experiment to any religious philosophy whatsoever, and it will equally disappear under the process. Thought lies under a fatal disability with regard to Divine things, and is doomed to frame its religion out of hopelessly incompatible beliefs.

There is something very tempting to a reasoner in a principle of this kind, — the discovery of a subjective incompetence. It does great execution on very easy terms. It saves all trouble of external reconnoitring and comparison of evidence, and serves for every case alike. It despatches all enemies with one instrument: a sort of unicorn polemic that, like the beast in the book of Daniel, "pushes" impartially against all the cardinal points. Dr. Mansel, accordingly, by a single operation, clears the field of all opponents at once; he has only to wave his metaphysical wand, and pronounce his universal incantation, and they turn into phantoms, and disappear into his appendix; — a miscellaneous prison-house, where all evil spirits are reserved for judgment. There would seem to be some little difference between the springs of doubt in ethical minds like Theodore Parker's or Francis Newman's, and in mystical, like Bruno and Schelling, — between the akosmism of Spinoza and the atheism of Comte, — between the historical scepticism of Strauss or Baur and the speculative dialectic of Hegel, — between the business-like rationalism of the Socini and the impersonal theology of Schleiermacher: and he indeed must be a fortunate divine who has found an answer that will serve for all. The danger of such a comprehensive refutation always is, lest it should inadvertently include yourself. It is difficult to set so large an appetite to work, and stand yourself out of reach of its voracity. And we have serious fears that Dr. Mansel must sooner or later fall a victim to the hunger of his own logic.

The mighty spell which is to paralyze all heretical critics at a stroke is no other than Sir William Hamilton's principle, that the Infinite cannot be known, because to know is to discriminate, and what is discriminated is finite; or, again, to state the matter in another form, that the Absolute cannot be known, because to know is to apprehend relations, and what is related is not absolute. The rule may be expressed in the terms of various other antitheses: that thought, as such, can deal only with that which is *conditioned*, and which is *plural;* and must therefore find unconditioned and unitary being inaccessible. This inability to think or apprehend, except by relation and difference, is assumed to be a human limitation of faculty, a provincial incompetency, a negation of mental light and power. And the realm from which it excludes us is precisely, we are told, the religious realm: for God is that infinite, absolute, unconditioned unity, the knowledge of whom contradicts the very nature of thought. Hence there can be no philosophy of religion. Every attempt to construct such a system has to substitute spurious counterfeits of the genuine Divine essentials: for positive "Infinitude," the simply *Indefinite;* for the "Absolute" *per se*, the mere ground-term of a Relation; for the "Unconditioned," the conditioning antecedent. Not only are these ambitious impostures in contradiction with the legitimate originals (the "indefinite," for instance, being susceptible of increase, while the "Infinite" is not); but they are themselves only illusions, — negations of thought rather than thoughts, — the mental background on which our positive conceptions rise and display themselves. No ingenuity can avail to rescue us from this inherent disqualification: no spasmodic spring can carry us over the chasm that parts our intellect from all divine knowledge: no cautious steps and steady eye can find a bottom to the cleft between. A critique of religion is impossible to a mind which is condemned by its constitution to a faith composed of contradictions.

In order to show the different forms in which these inevitable contradictions crop up, our author reviews, first, the metaphysical systems which form themselves, like Spinoza's and Hegel's, by evolution from the supreme terms of thought, — the Infinite, the Absolute, the Causal, — as their data, and endeavor from this ontological beginning to find a deductive path into and through the phenomenal world of nature and humanity: and then, the Psychological systems which, inversely, commence from the laws of human consciousness, — the sense of dependence, the belief of origination, the feeling of obligation, — and attempt thence to explore a passage into the hyperphysical and divine world. In the former, the finite can never attain to its rights or at all emerge from the pantheistic whole; nor can any predicates be attached to the Infinite: for, on the principle that *omnis determinatio est negatio*, it parts with its essence by gaining an attribute, and, unless it is to lose its affirmative reality, must for ever remain the blank of Being. In the latter order of systems, on the other hand, we can never escape from the finite: if we wait for logical stepping-stones to the other side, we shall wait for ever, and have no resource but to lodge in an atheistic world; and if, rather than this, we convey into a presumed Infinite our ideas of Personality, Intellect, and Character, we do but deny the essence we mean to enrich, and in the same breath affirm limitation and disclaim it. The self-destructive nature of the fundamental conceptions of rational theology is thus exhibited:

"These three conceptions, — the Cause, the Absolute, the Infinite, — all equally indispensable, do they not imply contradiction to each other, when viewed in conjunction, as attributes of one and the same being? A Cause cannot, as such, be absolute; the Absolute cannot, as such, be a cause. The cause, as such, exists only in relation to its effect; the cause is a cause of the effect; the effect is an effect of the cause. On the other hand, the conception of the Absolute implies a possible existence out of all relation. We attempt to escape from this apparent contradiction, by introducing the idea of succession in time. The Absolute exists first by itself, and afterwards becomes a Cause. But here we are checked by the third conception, that of the Infinite. How can the Infinite become that which it was not from the first? If causation is a possible mode of existence, that which exists without causing is not infinite, that which becomes a cause has passed beyond its former limits. Creation at any particular moment of time being thus inconceivable, the philosopher is reduced to the alternative of pantheism, which pronounces the effect to be mere appearance, and merges all real existence in the cause. The validity of this alternative will be examined presently.

"Meanwhile, to return for a moment to the supposition of a true causation. Supposing the Absolute to become a cause, it will follow that it operates by means of free-will and consciousness. For a necessary cause cannot be conceived as absolute and infinite. If necessitated by something beyond itself, it is thereby limited by a superior power; and if necessitated by itself, it has in its own nature a necessary relation to its effect. The act of causation must therefore be voluntary; and volition is only possible in a conscious being. But consciousness, again, is only conceivable as a relation. There must be a conscious subject and an object of which he is conscious. The subject is a subject to the object; the object is an object to the subject; and neither can exist by itself as the Absolute. This difficulty, again, may be for the moment evaded, by distinguishing between the Absolute as related to another and the Absolute as related to itself. The Absolute, it may be said, may possibly be conscious, provided it is only conscious of itself. But this alternative is, in ultimate analysis, no less self-destructive than the other. For the object of consciousness, whether a mode of the subject's existence or not, is either created in and by the act of consciousness, or has an existence independent of it. In the former case, the object depends upon the subject, and the subject alone is the true absolute. In the latter case, the subject depends upon the object, and the object alone is the true absolute. Or, if we attempt a third hypothesis, and maintain that each exists independently of the other, we have no absolute at all, but only a pair of relatives; for co-existence, whether in consciousness or not, is itself a relation" (p. 47).

The general conclusion which Dr. Mansel draws from this *Streit der Facultäten* is hardly what the premises would lead us to expect. Our idea of the "Infinite," being merely negative, would seem to be the index to no positive reality. Our idea of "Personality," being a mere reflection of our limited consciousness, is declared to be incapable of application to a nature not finite. Yet we are assured (p. 89) that it is "our duty to think of God as personal; and it is our duty to believe that He is infinite," though the two conceptions contradict each other. The notion of "Infinitude" is at once "inadmissible" in theology, and yet "indispensable." Nor is this humiliating necessity of compounding a faith out of contradictories at all peculiar to our *Religion*. All the fundamental postulates of thought, — Time, Space, Substance, Power, — are in the same plight; introducing us to entities which we cannot harmonize with our experience of phenomena. In all these cases nothing is left to us but to accept the ontological ideas as *true relatively to us*, — given forms of *our* thought, — but to beware of regarding them as valid for things in themselves, or for any point of view beyond our own. Whether they do or do not represent realities as they are, we cannot tell: but as we are imprisoned within them, they are *regulative* truth for our minds, though having no claim to the character of *speculative* truth, imaging what lies in the outer daylight of the universe beyond our dreams.

Our readers will at once recognize in this sketch a revival of the principles of Kant; who, by resolving into subjective conditions all our ontological and perceptive assumptions, left the intellect in idealistic insulation, and blew up every bridge by which thought could pass to the mainland of real Being. Dr. Mansel, however, is more thorough-going still. Kant, it is well known, recovered in his treatise on the Practical Reason the ground he had abandoned in his analysis of the Speculative: and authorized the resumption, as presuppositions of conscience, of the very faiths, in moral freedom, responsibility, and absolute divine law, which no dialectic was able to guarantee. Our author complains of this as an inconsequence; and carrying his own scepticism steadily through, involves Morals with Theology in the same sentence of mere subjectivity, rendering their ideas inapplicable, except in condescension to our incapacities, to any sphere beyond the human.* We may indeed — perhaps must — *speak* of an Absolute Morality: but the phrase involves a contradiction in terms; for the moment we try any ethical conception upon an Infinite nature, it is swallowed up and disappears. Emotion and change, such as are inseparable from disapproval or compassion, from either free forgiveness or conditional reconciliation, and from openness to prayer, are incompatible with immutable self-identity: yet, on the other hand, the alternative suppositions, of an ethical neutrality or an optionless and necessitated justice, no less impose limits on the perfection of Being. On this side also, our author contends, all religious belief is necessarily a tissue of contradictions, protected only by the existence of equal contradictions in any scheme of unbelief. The conclusion from the whole is, that, in our natural Theism, we must hold to *both* of the incompatible terms, the existence of the Infinite that can have no predicates, and the truth of the Finite predicates he cannot have; and that, bringing this state of mind to the scheme of Redemption, we are in no condition to

* It is with great diffidence that, speaking from memory alone, we call in question a statement respecting Kant, repeatedly made or implied by so studious and careful a writer as Dr. Mansel. But we know of no authority for the following representation, and cannot persuade ourselves that Kant has anywhere exposed himself to so reasonable a criticism: "Kant unquestionably went too far, in asserting that things in themselves *are not* as they appear to our faculties; the utmost that his premises could warrant him in asserting is, that we cannot tell whether they are so or not" (p. 348). Dr. Mansel produces no citation, and affords no means of verification. Certainly, if Kant ever said such a thing, he not only "went too far," but fell into variance with the whole spirit of his philosophy.

cast the first stone at its seeming inconsistencies, but are bound to content ourselves with estimating its evidences, without attempting a critique of its doctrines. Taken at their worst, they are as good as ours.

This line of thought, we must confess, appears to us even painfully precarious. Suppose, for argument's sake, that we grant the premises, and say, with Sir W. Hamilton, that only the Finite can be given us in thought; that the Infinite is for us only a negation,— a subjective inability to think; and that relative conceptions, on such a subject, are equivalent to ignorance. How far do these assumptions bear out Dr. Mansel's conclusion, that we must throw ourselves on Revelation? They establish conditions which make all revelation impossible.

Let us allow for the moment that, by the constitution of our faculties, we have (as our author says) a legitimate belief in the *existence* of the Infinite, but a total inability to attach any predicates to this subject. How can such a Being, so cut off from all possible access to our minds, *reveal* himself to us? As well might you say that Silence can make a speech. An existence without predicates is a non-existence: as Dr. Mansel himself admits, "pure being is" *to us* "pure nothing" (p. 328). That negation should send a message to nescience appears not readily conceivable; nor can we imagine in what the "evidences" of such a communication could consist.

But do the premises really guarantee to us even the bare *existence* of the Infinite? We cannot see how. The only ground for this faith which Dr. Mansel ever presents is, "that our whole consciousness is compassed about with restrictions, which we are ever striving to pass, and ever failing in the effort" (p. 121). But the bird in the cage and the captive in his cell learn nothing, by their vain efforts, of the world beyond. It is a marvellous thing to affirm that every incompetency implies an Infinitude. Our mental limits are evidence of no more than that the intellect is less than the intelligible. If, moreover, we are capable of discovering, with Hamilton and Mansel, that this "Infinite," which we are to endow with "existence," is but a subjective negation, the mocking shadow of our own impotence, we lose every ground for holding to its objective reality. The very discovery itself consists in nothing else than the detection of untrustworthiness in the belief. What does it amount to but this,—that our cognitive faculties are constructed without provision for any thing beyond phenomenal knowledge,—that we are made exclusively for the finite, not for the infinite? And this is only to say that, whether there be an Infinite or not, is a question beyond our affirmation or denial.

Turn the matter which way you will, this much is certain: to a mind disqualified in its structure for a "Philosophy of the Infinite," there can be made no Revelation of the Infinite; in older form of phrase, if natural religion be impossible, *through incapacity in the subject*, so is supernatural. Religious ignorance arising from defect in the attainable evidence, or from an undeveloped state of the faculties, may be remedied by supplementary information or an awakening discipline. But if the very instrument of intelligence carries its own darkness with it, and is fated ever to turn its blind side to God, then it stands similarly related to all possible media of expression, and there are no terms on which Divine light can be had. Where the receptive power is at fault, it is vain to multiply and intensify communication: as well might you hang a blind asylum with chandeliers, and expect that, though the daylight was useless, the brilliancy at night would tell. If there are no predicates of God assured to us by Reason, or only such as contradict each other and open the way to opposing possibilities; if we have only such knowledge (?) of Him as either may or may not represent Him as He is (p. 146); if we can affirm nothing of Him that might not with equal reason be denied; — there are no discriminative marks by which He and His agency may be recognized: for the unknown has no characteristics. Our incompetency extends therefore further than Dr. Mansel contemplates, — to the signs and evidences of Revelation, as well as its contents; and the paralysis of Natural Religion is the suppression of Revealed.

Our author's logic, then, in mowing down its thistle-field, inconsiderately mows off its own legs. He cuts away the only supports on which religious thought can rest or move; and nothing short of an unqualified ontological scepticism is in agreement with his premises. We cannot in the least discover *why*, on his principles, we are to believe *either* of the two contradictories which he requires us to hold in combination, — that God is infinite, that God is personal. He disparages the sources of cognition from which we receive these propositions, yet keeps their allegations on his books.

If the witnesses are untrustworthy, why let their testimony fix the main points of the case? The "infinite" being unmeaning for us, and the "personal" unmeaning in God, what title can they show to joint hold on our belief? No intellectual intuition, no consciousness, no legitimate inference, can assure us of either; where, then, are their credentials? To these questions we find no reply except that disbelief, if we choose to try it, will bring no logical gain. This is a good argument for a Pyrrhonist, who would maintain us in indeterminate equipoise, but is inconvertible to the purposes of the Christian philosopher and divine. The habit of dealing with derivative steps of thought is not favorable to a firm grasp of the primary data; and we cannot help thinking that Dr. Mansel's own mind is not clear with regard to the ultimate roots of religious belief. He cleverly pursues and breaks the track of many a system of erratic metaphysics; but, fascinated with the hunt of delusion and incompetency, he pushes the rout too far, and, as it seems to us, rides over the brink of the solid world, and falls into the abysses.

And now, having argued the matter from our author's premises, we must confess and justify our discontent with them. We cannot admit the doctrine of the religious incompetency of the human faculties; and the wide concurrence in it of schools apparently opposite, — of Mill and Comte, of Hamilton and Mansel, — will hereafter, we conceive, be looked upon as no less curious a phenomenon than the ovation with which, in the last century, the Critical Philosophy was carried off along the most divergent paths of thought. Undeterred by the fashion of the day and the influence of authoritative names, we do not hesitate to believe with Cousin, that there is a legitimate "passage from psychology to ontology," and to protest against the paradox that human intelligence, in its highest exercise, can only mock us with impossibilities and contradictions.

To put the matter into the shortest formula, let us say, we admit the *relative character* of human thought as a psychological fact; we deny it as an ontological disqualification. All acts of the mind, whether creative or apprehensive, are undoubtedly discriminative, a procedure from a less to a more determinate state. As self-conscious, they carry with them the distinction between subject and object; and as directed upon this, and not on that, they cut out a definite from an indefinite. To conceive, to know, to reflect, is in every case to deal exclusively with difference and relation; mental action is dualistic, not monistic. So far we are agreed.

Is, then, this *relativity* an incompetency or a qualification for thinking? a cognitive limitation, or a cognitive power? Our author, following Sir W. Hamilton, treats it as a provincial restriction imposed upon our nature, barring us from escape into the realm of real rather than seeming knowledge, and under the show of science dooming us to nescience. Is there any plea for such disparagement and distrust beyond the argument which, in parallel case, Hegel wittily attributed to Kant: "It cannot be true, because *we* think it"? What reason is there to suppose that in natures higher than ours there is another sort of knowledge in which nothing is differenced, and even the knower is not separated from the known? And if such a condition of being existed, would it legitimately rank as *more* intelligent or *less* intelligent than ours? And again, where is the field of otherwise possible knowledge from which this relativity excludes us? Drop the limit, and what new reaches of being do you bring within the intellectual horizon? Nothing surely can be more arbitrary than to treat the very essence of a faculty as the negation of faculty, and complain of the eye as enabling us to do nothing but see, and condemning us to see only what is visible. That we cannot think except by differencing, means only that we cannot know where there is nothing to be known, or that we cannot use a function without having it. If intelligence consists in distinguishing, how can distinguishing be an incompetency to understand? And does the "competency" of the most perfect intellect consist in this, — that it dispenses with differences, and sees all things to be equally true, and truth itself identical with falsehood?

But, it will be said, this relative character of knowledge at all events limits you to the finite, and precludes access to God as Infinite. On the contrary, we submit that relative apprehension is always and necessarily of two terms together: if of sound, then also of silence; if of succession, then also of duration; if of the finite, then also of the infinite. It is the πρῶτον ψεῦδος of Spinoza, of Schelling, of Hegel, of all monistic speculative systems, that they set up in isolated supremacy one of two inseparable data of thought, and then endeavor to educe the other out of it; and Dr. Mansel falls, we think, into the same snare. He strains after an Infinite that shall exclude the Finite; an Absolute that shall emerge from all Relation; a Causality that shall be pure of all conditions. If Theism were staked on his finding such things, his despair of it would be natural enough. For these conceptions, which he denies to be on speaking terms, are in each case Siamese twins, between which any affectation of estrangement cannot fail to be highly inconvenient. They come into existence before our thought together, and have their living meaning only *in pairs;* one of the two giving us the constant and ontological ground, the other the phenomenal manifestation. The attempt to think away the finite from the presence of the infinite, or *vice versâ*, must inevitably fail; and of the two schemes to which the attempt gives rise, viz. that which says "entities only can be known," and that which says "phenomena only can be known," both are to be unhesitatingly rejected. Two other possibilities remain, viz. the Idealism which, treating all "relation" as a subjective economy of ours, pronounces that we know *neither;* and the Realism which, taking relations in the mind as exponents of relations out, decides that we know *both*. It is on this last alone that, in our view, a sound philosophy can take its stand.

The position taken up against this doctrine rests on the distinction between positive and negative ideas. Of the finite, it is said we have a positive idea; of the infinite, except as the negative of this, we have none at all: the one, therefore, is the exponent of an objective reality, the other is only a subjective incapacity. The term which is given to us by experience is reliable: its concomitant, which is supplied in thought, is an empty form. In every case of relation between presumed entity and perceived phenomenon, — Space and position, — Time and succession, — Substance and quality, — Infinite and finite, — the more ambitious term is unaccredited, — a mere metaphysical impostor; putting on the airs of demonstration and universal validity, and pretending to hold good for all possible worlds; but, by this very mark, betraying its close confinement to our own mind as the mere shape and shadow of our faculty. So far does Dr. Mansel carry this Kantian Idealism, that he pronounces all judgments insecure and personal in proportion as they are self-evident, and, like the exact sciences, exhibit the characteristics of Universality and Necessity (p. 203). Now we will not enter here on the question whether those pairs of ideas are or are not valid beyond the enclosure of our nature; *that* falls into the general controversy with the Idealist. But this we venture to affirm, that, valid or invalid, the two terms of each pair must stand or fall *together;* and that, except by an arbitrary *coup-de-tête*, one cannot be taken and the other left. Both are given to us, — *e. g.* a limited figure and the boundless Space from which it is cut out, — in one and the same mental act, and are equally secured by the veracity, or vitiated by the unveracity, of our intellectual constitution. There can be no objection to call the one "positive" and the other "negative," provided it be understood that *each* is so with regard to the other, and that the relation is convertible; the finite, for instance, being the negative of the infinite, not less than the infinite of the finite. If more than this be meant, if the word "negative" is immovably fixed on the ontological term, as a disparagement of its trustworthiness and an assertion that it is obtained by mere thinking-away of sterling elements, then we dispute the doctrine as false alike to psychology and to logic; and with Dr. M'Cosh, whom our author unsatisfactorily criticises (p. 333), contend for a "positive" idea of the infinite. The attempt to resolve this idea into that of the "indefinite," does but mock the feeling of every precise thinker. That is "indefinite," to which we know no end; that is "infinite" which we know to have no end. The belief in the one is attainable by simply thinking limits away; the belief in the other rests on the positive deposition of our own faculties, which must be either taken at their word or dismissed as cheats.

It is perfectly true that of the Infinite, whether of Space, Time, or other mode of Being, we can form no mental *representation;* and that, when we try to do so, we can only resort to a vain stretching of the finite till we are tired and give it up. We suspect that this is what is meant when the idea is identified with a mere inability to think; for certainly many of the "contradictions" charged upon it are simply cases of baffled imagination. But it is no objection to either the reality or the legitimacy of a thought, that it is not of a kind to be brought before "the mind's *eye*." We *believe*, though we cannot *conceive*, the infinitude of space and time: and these beliefs take their place and perform their proper intellectual function in processes of rigorous scientific reasoning; not only without vitiating the result, but with indispensable aid to its true evolution. If this is not a "*thinking*" the infinite, — this letting it into a procedure of thought with operative power on the final product, — we know not what thinking is.

We confess a total insensibility to most of the alarming perplexities which our author endeavors to fix on the Idea of the Infinite. They all arise out of the spurious Spinozistic demand, that this idea shall be kept out of relation to any thing, and the false assumption that, unless this is done, the idea is sacrificed. Except in personal argument with opponents making this demand, there is no reason for giving way to it. No religious truth or moral interest requires us to identify God with any infinitude but that which stands in ontological relation to the finite. When we are asked whether, in creating the world, God increased the quantity of being, and are reminded that, if He did, infinitude received addition, and if He did not, the finite world is nothing at all, — the consequences do not in either case distress us as might be expected: an Infinitude that supplies its own completion was potentially without defect; and a world that manifests an Infinitude other than its own atones for its nonentity. As well might you ask whether the sun, on first appearing, added any thing to the extension of the universe; because, if he did, it was not infinite before; if he did not, he could have no size. These puzzles (which, be it remembered, remain after Revelation precisely what they were before) arise in great measure from the application of quantitative ideas to qualitative existence, and the attempt to solve all problems of genesis and change by the formulas of addition and subtraction. In order to be added together or to limit one another, objects must be homogeneous and must be magnitudes; and to speak of "quantity of *being*" in the abstract, or to discuss such a combination as God + World, appears to us not less unmeaning than to ask about the temperature of duration, or to debate whether sleep + dream is larger than sleep alone. In forgetfulness of this principle, our author pronounces the co-existence of the Divine attributes inconceivable without contradiction, because involving a plurality of infinitudes, side by side. If the attributes were not each *sui generis*, and if they wanted room, the remark would be true. But if, according to Spinoza's rule, "thinking is not bounded by body, or body by thinking," there is no need for heterogeneous attributes to become finite in order to co-exist.

These things being borne in mind, it is truly astonishing to find Dr. Mansel treating as perfectly parallel mysteries the co-existence of Attributes in the Divine substance, and the co-existence of Persons in the Divine Unity. For the cases differ precisely in that which turns the scale from possibility to impossibility. No two *attributes* of the same substance are alike; there is no tangential relation between them; therefore no mutual interference. But with *personalities* it is otherwise; as so many distinct *subjects* they are generically the same, with differences only attributive; and are therefore mutually exclusive and limit each other. It is only by attenuating the conception of personality till it melts away into that of attribute or function, that this doctrine becomes at all presentable in thought; and so, to the very relation which our author adduces as the counterpart of its contradiction, we habitually resort to relieve it of its mystery. In like manner,

Dr. Mansel's remark that the doctrine of the God-Man is neither more nor less perplexing than any other co-existence of a finite object with the infinite overlooks the real seat of the difficulty, which lies not in the relation of magnitude between the two natures predicated, but in the fact that both of them are *Personal* essences, — the second Person in the Godhead and the "perfect man" Jesus, — and therefore, by the rule of mutual exclusion in such cases, incapable of union in the same subject. It is a bold paradox to assert that the tormenting and intricate subtleties of the Eutychian and Monophysite controversies concerned a matter no harder to understand than the co-existence of the finite Moon with the infinite Space.

On the whole, then, we cannot follow Dr. Mansel in his scepticism respecting the natural springs of religion in the human mind; and if we could, we should feel that the possibility of revelation was gone too. We have entire faith in the veracity, and in the consistency, of the reports given in by our highest faculties; and think it possible, even within our segment of a life, to trace their convergence towards one Divine and Holy Reality. The causal instinct of the intellect, the solemn suspicions of the conscience, the ideal passion of the imagination, the dependent self-renunciation of the affections, are all, we believe, so many lines of attraction to the same Infinite Object. And however numerous the aspects under which that transcendent Being may present Himself to the different sides of our nature, we see no reason to doubt their consonance, or to despair of the noble and pious attempt to exhibit them in harmony. Nor do we think it should be a congenial task, for a divine versed in philosophy, to enlist his skill in the defeat of this attempt, — in widening the discrepancies, reducing the approximations, and making the most of the failures of the religious reason. We have no tenderness towards the metaphysical pantheism, — from Spinoza to Hegel, — which Dr. Mansel criticises in his earlier lectures. But we should give it up to him with more satisfaction, did he not, in his doctrine of the Infinite, appropriate its chief feature, and so, in the very act of putting it to death, transfer to himself its most fatal weapon. The effect of his essential sympathy with these systems in their conception of the problem to be proposed, shows itself especially when he ceases to contend with them, and addresses himself to the *moral* difficulties of faith, the doctrine of forgiveness, the grounds of prayer, the possibility of character in God. His treatment of these great subjects makes us forget the philosopher and recognize the divine: inventing imaginary difficulties, and removing them by fictitious solutions; implying slighter acquaintance than in the previous discussions with the literature of the subject; and missing, as it seems to us, the essential bases of ethical theory.

The general spirit of this book is scholarly and liberal; and probably the deviations from this tone are involuntary and intellectual merely. But there are examples of controversial unfairness, which, though sanctioned by usage, we deeply lament to see. In notes giving some account of the works of Strauss and of Baur, Dr. Mansel thinks it allowable to bring together, as an anthology of absurdities, all the extreme results and most amazing hints which the Hegelian dialectic of these writers supplies, without noticing the fact that their philosophy is an insignificant accident, which, if entirely removed or replaced by a different scheme, would leave the mass of their historical criticism unaffected. The consequence is, that these notes present a gross caricature, and leave an impression utterly false of two writers, both of whom, in spite of great aberrations of ingenuity, have produced an ineffaceable impression on Christian theology; and one has furnished contributions of extraordinary value to the solution of the grandest of historical problems. How decidedly we are opposed to their main theories, our habitual readers well know; and from their philosophy we stand at a greater distance probably than Dr. Mansel. But no orthodoxy can consecrate the spirit of polemic detraction, or excuse a scholar from recognizing scholarship and a Christian from observing justice. A writer, however, who thinks (p. 247) that Christianity is all lost, if once you admit the slightest human element in the teaching of Christ, belongs to a stage of theological opinion at which genial admiration and judicial estimates of modern critical learning are hardly possible. Few things, indeed, are more striking in this volume than the contrast between the acuteness and refinement of its metaphysics, and the purely popular and elementary character of its biblical ideas.

CEREBRAL PSYCHOLOGY: BAIN.*

It is rare to find an Englishman, not a graduate in Arts, who believes in the existence, — or even the possibility, — of what are called the "Mental and Moral Sciences." The average national intelligence looks on them as the showy shams of Academic discipline, and is as suspicious of their solidity as of Mr. Gladstone's. The Scotchman, on the other hand, — by ordination of nature and University charter, — takes kindly to these studies; discusses their problems everywhere, at church, on the platform, even in the public-house; and, migrating South of the Tweed, re-introduces them, from time to time, into our literature and life. In their pure form, however, he would hardly succeed in gaining our ear for them. But, himself catching the infection of our scepticism, he adapts them to the level of our belief, surrenders their distinctive characteristics, assimilates them to physical knowledge, and reduces them from their autonomy to a mere province of the "Natural Sciences:" and then, for the first time, when he has construed all that is "mental" in the

* The Senses and the Intellect. By Alexander Bain, A. M. London, 1855.

The Emotions and the Will. By Alexander Bain, A. M., Examiner in Logic and Moral Philosophy in the University of London. London, 1859.

National Review, April, 1860.

phenomena into physiology, and all that is "moral" into the chemistry of ideas, we begin to suspect his doctrine of something better than metaphysic moonshine. Both the elder Mill and Mr. Bain owe their English laurels to the remarkable skill with which they have negotiated away the claims of the native Scottish philosophy, and saved or sacrificed their science by putting it under protection of a stronger power. In saying this, we refer, not so much to their doctrines as to their method; and especially to the preconception from which they set out, as to the nature of their study and its relative place in the scheme of human knowledge.

What is "Psychology"? Nobody would think of putting it among the Physical Sciences, or would hesitate to admit that it stands, in some sense, at the remotest point from them. Nor would the most enthusiastic disciple of Faraday or Liebig pretend that it dealt with phenomena reducible to Chemical Law; though perhaps he might claim a less distant relationship to them than that of the mere Natural Philosopher, and might even reserve, on behalf of his favorite pursuit, some contingent reversionary right of interest in them. To judge from the habitual language of medical literature, the Physiologist considers himself to be treading close upon the heels of the Mental Philosopher, and to be heir-presumptive, if not already rival claimant, to the whole domain. Between the facts of life, as manifested through the lower grades of organized existence, and the facts of mind, special to our race, he recognizes no ultimate distinction, and confidently looks for evidence of essential identity. And whatever be the destination of Intellectual Philosophy, draws with it that of Ethics and Religion: for, once within the enclosure of the distinctive human faculties, it is impossible for the inquirer to insulate the Reason, whilst relegating Conscience and Faith to quite another field. In this view, therefore, the study of humanity constitutes only the uppermost stratum of scientific Natural History: it deals with certain residuary phenomena left on hand when the lower organisms have been exhausted: and its separation is no less provisional and artificial than that of any one branch of zoölogy from any other. It is thus the crown and summit of the hierarchy of Natural Sciences; emerging from physiology, as physiology from chemistry, and chemistry from physics; and differing only, as each superior term differs from the subjacent, in the greater complexity and more restricted range of the attributes it contemplates. Psychological studies, prosecuted with this preconception of their position, will naturally borrow, as far as possible, the resources of the nearest science, will seek explanation of human facts in the simpler animal analogies; and in proportion as these fail, will feel baffled, and anxious to reduce the variance to the lowest point. To bring the higher phenomena under the rule, or close to the confines of the lower; to exhibit them as woven in the same loom, only of finer web and more complicated pattern, — will be the instinctive aim of researches begun from this side. Nor will the aim be wholly unsuccessful in regard to the border phenomena, — of Sense, Propension, and Habit, — which retain us in affinity with other living kinds. If it incurs the risk of failure and harm, it will be at the upper end, among the extreme human characteristics: where, to say the least, it is strongly tempted to repeat upon psychology the same violence of which Comte complains as committed by the physicist on chemistry, and the chemist on physiology, — a coercive assimilation of ulterior to prior laws.

There is certainly a captivating simplicity in this pyramidal arrangement of all our possible knowledge around a single axis; with the base broadly laid in the universal properties of matter, and the apex rising to the solitary loftiness of Man and even crowned with his highest symbol, — the cross. It seems to promise that, by merely repeating our steps and not growing dizzy, we shall surmount all our ignorance, and find Thought and Love, as well as Force and Matter, beneath our feet. At the same time, it seems to warn us, that the special endowments of our own being are utterly inaccessible to our apprehension, till we have ascended through tier after tier of previous sciences. The promise and the warning, if reliable, are of superlative importance. Is it true, then, that, simply and only by ascending the stair of natural knowledge, — by persistent prolongation of its familiar processes, — we reach the stage of Mental and Moral Science? Is that stage really to be found along the same line of method, only ranged around its furthest segment? We utterly disbelieve it: and venture to affirm that no refinement of growth in the other sciences has any tendency to blossom into knowledge of the Mind; and that such knowledge, instead of being doomed to wait till the alleged prior terms in the series have been built up, begins with them at the beginning, proceeds with them *pari passu*, and can no more be put before or after them than the image in the mirror before or after the object it reflects.

The ground of these assertions is simply this: — Mental Science is Self-knowledge: Natural Science, the knowledge of something other than Self. Their spheres are of necessity mutually exclusive; yet so related that, like all true opposites, they come into existence together. Wakened up by some phenomenon from the sleep of unconsciousness, we discover two things at once, viz. ourselves as recipient and the phenomenon as given: we are in possession of an external fact and an internal feeling; and have already had our first lesson in both physical and mental knowledge. Every event, in like manner, has its outer and its inner face, and is apprehended by us as existing and as felt; contributing an element, in the one aspect, to our familiarity with nature, in the other, to our acquaintance with our own mind. The same relative fact which, in the external space, is called Light, when brought home to us, is called Vision: and whilst Optics take charge of it in the former case, it belongs to Psychology in the latter. Not a single predicate attaching to it is common to both sides of the relation: on the one, it is cause, — it is in space, — it has dimension and local movement: on the other, it is effect, — it is in time, — it is a feeling, exempt from the laws of size and measurement. This divarication of the phenomenon into two opposite directions is inherent in the cognitive act itself, and goes wherever it goes, constant as focus to focus in the ellipse: and this it is which constitutes the indestructible antithesis between physical and mental science, making them twins in their birth but without contact in their career. In the play of life, — the action and re-action, — between ourselves and the surrounding scene, attention may pass outward, and forgetting itself, may look at this or that; or may turn inward, and forgetting the world, may count the beads of thought and note the flush of feeling: and the results, of natural knowledge in the first instance and psychologic in the second, are absolutely parallel and co-ordinate, and can never be transposed into linear subordination. Self-consciousness has one realm to construe; Perceptive observation, another. Could we always forget ourselves, and use our faculty upon objects without knowing it, we should still be competent to the "interpretation of nature:" could we always forget the world, and scan the inner history alone, we should still be competent to register the laws of thought. The necessary duality of all intellectual action happily excludes this extreme, and preserves some approximate equipoise between the two momenta of our knowledge: but it is none the less true that they are perfectly distinct, however concurrent; that interchange between them is impossible; that, though they hang and balance from the same beam, the weights which are heaviest in the one have no effect upon the other; and that the attempt to treat them as homogeneous can but upset and confound the conditions of human intelligence. What is shown to us by the outer daylight of objective discovery must always be other than that which we see by the inner light of self-knowledge: and could the rays of either fall upon the other's field, there is nothing there which they could fetch out of darkness.

We submit therefore that a dualistic grouping of the Sciences, in place of a monistic, is prescribed by the fundamental conditions of Intelligence itself; that without a firm and absolute reliance on the postulates and resources of objective experience, Natural knowledge can make no way; that without equally firm and absolute reliance on the postulates and resources of self-consciousness, Mental and Moral philosophy must remain impossible; and that whilst neither can question, not either may borrow, the language and methods of the other. So long as we look at the extreme cases of contrast in the two series, — Astronomy, for instance, and Psychology, — this statement will perhaps challenge little objection: star-gazing taking us out pretty far, and thought-analyzing keeping us pretty close at home. There are however several intermediate departments of knowledge which seem to give us insight into the workings of the human mind, not by introspection, but distinctly by the study of external data. Jurisprudence and Politics, History, Philology, and Art, all engage themselves upon visible and tangible products of the past, and have no less objective a look than Botany and Geology themselves; yet all issue in deeper acquaintance with humanity: they appear to be physical in their procedure, and moral in their result. Nevertheless, they do not disturb, they even confirm, the principle of our dual arrangement. What are the "external phenomena" with which they deal? Laws and States, — the embodiment of the social Conscience; Language, — the crystallization of human Thought; Poetry, Painting, and Sculpture, — the witnesses of human Ideality; Action and Suffering, — the outcome of human Life and Passion. For the purpose of our present argument, it is an abuse of terms to call these "external" facts. They are so, in the sense in which tears are drops of water, or a ship's colors a few yards of cotton rag: but their whole essence lies in the internal meaning of which they are the record and the sign, in the invisible and spiritual facts of which they compel the very elements to take charge. And all such simply *expressive* phenomena speak to us only to the extent of our sympathy, and through the medium of our self-consciousness: did they not hold up the mirror to our inner life, and enable us better to read ourselves in their reflex image, they would tell us nothing, and would drop from the catalogue of human studies. Here, and here alone, does the maxim hold, that "like only can know like," — that the cognitive process requires community of nature between the knower and the known. In physics, it is rather the opposite rule that prevails, — of contrariety between subject and object: — at all events I need not, in order to estimate color, have my faculty prismatically painted; or, to appreciate acids, be sour myself; or, to examine the magnetic laws, be personally liable to dip. But, if I am to know humanity, human I must be; and all its memorials, so far as they are not dumb to me, are but the extension of my self-conscious being. In this distinction we have the true dividing-line between the departments of Science and Literature, and the principle of their profound difference of operation on the minds exclusively occupied with either. It would take us too far from our proper path to work out this hint at present: it is intended only adequately to carry out the dual arrangement of our intellectual pursuits, and justify the appropriation of all the "literæ humaniores" to the side of self-knowledge.

Mr. Bain's book opens with an account, lucid, exact, and compendious, of the nervous system in man. In its proper place, beside the volumes of Bell, of Quain, of Sharpey, of Carpenter, nothing could be better: and in a practical manual for students, especially when they are to be examined by the Author himself, we do not question the utility of such an exposition. It is a serviceable key to much that would else be obscure in the language of psychological writers: and just as a musician may reasonably feel some curiosity respecting acoustic laws, so is it natural that an interest in mental processes should extend itself to their organic antecedents. But, tried by any strict test of logical right, the disquisition is, in our view, altogether foreign and intrusive: and we prefer the practice of the older writers, — Reid, Stewart, and Mill, — who take up their subject no earlier than the conscious phenomena, and leave the medullary conditions entirely out of view. It is not that we doubt the physiological importance of the modern cerebral researches, or feel any thing but regret at their hitherto scanty achievements. But if they were ever so successful, — if we could get to look at all that we want, — if we could turn the exterior of a man's body into a transparent case, and compel powerful magnifiers to lay bare to us all that happens in his nerves and brain, — what we should see would not be sensation, thought, affection, but some form of movement or other visible change, which would equally show itself to any being with observing eyesight, however incapable of the corresponding inner emotion. Facts thus legible from a position foreign to the human consciousness are not mental facts, are not moral facts, and have no place in the interior of a science which professes to treat of these, and reduce them to their laws. All that could be done with such outwardly perceived phenomena, at their point of nearest approach to the pyschologist, is to note down their order of succession, in parallelism with the corresponding order of the series known to self-consciousness. Supposing two such co-ordinated trains to be established, we may admit that the physical, if the better ascertained and distincter in its terms, might help us, like the clearer column of a bilingual inscription, to identify or discriminate the parts of the other. But it cannot be pretended that our acquaintance with the nervous system supplies us with any secondary ratios of this kind by which the primary can be construed into truer order. The cerebral phenomena are in an immeasurably darker state than the mental, and are even indebted to these for every hypothetic clue by which the fancy of physiologists could find a way through their relations. The grand discovery itself (still not undisputed) of separate motory and sensory nerves only follows at a vast distance, in respect of certainty and perspicuity, the conscious difference between action and receptivity. Dr. Hartley's theory of Vibrations was not, in our judgment, a more questionable incumbrance on his doctrine of Association, than Mr. Bain's correcter physiological exposition on his subsequent intellectual analyses. While it throws not a ray of real light into them, it tinctures them with a language of materialistic description, at once unphilosophical and repulsive. When we are told of the "high charge of nervous power" needful for "susceptibility to delicate emotions,"—of the "numerous currents of the brain" involved in "wandering of the thoughts,"—of the "full development of a wave of emotion" from "the cerebral centres,"—of the "eminently glandular" nature of "the tender affections;"—when it is observed that "Irascibility may draw to itself a large share of the vital sap;"—and that "the tender emotion usurps largely a great portion of mankind, being so alimented by the natural conformation of the system as to maintain its characteristic wave with considerable persistence," and that "this gives great capacity for the affections," especially with "requisite support" from "the structure of the glandular organs;"*—we lose all sense of psychological truth, and no more know ourselves again than if, on looking in the glass, we were to see an anatomical figure staring at us. There is no more occasion for such phraseology, than for an artist to paint his Madonna with the skin off. It is recommended neither by scientific precision, nor by illustrative good taste. The one only excellence of psychological description is to speak truly and searchingly to our self-consciousness: and of vital sap, and high charges, and powerful currents, and diffusive waves, we certainly are not conscious: nor do we know of any writer resorting to this style of exposition, without forfeiture of all fineness and sharpness in his delineations of spiritual facts, and quite degenerating from the purity of Berkeley, the neatness of Stewart, the severity of Kant, the transparency of Jouffroy.

* The Emotions and the Will, pp. 32, 193, 230, 94, 233, 232.

We have said that the psychological difference between active power and the passive susceptibilities of Sense was familiar to mental philosophers, and was treated as fundamental, long before the physiological separation of motory from sensory nerves. Of the vast majority of writers the remark is so true, that this distinction is seldom absent from the leading divisions and even titles of their works. But there is one important class of exceptions. The Sensational psychologists have steadily resisted the claims of this distinction; have denied its ultimate reality, and by various ingenuities resolved it away; have contended that activity means only muscular movement, and that this is both set a-going and made known exclusively by sensation. From this sole source, followed by the clinging together of connected movements and the vestiges of contiguous sensations, they have explained all the phenomena of human nature. Of all the difficulties of this undertaking, no one has been more pressed upon them, and more in vain, than that of extracting from a primitive passivity the various forms of energy and struggle. At last however the conviction, which has so long stood out against psychological appeal, is yielded to physiology: and Sir Charles Bell having detached the nerves, Mr. Bain separates the functions, of action and sensation. He admits as original, along with the susceptibilities of sense, a spontaneity of movement, — a start into energy without any prefix of feeling: and this is the capital new feature, — certainly a marked improvement, — which he has added to the resources of his school. In order to turn this spontaneity, — quite random at first, — into volition, he assumes an inherent tendency to persistence in every muscular adjustment which procures a pleasure or relieves a pain: in virtue of which this class of movements, once hit upon, disengage themselves from the heterogeneous mass of possible combinations, and fall into the track, and come under the command, of regulated associations. This mode of deriving the voluntary from the involuntary phenomena is essentially the same with that of Hartley and James Mill: and, though carried out with much fuller elaboration, and addressing itself more carefully to the grand *nodus* of the problem, — the process of deliberate preference and decision, — will probably convert no one who has been left unsatisfied by the previous expositors. The real novelty lies higher up: in freeing the first involuntary movements from their dependence on any sort of feeling, and so creating a fund of spontaneity to set off against the stores of sensation, and make acquaintance with them.

This doubling of the established data of his school, by the introduction of a term distinctly antithetic to sensation, seemed to us at first to offer the means of reconciliation with the opposite philosophy. Nothing could look more like a surrender of the monistic for a dualistic principle. But, we regret to say, the promise is for the present illusory. The reason is this. Though Mr. Bain grants us a spontaneity, he plants it where we have nothing to do with it, any more than if our limbs were spasmodically stirred by a galvanic touch. In his zeal to cancel Hartley's prefix of a sensational stimulus, he forgets to leave any attendant consciousness at the fountain-head at all, and makes the movement come, *psychologically*, out of nothing. The first thing we feel is the series of muscular sensations in the execution of the act: there it is, accordingly, that our conscious life begins, and the prior word of command for the initiation of the act took place outside. The dynamics of the case are thus quite numb and foreign to us: and our experience still dates from the earliest sensation, and includes no counter element. So far as our mental history is concerned, this novelty of Mr. Bain's is therefore inoperative, and lapses back into that mere emphasizing of the muscular feelings so familiar to the readers of Dr. Thomas Brown. Could he only have burst through the enchantments of this paralyzing sensational circle, we believe him to have been on the eve of an important advance. By simply drawing his "spontaneity" and its force within the limits of consciousness, instead of leaving it beyond the threshold, solutions arise of problems otherwise unmanageable. On one of these we will dwell for a few moments, — the origin of the beliefs respecting Externality and Space.

It is admitted on all hands, — or, at least, we shall freely concede it to our author's philosophy, — that if, like Condillac's sentient statue, we simply stood still and felt this and that sensation of smell, taste, or sound, we should have no knowledge of an outward world. The conditions of this belief first enter in connection with the muscular system; in the exercise of which we gain our apprehensions of objects distinct from ourselves, of their dimensions, forms, positions, and of the circumambient field in which they lie. So far we are agreed. But now comes the question, how are the muscles qualified to give us this special instruction? and by what process do they impart it? Brown, Mill, Bain, all concur in their answer. First, we gain the idea of *linear extension* by muscular feelings of various range, as in the slight or greater closing of the fingers, or sweep of the arm, or exploring a wire: part of a given series of sensations not being the same to us as the whole, or a less part as a more considerable, we have differences for every degree of continuance; and these are so many *lengths*. Next, we have but to give this idea numerical increase, *i.e.* conceive of *co-existing lengths*, whether by joint action of a plurality of fingers, or by combining the movements of one over a surface, as of a pane of glass, — and we are introduced to *superficial extension*. And lastly, by letting our fancy go out with its length-idea on all radii from any point, we win at once the conception of *Space;* or again, by embracing a solid object between the two hands, we discover co-existing surfaces separated by lengths, and complete our triad of dimensions. Thus our idea of Extension is built up, bit by bit, one dimension at a time; and the last to come, in the order of our knowledge, is geometrical solidity.

Every thing, in this exposition, depends on the soundness of the first step; the others, being little else than contrivances for multiplying lengths, disappear of themselves if the lengths are yet to seek. How, then, are they got? Merely, it is said, by our experiencing in the muscles a train of sensations, coming to an end, now sooner, now later; this variation in the protraction of the series being the gist of the whole matter, and giving us our *quæsitum* of *length*. If so, however, *any* succession of feelings susceptible of similar variation would do as well: a melody heard, now complete, now broken off; a cycle of odors, at one time half administered, at another cut short near the beginning, would meet all the prescribed conditions, and ought to furnish us with the Knowledge of Extension. The liability to more or less abbreviation of the sensational thread is no peculiarity of the muscular sense: and to pitch upon this circumstance as giving us our comparison of lengths is fatal to the exclusive claim which is set up for this class of feelings. What can be more inconsistent than, first, to single out the locomotive organs as alone competent to the phenomenon, and then to refer the phenomenon to something in them which is no speciality of theirs at all? Do you fly then to the distinctive *quality* of their feelings, rather than their mere interrupted succession? Different, of course, the muscular feelings are from smells, as tastes also or sounds are from both; but so long as they are *only* sensations, delivered upon our consciousness one after another, they win no advantage, for purposes of objective disclosure, over their companions. Even could we know them by ever so perfect an introspection, they would be found in us, not out of us, and would not help us to step beyond the subjective world: their succession would be in *duration*, not in *space*, and would give us the sequent parts of time, not the synchronous parts of linear extension. Ring the changes as you will upon mere Sensation, these difficulties will shut you in. The only reason why the passive reception of odors would not reveal the outward world is, that it does not go beyond sensation; and so long as you stop at that stage, the muscles will serve you no better than the pituitary membrane.

In what, then, really consists the prerogative distinction of the muscular system? It has an obvious and important peculiarity. In our experience of smell, hearing, &c., the first thing that happens is the sensation, which arrives at us out of the unknown, and wakes us up in an unexpected way; and any cognitive act, when we are in a condition to have one, follows on the sensitive phenomenon. But the muscular sensations occur in executing an act already ordered by mandate from ourselves; the signal for them is passed before they arise, and this mental prefix, name it as you will, prevents our being taken by surprise with the phenomenon, and provides an incipient cognitive element at the fountain-head. This inverse order of procedure in the locomotive faculty redeems it altogether from the category of the Senses. It starts from a point that is no more "Sensation" than the cognitions in which the proper Senses terminate; call it volition, or call it spontaneous energy, it is the putting forth of personal causation. This is a function beyond the province of mere Sense. A *Sense* cannot *make efforts;* nor are its phenomena causes, but effects. Not even, we believe, are sensations an essential feature in the executive stage of the operation; if the muscles were made of india-rubber, or paralyzed in their sensory nerves, their system, we conceive, would not be disqualified, provided it obeyed the mandates from head-quarters, for giving us knowledge of an objective world. This knowledge breaks on us from the collision of our own conscious force with impeding resistance: and so long as the two extremes retain this relation, the intermediary members may be many or few, sensible or insensible, without hindering our discovery of the antithetic Subject and Object: the one *here*, the other *there;* the one *Causal hence*, the other *Causal hither*. By removing the dynamical commencement of this experience out of consciousness, and beginning our psychological history lower down, in the sensations of the executive muscles, Mr. Bain appears to us to have missed the true germ of our ideas of Personality, of Space, and of Causation.

No doubt, the accurate *measurement* of our force against variable resistances, and of the several intervals between objects, is largely dependent on the proper muscular sensations, which are invaluable as a scheme of graduated signs. But the *things measured and signified*, — apart from the appreciation of their degrees, — are cognizable through an energy behind the muscles. The collision of that energy of ours with the counter-energy of the world, as attested by Sensation, reveals to us, by the crossing lines of direction, the contrast of the Self and the other-than-Self, and gives us, as Categories for all phenomena, the two centres of Personality and Externality. The antithesis of these mutually excluding terms carries in itself both a geometrical opposition of Place, and a dynamical opposition of Force. Instead of our having to go to school for a long experience, in order to be trained into these ideas, our whole experience constitutes itself around these apprehensions, as its three grand axes; and of the two sides of each pair, neither has any advantage over the other: the outer and the inner both are given in the same act, and known by the same self-light, or rather reciprocal light; and there is no more propriety in saying, that we know the external world only through our own feelings, than in saying that we know our own feelings only through the external world. To know at all involves both terms: and the attempt to establish a subordination between them, and resolve objective cognition into subjective consciousness of our own phenomena, is nothing else than, in the very act of patronizing experience, to destroy its fundamental postulates, and open the way to every idealistic dream. The following passage is therefore, in our view, far from satisfactory:

> "As our belief in the externality of the causes of our sensations means, that certain actions of ours will bring the sensations into play, or modify them in a known manner, this belief is easily furnished to us by experience; it is no more than our experience entitles us to entertain. Having felt, again and again, that a tree becomes larger to the eye as we move; that this movement brings on at last a sensation of touch; that this sensation of touch varies with movements of our arm, and a great many other similar coincidences; the repetition of all this experience fixes it in the mind, and from the sight alone we can anticipate all the rest. We then know that our movements will bring about all the changes and sensations above described, and we know no more; but this knowledge is to us the recognition of external existence, the only thing, so far as I see, that external existence can possibly mean. Belief in external reality is the anticipation of a given effect to a given antecedent; and the effects and causes are our own various sensations and movements." (*The Senses and the Intellect*, p. 373.)

According to this, to see the sun in the heavens is to believe that, if we could only keep on walking long enough, we might burn our fingers; to descry the lark aloft, is to recite by muscular sympathy the beating of its wings since it left its nest; to think of any distant space is to run over our locomotive sensations in reaching it, and the opportunity of thrusting out our arm when we have got there. Emptiness means simply scope for muscular exercise; and the Infinitude of Space imports only potential gymnastics for us under all conceivable circumstances. This kind of "analysis" of our ideas seems to us, we must confess, a cruel operation, — a cold-blooded dissecting of them to death. The *disjecta membra* given as their equivalents, and strung together in succession to replace the original whole, defy all identification. Look down an avenue of trees, and consider whether, in appreciating its perspective, you are engaged upon the mere imagination of touches, or the computation of fatigue? Watch a lighthouse from a ship's deck, by night, laying its long line of beads towards you upon the waves, and say whether the thing denoted by this "visual sign" has any thing to do with either your legs or your finger-ends. Can you believe that even to a blind geometrician diagrams and areas present themselves, not as simultaneous existences beyond his personality, but as possible series of tactual impressions in himself? or, that when James Mitchell, the blind deaf-mute, amused himself with picking stones out of the brook, ranging them in a circle on the grass, and then assuming the centre as his own seat, the figure of his environment did not lie in his dark imagination complete at once? For our own part, we utterly distrust this whole doctrine, which construes back the grand synchronous unity of Space into trains of muscular successions in our Sense, and interprets the objective world into cohesive relations among our subjective phenomena. How completely all externality disappears in the *Ego*, when this psychology is fairly carried out, will be evident from the following passage, in which the existence of light is made contingent on the visual feelings, and the whole language of outward being and causation is treated as an empty product of "abstraction:"

"We seem to have no better way of assuring ourselves and all mankind that with the conscious movement of opening the eyes there will always be a consciousness of light, than by saying that the light exists as independent fact, with or without any eyes to see it. But if we consider the case fairly, we shall see that this assertion errs, not simply in being beyond any evidence that we can have, but also in being a self-contradiction. We are affirming that to have an existence out of our minds which we cannot know but as in our minds. In words we assert independent existence, while in the very act of doing so we contradict ourselves. Even a possible world implies a possible mind to perceive it, just as much as an actual world implies an actual mind. The mistake of the common modes of expression in this matter, is the mistake of supposing the abstractions of the mind to have a separate and independent existence. This is the doctrine of the Platonic 'ideas,' or 'forms,' which are understood to impart all that is common to the particular facts or realities, instead of being derived from them by an operation of the mind. Thus the actual circles of nature derive their mathematical properties from the pre-existing 'idea,' or circle in the abstract; the actual men owe their sameness to the ideal man. So instead of looking upon the doctrine of an external and independent world as a generalization or abstraction grounded on our particular experiences, summing up the past, and predicting the future, we have got into the way of maintaining the abstraction to be an independent reality, the foundation, or cause, or origin, of all those experiences." (*The Senses and the Intellect*, p. 376.)

This is the old pitfall, where philosophy, too boldly stepping on its solid-looking sensational ground, has so often tumbled through into a bottomless Idealism. We are not to say, it seems, that light exists as an "independent fact." Then it exists either as a dependent fact, or not at all. If the former, it is dependent on vision, that is, on its own effect, which is absurd. If the latter, then vision exists by itself; that is, effect without the cause, perception with nothing perceived. Our author plainly confounds the two inverse kinds of "dependence,"—logical, in the order of knowing,—real, in the order of being;—the *causa cognoscendi* and the *causa essendi*. The *knowledge* of light is dependent on vision, its effect; the *being* of vision is dependent on light, its cause: whose relative "inde pendent existence" is so far from being "contradicted," that it is directly implied, by its dependent logical position:—the two things being indeed but one and the same relation read from opposite ends. Our author, it is true, affirms that "we cannot know light, *but as in our minds*." But how so? Because, we presume, it is known by *seeing it*, and that is an act of the mind. Yes, certainly; *the seeing:*—but, on that very account, not the *things seen:* for the cognitive act, instead of implying coalescence and identity, is conditional on separation and mutual exclusion, of the knower and the known, and can reveal neither except as over against the other. Were it otherwise,—were all that we know to be on that account seated at the cognitive point,—knowledge and being must coalesce, and could never look each other in the face: nothing could be known as existing: and nothing could exist as known. The intellectual power itself would constitute a disqualification for intelligence. If there really were external objects, and a faculty in us for their apprehension, Mr. Bain's argument would still apply: if where they are known, there we must presume them to be, our cognizance of them as external ought to be treated as false; its truth would be a proper ground for disbelieving it; and the perfect knowledge of a thing would be its absolute disproof.

A psychology which allows us cognizance only of the thread of our own feelings is obliged to account for the objective look and substantive pretensions of some portions of our knowledge, by making up aggregates of feelings, and assuming that their chemical union gives them the fallacious aspect of being more than feelings, — of being elsewhere than in ourselves, — of being one instead of many. The grand instrument of this metamorphosis, we need hardly say, is the Association of Ideas, — or, more properly, of actions and mental states; among which, either contiguous terms, or resembling terms, have a tendency to revive each other. This is a veritable and universally recognized psychological law: and to the great merits of his school in vindicating its importance and extending its application Mr. Bain has made large additions in his copious and elaborate exposition. Without the originality of Hartley (whose work, after every deduction, still stands in the highest rank of psychological literature), and without the severe precision of James Mill, our author opens a fuller storehouse of illustration, and spreads out its contents in a more telling and agreeable way. He is master of all the dexterities of this law, and prepared to show the utmost that can be done with it. Whether it is not overtasked is perhaps a natural question with even the most trustful reader. Its requirements are so modest, and its achievements so grand, that it is apt to be suspected for the very scale of its apparent victories. 'Given the rudiments of any brute,'— so it seems to state its problem, — 'to construct the perfection of any angel.' The five senses and ganglionic spontaneities are briskly stretched upon the Jacquard-loom: the cards, perforated according to theory, are hung upon the beam: and after a few chapters of cheerful weaving, the divine form is finished off; and you have the satisfaction not only of admiring it, but of knowing exactly what its reason, love, and goodness are made of, and how put together. The doctrine, appealing as it does chiefly to the earliest experience, and making rapid use of the years of infancy, rests, to a dangerous extent, on a conjectural psychology. It has already got over all its difficulties before the age when reflection can put it to the test: and when called in question by the mature and practised self-consciousness, glibly answers that it is too late in the day to bring up any inner evidence against it; that its wonders are all wrought within us, and can no longer be unravelled; that we have been so transformed by it as not to know ourselves, and to be decipherable only by its light; that what we take to be the simplest mental states it knows to be superlatively complex; — what, the primary truths of reason, to be the ultimate tricks of language; — what, the native insight of conscience, to be the artificial imposition of social opinion. It is always difficult, for want of recognized criteria, to criticise hypothetical history; as, for want of common substance, to fight a duel with a ghost. Being, however, to no small extent, at one with this doctrine, we may perhaps hope to explain a scruple which checks our complete assent to it. For the sake of distinctness we limit ourselves to a certain point.

All the langage of the doctrine is framed on the supposition that, a number of elements being given, and laid detached before the mind, it cements them together in groups and trains, in ever-increasing complexity. The mental history is, in this view, a perpetual formation of new compounds: and the words, "Association," "Suggestion," "Cohesion," "Fusion," "Indissoluble Connection," all express the change from plurality of data to some unity of result. An explanation of the process therefore requires two things; — a true enumeration of the primary constituents, and a correct statement of their laws of combination: just as, in chemistry, we are furnished with a list of the simple elements, and then with the principles of their synthesis. Now the latter of these two conditions we find satisfied by the Association psychologists: but not the former. They are not agreed upon their catalogue of elements, or the marks by which they may know the simple from the compound. The psychologic unit is not fixed; that which is called *one* impression by Hartley is treated as half-a-dozen or more by Mill: and the tendency of the modern teachers on this point is to recede more and more from the better chosen track of their master. Hartley, for example, regarded the whole present effect upon us of any single object, — say, an orange, — as a single sensation; and the whole vestige it left behind, as a single "idea of sensation." His modern disciples, on the other hand, consider this same effect as an aggregate from a plurality of sensations, and the ideal trace it leaves as highly compound. The "idea of an object," instead of being an elementary starting-point with them, is one of the elaborate results of repetition and experience; and is continually adduced as remarkably illustrating the fusing power of habitual association. Thus James Mill observes:

"It is to this great law of association that we trace the formation of our ideas of what we call external objects; that is, the ideas of a certain number of sensations, received together so frequently that they coalesce as it were, and are spoken of under the idea of unity. Hence, what we call the idea of a tree, the idea of a stone, the idea of a horse, the idea of a man. In using the names, tree, horse, man, the names of what I call objects, I am referring, and can be referring, only to my own sensations; in fact, therefore, only naming a certain number of sensations, regarded as in a particular state of combination; that is, concomitance. Particular sensations of sight, of touch, of the muscles, are the sensations to the ideas of which, color, extension, roughness, hardness, smoothness, taste, smell, so coalescing as to appear one idea, I give the name, idea of a tree."*

To precisely the same effect Mr. Bain remarks:

"External objects usually affect us through a plurality of senses. The pebble on the seashore is pictured on the eye as form and color. We take it up in the hand and repeat the

* Analysis of the Phenomena of the Human Mind, vol. i. p. 71.

impression of form, with the additional feeling of touch. Knock two together, and there is a characteristic sound. To preserve the impression of an object of this kind, there must be an association of all these different effects. Such association, when matured and firm, is our idea, our intellectual grasp of the pebble. Passing to the organic world, and plucking a rose, we have the same effects of form to the eye and hand, color and touch, with the new effects of odor and taste. A certain time is requisite for the coherence of all these qualities in one aggregate, so as to give us for all purposes the enduring image of the rose. When fully acquired, any one of the characteristic impressions will revive the others; the odor, the sight, the feeling of the thorny stalk, — each of these by itself will hoist the entire impression into the view." (*The Senses and the Intellect*, p. 411.)

Now, this order of derivation, making our objective knowledge begin with plurality of impression and arrive at unity, we take to be a complete inversion of our psychological history. Hartley, we think, was perfectly right in taking no notice of the number of inlets through which an object delivers its effect upon us, and, in spite of this circumstance, treating the effect as one. Had he explicitly drawn out the principle which implicitly guided him, it would have assumed perhaps something like this form: 'That each state of consciousness, whether awakened through more or fewer channels, is, during its continuance, originally simple; and can resolve itself only by change of equilibrium.' No psychological law appears to have higher evidence than this; and, little as the range of its consequences has been perceived, there are probably few who would dispute it when stated in a general form. Were it not true, the feeling of each moment, determined as it is by innumerable conditions in our organism, not one of which could change and leave our state the same, would seem to us, or must once have seemed, infinitely intricate. But the constancies of our system, however numerous, never disclose themselves till they break up; the functional sensibilities of the organic life first report their character when they go wrong; the muscles, blended in a state of rest, detach themselves by the permutations of motion, and acquire, as in learning the use of a keyed instrument, more and more delicate discriminations of feeling and action; and if the special senses less obviously converge upon one psychologic point, it is only because their relations are perpetually shifting *inter se*, and disappointing our experiments of the requisite statical conditions. But even now, after life has read us so many analytic lessons, in proportion as we can fix the attitude of our scene and ourselves, the sense of plurality in our impressions retreats, and we lapse into an undivided consciousness; losing, for instance, the separate notice of any uniform hum in the ear, or light in the eye, or weight of clothes on the body, though not one of them is inoperative on the complexion of our feeling. This law, once granted, must be carried far beyond Hartley's point. Not only must each object present itself to us integrally before it shells off into its qualities, but the whole scene around us must disengage for us object after object from its still background by emergence and change; and even our self-detachment from the world over-against us must wait for the start of collision between the force we issue and that which we receive. To confine ourselves to the simplest case: when a red ivory-ball, seen for the first time, has been withdrawn, it will leave a mental representation of itself, in which all that it simultaneously gave us will indistinguishably co-exist. Let a white ball succeed to it; now, and not before, will an attribute detach itself, and the color, by force of contrast, be shaken out into the foreground. Let the white ball be replaced by an egg: and this new difference will bring the form into notice from its previous slumber. And thus, that which began by being simply an object, cut out from the surrounding scene, becomes for us first a *red* object, and then a *red round* object; and so on. Instead, therefore, of the qualities, as separately given, subscribing together and adding themselves up to present us with the object as their aggregate, the object is beforehand with them, and from its integrity delivers them out to our knowledge, one by one. In this disintegration, the primary nucleus never loses its substantive character or name; whilst the difference which it throws off appears as a mere attribute, expressed by an adjective. Hence it is that we are compelled to think of the object as *having*, not as *being*, its qualities; and can never heartily admit the belief of any loose lot of attributes really fusing themselves into a *thing*. The unity of the original whole is not felt to go to pieces and be resolved into the properties which it successively gives off; it retains a residuary existence, which constitutes it a *substance*, as against the emerging quality, which is only its *phenomenal predicate*. Were it not for this perpetual process of differentiation — of self from the world, of object from its scene, of attribute from object, no step of Abstraction could be taken; no qualities could fall under our notice; and had we ten thousand senses, they would all converge and meet in but one consciousness. But if this be so, it is an utter falsification of the order of nature to speak of sensations grouping themselves into aggregates, and so composing for us the objects of which we think; and the whole language of the theory, in regard to the field of synchronous existences, is a direct inversion of the truth. Experience proceeds and intellect is trained, not by Association, but by *Dissociation*, not by reduction of pluralities of impression to one, but by the opening out of one into many; and a true psychological history must expound itself in analytic rather than synthetic terms. Precisely those ideas,—of Substance, of Mind, of Cause, of Space,—which this system treats as infinitely complex, the last result of myriads of confluent elements, are in truth the residuary simplicities of consciousness, whose stability the eddies and currents of phenomenal experience have left undisturbed. The same inversion of the real mental order has exercised, we think, an injurious influence on the whole Logic and Philology of the Association philosophers; the organism of speech requiring, for its due interpretation, to be read *downward* from its wholes into its parts; and, without this, being hardly capable of construction *upwards* from the atoms of predication to its life. We cannot at present expand these hints; but they will suffice to show the wide sweep which a fundamental psychological truth or error cannot fail to have, and how the whole configuration of philosophy may be affected by even a slight want of precision in its first lines. Mr. Bain often approaches very near the important principle (as it seems to us) of the Unity of original consciousness; speaking, for instance, of "the concurrence of Sensations in one common stream of consciousness, in the same cerebral highway" (*The Senses and the Intellect*, p. 359); and in the following passage not only recognizing, but enforcing, the necessity of differentiation by change:

"Were it not for the primitive shock that difference gives, there would be no basis for the intellect. All colors would be alike; sounds would not be distinct from touches or smells, and there would be no cognition possible in any sense. The feeling of difference, therefore, is the first step; the impressing of that, under the plastic property of the mind, into an enduring notion is the next. We begin by being alive to the distinctive shocks of red and green, of round and oval, small and large; by and by, we attain to the fixed notion of a rose on its stem; thence we go on combining this with others, until the mind is full of the most variegated trains of imagery. The laws of association follow up, and do not necessarily imply, or contain in themselves, the primordial sense of difference, which is the most rudimentary of all the properties of our intellectual being. Analysis can descend no deeper, explanation can go no farther; we must make a stand upon this, as the preliminary condition of all intelligence, and merely seek to place its character in a clear and certain light." (*The Emotions and the Will*, p. 626.)

Whilst insisting, however, on the indispensableness of change of impression, Mr. Bain apparently thinks this condition sufficiently provided for by the mere co-existence of sensations through a plurality of Senses; the power of discriminating which he attributes to the Intellect as an ultimate and fundamental prerogative:

"The basis or fundamental peculiarity of the Intellect is discrimination, or the feeling of difference between consecutive, *or co-existing* impressions. Nothing more fundamental can possibly be assigned as the defining mark of intelligence, and emotion as such does not imply any such property." (*The Emotions and the Will*, p. 614.)

"Consecutive impressions" involve change; but "co-existing impressions" do not: and if the discriminative power is equally related to both, it is not dependent on the occurrence of change. And conversely, if it demand change, it can do nothing with mere co-existing impressions. This last position we believe to be the true one; and we cannot assent to Dugald Stewart's statement: "Although we had never seen but one rose, we might still have been able to attend to its color, without thinking of its other properties." * Mr. Bain, in concurring with this opinion of Stewart's, and attributing plurality to the original effect of a single object, appears to us to forget his own doctrine as to impossibility of any sense of difference without change, and to let slip a psychological clue already familiar to his hand.

We have lingered near the *incunabula* of the opposite psychologies in the hope that, by scrutiny of their development at its initial stage, some approximate lines might be found for them to prevent their rapid divergence. The only hope of improved mutual understanding lies at the beginning. To discuss the ulterior questions into which they run is a far easier and more attractive task; but, at the same time, utterly useless, till the logical preliminaries are determined — a mere race from different starting-points over incommensurable

* Elements of the Philosophy of the Human Mind, part ii. chap. iv. sect. 1.

fields. The enormous differences which open out as the two methods pursue their way suffice, for those who know them, to throw an interest around the finer distinctions at the commencement. If the dualistic method be admissible, we obtain at the fountain-head, unless our ultimate constitution be unveracious, direct authority for a few primitive cognitions, accurately corresponding with the most rooted and universal beliefs of mankind — viz. the substantial existence of ourselves as knowing Subject, and of the external world as known Object; the reality and infinity of Space as the seat of the latter with its contents, and the reality and infinity of Duration as containing the successions of the former; the origin of all phenomena from a causality not phenomenal. In such judgments, accepted as the inherent postulates of all intelligence, we have a few first truths to render experience possible, and to form a basis for reliable knowledge. If the monistic principle holds, if the only thing accessible to us is our own phenomena, if they are but transformed sensations, if, moreover, they are phenomena of nothing and nobody, — it is idle to speak of cognition at all; there is neither outer world to be known, nor any "we" to know it: the inner history alone is fact; and it can furnish no rational propositions, except about the groupings, the successions, or the resemblances *inter se*, of the feelings and ideas composing it. Body means the experience of certain muscular sensations; Space, the experience of their absence; Infinity, the conception of their possibility; and what we say of these can be only autobiographical, without validity beyond. Causality denotes the constant priority of one of our states to another. Belief means an association of ideas and feelings, strong enough to stir muscular sensations. Perception is a very misleading word; pretending to refer some sensation to an object that gives it, but properly referring it only to the group that has it. Personality is the sum-total of all the feelings in any one conscious life up to its present moment, — in common language, rather aristocratically limited to human beings; and to say, 'I committed this sin,' is to tack on a new phenomenon at the end of a train and lengthen its thread. There can be no first truths; for we form no judgments till we have got language, and must have the parts of speech before we can predicate any thing; and then any stiff association of ideas, however arbitrary, is ready to set up for self-evidence. The propositions which assume this look are about nothing except empty abstractions of the mind's creation, yielding only an illusory certainty; and it is a rule that a Science, to be demonstrative, must be hypothetical; and, to be pure, its hypotheses must be false. The steadiness with which the thorough-paced Hartleyan walks through these startling paradoxes, — the rigor with which he follows out their lines, with a pleasant sense of beauty and discovery, — we cannot but regard as curiously expressive of the mind logical rather than psychological. The skill and ingenuity are often marvellous; but to a very large extent are expended, not in interpreting, so much as in explaining away, your actual consciousness; in converting it into some strange, uncomfortable coin, declared to be its change in full; in apologizing for the imperfect evidence of their equivalence, and showing that it could not well be greater, considering all that they have had to go through. Just as Mr. Darwin, on finding fossil species disinclined to help him, fixes on them an *ex-parte* character, and urges that his genuine witnesses must have disappeared and become indistinguishably worked up into the very grain of the world; so does the Association psychologist feel no discouragement from the refractory look of mental facts as they are, whilst he can plead that the rudimentary forms are compelled by the very hypothesis to vanish, and lie mingled invisibly with the containing strata of the mind. There is obviously a limit beyond which this kind of plea cannot be carried without withdrawing the doctrine it is meant to benefit from all rational test: and the extent to which it is urged, measures the degree in which conjecture takes the place of the *vera causa*. Now, when it is remembered that almost every one of the *distinctively human* phenomena presents a *crux interpretum* to this school; that the points at which suspicion of psychological tampering arises include the Ideas of Space and Time, the ground of the Mathematics; of Substance and Causality, implied in Physics; of Personality and Obligation, the conditions of Morals; of Right, the basis of Law; of Beauty, the essence of Art; of Supreme Goodness, the inspiration of Religion; that whilst Memory and Conception and Habit are fairly explained, Belief and Volition are analyzed out of their identity; the disproportion becomes striking between the assured value of the doctrine and its cost. At every one of these points, Mr. Bain's exposition has, to our feeling, the peculiar character of ingenious unreality which is so common in all the later writings of his school, and which so markedly distinguishes the subtle misconstructions of Brown and Mill from the faithful half-analysis of Locke. We find ourselves entangled continually in mere *quasi-psychology*, which does not in the least speak to any thing within; but shows how, under certain enumerated conditions, an equivalent to the actual state of mind might be produced. This is more especially the case in the second volume, where the author's description of the *moral* phenomena seems to us to be drawn from some quite imaginary human nature; and to have no relation to the real experiences and faiths of tempted and struggling men. Highly significant of his method in this respect is his habitual discontent with the *language* in which men have embodied their ethical feeling and thought. The great question of Moral Liberty is got rid of by a wholesale objection to every one of its leading terms: "Freedom" is inappropriate; "Necessity" is an incumbrance; "Self-determination" is a bad name for motive pleasures and pains; "Choice" can mean nothing but the ending of suspense in a single line of activity; and so on. These terms "have weighed like a nightmare upon the investigation of the active region of the mind." Does the suspicion never cross Mr. Bain that to cancel the vocabulary of moral thought and feeling is to discharge the phenomena from his philosophy? We refrain, however, from following him at present into this great field; his elaborate treatment of which would require an independent discussion.

REVELATION; WHAT IT IS NOT AND WHAT IT IS.*

As there is a substance, we believe, which not only burns in water, but actually kindles at the very touch of water, so there certainly are insatiable doubts, which not only resist the power, but seem to kindle at the very centre of Christian faith. There is one question which we should have supposed set at rest for ever in the mind of any man who believes either in the revelations of conscience or those of Scripture, — the question whether or not it is permitted to man to *know*, and grow in the knowledge of, God. If that be not possible, we, for our part, should have assumed that religion was a name for unwise, because useless, yearnings in the heart of man; and the Revelation — whether natural or supernatural — which professes to satisfy those yearnings, simply a delusion. Yet so numerous and closely twined are the threads of human faith and scep-

* What is Revelation? A Series of Sermons on the Epiphany; to which are added "Letters to a Student of Theology on the Bampton Lectures of Mr. Mansel." By the Rev. F. D. Maurice, M.A. Cambridge: Macmillan, 1859.

Preface to the Third Edition of Mr. Mansel's Bampton Lectures on the Limits of Religious Thought. London: Murray, 1857.

Characteristics of the Gospel Miracles: Sermons preached before the University of Cambridge. By F. B. Westcott, M.A. Cambridge: Macmillan.

National Review, July, 1859.

ticism, that probably half the Christian world scarcely knows whether to think God Himself the subject of Revelation, or only some fragment of his purposes for man; while professed apologists for Christianity are often, like Mr. Mansel, far firmer believers in the irremovable veil which covers the face of God, than in the faint gleams of light which manage to penetrate what they hold to be its almost opaque texture. And, as we have intimated, this doubt is not only not extinguished by the Christian Revelation, but it seems in some cases even to feed on its very essence. Mr. Mansel seems to regard the Christian revelation almost as express evidence that God is inscrutable and inaccessible to man, in that it only provides for us a "finite" type of the infinite mystery, and presents to us in Christ not, he thinks, the truth of God, but the best approximation to that truth — though possibly infinitely removed from it — of which "finite" minds are capable. In other words, he believes in the veil even more intensely than in the revelation: nay, he seems to think this profound conviction — that the veil is inherent in the very essence of our human nature, and indissoluble even by death itself, unless death can dissever the formal laws of human and finite thought — likely to enhance our reverence for the voices, so mysteriously "adapted" to finite intelligence, which float to us from behind it. "In this impotence of Reason," he says, "we are compelled to take refuge in faith, and to believe that an Infinite Being exists, though we know not how; and that He is the same with that Being who is made known in consciousness as our Sustainer and our Lawgiver." And again, in the preface to his new edition:

"It has been objected by reviewers of very opposite schools, that to deny to man a knowledge of the Infinite, is to make Revelation itself impossible, and to leave no room for evidences on which reason can be legitimately employed. The objection would be pertinent, if I had ever maintained that Revelation is, or can be, a direct manifestation of the Infinite nature of God. But I have constantly asserted the very reverse. In Revelation, as in Natural Religion, God is represented under finite conceptions, adapted to finite minds; and the evidences on which the authority of Revelation rests are finite and comprehensible also. It is true that in Revelation, no less than in the exercise of our natural faculties, there is indirectly indicated the existence of a higher truth, which, as it cannot be grasped by any effort of human thought, cannot be made the vehicle of any valid philosophical criticism. But the comprehension of this higher truth is no more necessary either to a belief in the contents of Revelation, or to a reasonable examination of its evidences, than a conception of the infinite divisibility of matter is necessary to the child before it can learn to walk."

The fact of Revelation, as it is conceived by Mr. Mansel, is, then, a mere adaptation of Truth to human forms of thought, whether it come through conscience or through Scripture; in both cases alike it is the formation in our minds of a "representative idea," or type, of God, not the direct presentation of the Divine Life to our spirits, which he believes that we could not receive and live. By conscience the vision of a holy but finite Judge, Lawgiver, Father, is borne in upon our hearts, namely, through the consciousness of our dependence and of moral obligation; by Scripture the historical picture of a finite law, a Providence adapted to finite minds, and lastly, a finite but perfect Son is presented to our eyes. Thus certain messages have issued from the depths of the infinite mystery, which have been mercifully translated for us into the meagre forms of human thought: some of them are spontaneously welcomed by human consciences; others, attested as they are by superhuman marvels, and not inconsistent with the revelations of the conscience, are accepted as convincing by human reason; and both alike help to teach us, — not what God is, — but how we may think of Him with least risk of unspeakable error. By these necessarily indirect hints, as the truest of which our nature is capable, Mr. Mansel entreats us to hold, and to guide our footsteps; calling them "regulative truths," by which he means the best *working hypothesis* we are able to attain of the character and purposes of God. They are the only palliatives of that darkness, to which the blinding veil of a human nature inevitably dooms us. Revelation, we are told, cannot unloose the "cramping" laws of a limited consciousness; it cannot help the finite to apprehend the infinite; but it can do something to guide us in our blindness, so that we may not unconsciously fall foul of the forces and laws of that infinite world which we are unable to know; it can give us a "conception" of God, which is quite true enough as a practical manual for human conduct. But, to use Mr. Mansel's own words, "how far that knowledge represents God as He is, we know not, and have no need to know."

With this theory of Mr. Mansel's we have already dealt in part.* We should rejoice that it had been given to the world if only for the reply which it has

* See page 213.

called forth from Mr. Maurice, — a reply which is not merely an embodiment of a completely opposite conviction, but the insurrection of an outraged faith, the protest of a whole character against a doctrine which pronounces that all the springs of its life have been delusions, and which tries to pass off human notions of God in the place of God. Books generally go but a little way below the outer varnish of men's individual culture; and it is not a little delightful to meet with any that has all the various life and complexity of the mind itself. The somewhat thin and triumphant logic of the Bampton lectures, the evident preference for analyzing the notions of man rather than returning to the study of the realities from which those notions were first derived; the dogmatic condemnation of human Reason to be imprisoned as long as it remains human in "the *Finite;*" and finally, and most of all, the gospel of God's inaccessibility, — might in any case probably have drawn from Mr. Maurice a solemn protest; but when all these instruments are used avowedly in defence of Christianity, and Christ is himself put forward, not as the perfect Revelation, but as the least inadequate symbol of the divine nature, we do not wonder that the tone of Mr. Maurice's reply is, if always charitable, often sad and stern. Mr. Mansel preaches that the sphere of Reason is the field of human things; Mr. Maurice, that every fruitful study of human things implies a real insight into things divine. Mr. Mansel holds that the human mind is "cramped by its own laws;" and that divine realities, therefore, so far as they can be the subject of its thoughts at all, must be stunted, or, as the phrase is, "accommodated" to the unfortunately dwarfed dimensions of the recipient: Mr. Maurice holds that the mind of man is "adapted" to lay a gradual hold of the divine truth it is to apprehend, and to grow into its immensity; instead of the divine truth being "adapted" to the little capacities of the human mind. Mr. Mansel holds, as we have seen, that Christianity tells us just enough to keep us right with a God whom we cannot really know; Mr. Maurice, that the only way we can be so kept right is by a direct and, in its highest form, *conscious* participation in the very life of God.

In attempting to discuss, with the help of our authors, the true meaning and objects of a divine Revelation, we shall not again travel over the ground which we have before disputed with Mr. Mansel. His position, that the so-called laws of human thought are 'laws' in the sense of arbitrary restrictions on intellectual freedom, and not qualifications for real knowledge of any thing deeper and wider than our own minds, we have already sufficiently examined. We saw every reason to think that the phenomena which induced him to despair of our capacity for any divine insight were phenomena inherent in all intelligence, human or divine, because describing the very essence of intelligence.* To this ground, therefore, we shall not now return; but assuming at once that there is nothing in the essential character of human thought to betray its own *a-priori*

* Mr. Mansel, in his new preface, quotes our observation, that "relative apprehension is always and necessarily of two terms together; if of sound, then also of silence; if of succession, then also of duration; if of the finite, then also of the infinite;" and replies: "This is true as regards the meaning of the words, but by no means as regards the corresponding objects. If extended to the latter, it should in consistency be asserted that the concep-

incapacity for venturing into every region into which human wants force us to gaze, let us take up the argument at once in its direct bearing on our communion

tion of that which is conceivable involves also the conception of that which is inconceivable; that the consciousness of any thing is also the consciousness of nothing; that the intuition of space and time is likewise the intuition of the absence of both." Mr. Mansel has here supplied us with an excellent illustration of the truth of our special position as to Finite and Infinite Space. No doubt the *general* law of relative apprehension, as applied to language, would require only that we should apprehend equally the meaning of the relative *terms*, and not the corresponding *objects*. To understand what I mean by "conceivable," I must understand what I mean by "inconceivable;" and perhaps the case of "sound" and "silence" is, as applied to the knowledge received by a special sense, a discrimination of the same kind. We insisted on this universal law, that the whole force of *apprehension* really consists in *discrimination*, only because Mr. Mansel seemed to us to represent this relativity of human thought as an imbecility requiring apology to those higher intelligences which, as he seems to suppose, can apprehend all things without discriminating one thing from another. But this general relativity of human apprehension was not the main fact referred to in the passage from which Mr. Mansel quotes. We were referring more particularly then to *special* pairs of relative apprehensions, which are not merely united together in logical significance, but which, as thus united, carry with them a conviction of objective reality, or in other words, which carry belief. In the case of "succession" and "duration," "change" and "cause," "Finite Space" and "Infinite Space," the tie is not logical, but real. No one can conceive "succession" without postulating infinite duration, nor awake to the consciousness of duration without an actual succession. No one can think of finite space without postulating infinite space, nor awake to the consciousness of infinite space without an actual experience of finite space. No one can think of a "change" without postulating a "cause," nor ask for a "cause" without consciousness of a "change." The "conceivable" and the "inconceivable" are mere logical correlatives, in which neither term carries any belief. "The conceivable" is not a district cut out of a Whole described as "the inconceivable," as Finite Space is with respect to the Whole of Infinite Space. The very word "finite" bears in itself testimony to the positive meaning in infinite, and therein alone differs from "definite," which would be fully adequate to express all that is expressed by "finite," if there were no more than an unsuccessful attempt to lay down a limit — if there were not an absolute denial of a limit — in the word Infinite. In the special cases referred to, then, the correlative is not formal and logical, but a real correlative in belief. We must say we cannot even understand what thinkers so accomplished as Sir W. Hamilton and Mr. Mansel mean when they talk of "Infinite" and "Infinitesimal" as purely negative ideas, implying only with God, and see whether Mr. Mansel has really any adequate ground for the assumption which his opponent, we think truly, regards as destructive of the very spring of faith, — that though able to convince ourselves that God does exist, the mere "infinitude" of his Nature renders it impossible for us to hold converse with Him. Passing as rapidly as may be over these somewhat artificial earlier difficulties, we shall reserve Mr. Maurice's help for the more positive and constructive part of our inquiry.

On what, then, does Mr. Mansel base his assumptions? Mainly on this, that if we really do hold direct and conscious converse with God, we should find the results of that converse, and of aptitude for it, inscribed on our mental constitution. "A presentative revelation implies faculties in man which can receive the presentation; and such faculties will also furnish the conditions of constructing a philosophical theory of the object presented." With the first part of this sentence every one must agree; if God can be present, as we believe, to the human mind, there must be faculties in us which enable us to discern that presence. But the latter assertion, that such faculties will also enable us to construct "a philosophical theory of the object presented,"

failures to think. Almost every one knows that mathematicians practically use these ideas, — distinguishing even between various *orders* of infinitude with accurate results. The merest schoolboy knows, for instance, that an infinitely small line, though of course impossible to picture, is a reality, and so different in kind from a point, that it can be shown geometrically to contain as many points as the longest line in Nature. Is this all a jargon without meaning, though it is a demonstrable certainty? As applied to "personalities," which are neither capable of increase nor diminution, the terms "Infinite" and "Finite" have either no meaning, or a totally different one; and hence much of Mr. Mansel's confusion.

seems to us a most amazing and gratuitous assertion. A philosophical theory is possible when we stand above our object, not when we stand beneath it. The learner has faculties by which to learn; but if what he studies is inexhaustible, he will never have a "philosophical theory" of it. Principles, no doubt, he will reach; certain truths to mark his progress he will discover; he will know that he *understands* better and better that which he can never *comprehend;* but a theory of the whole he can never attain unless the whole be within the limited range of his powers. Hence we entirely deny Mr. Mansel's assumption, that direct converse with God implies faculties for constructing "a theory" of God. This is the fundamental error of his work. He admits no knowledge except that which is on a level with its object. Nothing is easier than to prove that no plummet of human Reason can measure depths of the divine mind; nothing falser than to suppose that this incapacity shuts us out entirely from that Mind, and proves it to be the painted veil of "representative notions" of God, and not God Himself, who has filled our spirits in the act of worship.

We hold, then, that this is Mr. Mansel's first, and perhaps deepest, error. He sees that we have no "theory" of God which is not presumptuous and self-contradictory, and he argues therefrom that we have no knowledge. Surely he might have learned better from the simplest facts of human life. Have we any "theory" of any human being that will bear a moment's examination? Yet is our communion with our fellow men limited to a consciousness of our own notions of them? Are not "fixed ideas" of human things a sign of a proud and meagre intellect? Yet Mr. Mansel practically denies all knowledge of divine things, except knowledge through "fixed ideas." He mistakes that which hides God from us for that which reveals Him. "Notions," "fixed ideas," of God, no doubt, and very poor ones too, we have in abundance; but instead of being the media of our knowledge, they are more often the veil which every true moral experience has to tear aside. When we turn to Him with loving heart and conscience, we find half the crystallized and petrified ideas, professing to represent his attributes, dissipated like mists before the sun. To know is not to have a notion which stands in the place of the true object, but to be in direct communion with the true object. And this is exactly the most possible, where theory, or complete knowledge, is least possible. We know the "abysmal deeps" of personality, but have no theory of them. We know love and hatred, but have no theory of them. We know God better than we know ourselves, better than we know any other human being, better than we know either love or hatred; but have no theory, simply because we stand under and not above Him. We can recognize and learn, but never comprehend. It is therefore idle to argue that knowing faculties imply the means of "constructing a philosophical theory," when every case in which living beings share their life and experience with us adds to our knowledge and to our grasp of principles; whereas we can construct "theories" about only the most simple and abstract sciences.

But this point granted, Mr. Mansel takes his next stand in favor of a merely "notional" theology on the *infinite* nature of God. Admit, he says, that we cannot adequately comprehend our relations with finite realities, still such knowledge as we have of them may be direct, because our knowing power bears some definite proportion to the object known. But knowledge of an infinite being should either imply or generate, — so he reasons, — infinite ideas in your own intellect. Have you such ideas? If so, produce them. If not, admit at once that what knowledge you have of such beings is not direct, not first-hand at all, but at best only by representative ideas — miniature copies of the Reality on an infinitely reduced scale. The object to be known is unlimited; the intellectual receptacle a very narrow cell. There can be no room there for that which it professes to hold; if, therefore, any thing which gives a real notion of that object actually has managed to squeeze in, it can only be a minute image, a faint symbol, an "adaptation" to the poverty of human nature. Only a finite fraction of the infinite Reality could be apprehended by a finite intelligence at best; and that, of course, would give far less conception of the whole than a representative idea, reduced proportionately in all its parts to suit "the apprehensive powers of the recipient." Such is, as far as we understand it, the nature of Mr. Mansel's objection. "In whatever affection," he says, "we become conscious of our relation with the Supreme Being, *we can discern that consciousness only by reflecting on it under its proper notion*." Mr. Mansel does reflect on it, through many lectures, under several "notions," which he at least conceives to be "proper;" and finding them all what he terms finite, he ends by telling us that the human mind can only apprehend a finite type of God, and yet is compelled to believe that God is infinite: whence he argues we can have no direct knowledge of God at all, but can only study a limited symbol of Him, which He Himself has mercifully introduced into our minds, and reproduced in an objective and more perfect form in the incarnation of Christ. And if, still dissatisfied, any one suggests to Mr. Mansel that knowledge of God, like knowledge of human things, may be partial, but yet direct, and progressive, in short, a real and growing union of our mind with his, — he replies:

> "The supposition refutes itself: to have a partial knowledge of an object is to know a part of it, but not the whole. But the part of the infinite which is supposed to be known, must be itself either infinite or finite. If it is infinite, it presents the same difficulties as before; if it is finite, the point in question is conceded, and our consciousness is allowed to be limited to finite objects. But in truth it is obvious, on a moment's reflection, that neither the Absolute nor the Infinite can be represented in the form of a Whole composed of parts. Not the Absolute, for the existence of the Whole is dependent on the existence of its parts; not the Infinite, for if any part is Infinite, it cannot be distinguished from the Whole; and if each part is finite, no number of such parts can constitute the infinite."

Now what does all this prove? This, and this only: that if we take the words "Absolute" and "Infinite" to mean that He to whom they are applicable *chokes up* the universe, mental and physical, and prevents the existence of every one else, then it is nonsense and clear contradiction for any one else, who is conscious of his own existence, to use these words of God at all.

Surely this might have been said without so much circumlocution. And what does Mr. Mansel thereby gain? Simply, as far as we can see, that he has established the certain non-existence of any Being *in this sense* "absolute" or "infinite." Mr. Mansel denies this, and says, "No, I have only proved that a philosophy of the Absolute and Infinite is impossible to man." But if we ask, Why not to God also, and to all rational beings who do not believe in any philosophy of self-contradictions and chimeras? he will immediately turn upon us and say, "Because, after all, you must admit that there is an 'Absolute' and an 'Infinite,' and that these terms ought to apply to God. It is our incompetence to conceive that involves us in all these self-contradictions. If you are going to deny the existence of the 'Absolute' and 'Infinite,' you will get into as much trouble in another direction as if you admit and try to reason upon them. Suppose there is no Infinite and Absolute, and we must assume the universe to be made up of finites, and to be itself finite; which is the more inexplicable alternative of the two?"

Now, in reply to this reasoning, we must say very explicitly that it is a mere playing fast and loose with words. Mr. Mansel first wants the words "Infinite" and "Absolute" to exclude all limitation or order of all sorts. Every thing like essential laws of mind or character, — every mental or moral condition or constitution, self-imposed or otherwise, under which the Divine mind could act, — he calls a limitation, and excludes from the meaning of the words. When he has proved, what is exceedingly easy to prove on such an hypothesis, that we can only speak of the Infinite in self-contradictions, he says, "Well, then, here is an end of the Absolute and Infinite. Clearly we are unable to grasp this; but the only alternative is the 'relative' and 'finite;' an alternative still more inexplicable." And now, by "finite," we must remember, he means, not that which acts under given conditions, — under the limitations, say, of a Perfect Nature, infinitely rich in creative power, though of *ordered* Creative Power, issuing from the depths of an Eternal Holiness and Eternal Reason, — but limited in every direction; conditioned everywhere, not by the life-giving order of Character, but by the helplessness of external bonds. We have no hesitation in saying that between unlimited Infinitude, understood in that sense in which Mr. Mansel professes to think that less imbecile mental constitutions than ours would find no contradictions, and the absolutely cramped and fettered Finitude, understood in the sense in which there is no realm of unlimited development and free creation at all, — between these extremes, we say, the whole universe of mind, from the Divine to the human, is necessarily comprehended. The one alternative, which Mr. Mansel does not deign to admit into his religious dilemma even hypothetically, — that of unlimited energy, conditioned by definite laws, moral and spiritual, — is that which the Revelation of conscience and the Revelation of history alike reveal to us as the actual standard of perfection. The sense in which the "Absolute" and "Infinite" are really self-contradictory terms, is the sense in which we try to make them proof against every limitation; and they are so in that case for the very simple reason, that the *absence* of all positive characteristics is, as Mr. Mansel has himself admitted, not only as great, but really a far greater limitation than the presence of those characteristics would be. A vacuum is certainly not limited, like a human being, by any specific mode of life; but it must be said to be still more limited by the absence of all modes of life whatever. On the other hand, the sense in which the Conscience and Reason of man eagerly assert the reality of an "Infinite" and "Absolute" Being, is not in the least the sense in which they are self-contradictory terms. We are forced to believe in a being whose moral and intellectual constitution is, not vaguer and less orderly, but infinitely distincter and more rich in definite qualities and characteristics than our own; but whose free Creative Energies, as determined by those characteristics, are infinitely greater also. The mental constitution which impresses Order on the operation of Power is not, we are taught alike by conscience and inspiration, a true *limitation* on life, in the sense of a fetter; but is rather in itself a proper fountain of fresh life, and a conservation of Power which would otherwise neutralize itself. Our incapacity to conceive the "Infinite" and "Absolute," in the sense in which they repudiate all conditions, turns out to be a positive qualification for conceiving them as names of God. We want them as describing attributes in which we can *trust*, and we can only trust in the attributes of a perfectly holy, and therefore, in some sense, defined Nature.

We may be fully satisfied, then, as the great revelation of all experience, that the real fulness and perfection of character which we vainly strive to express by the word "infinite" is not gained by the absence, but by the expansion and deepening, of those defined moral qualities which Mr. Mansel wants to persuade us are to be considered mere *limitations* of nature. When, for instance, he applies the word "infinite," in its physical sense, to the divine personality, and asks if it does not exclude all other beings, because any other really free will must impose a limit on the operation of the divine will, — we ask if there would not be far deeper limitation in the denial to God of the possibility of that divine love which can exercise itself only on free wills. That only can be considered a real limitation which chokes the springs of spiritual life; and all self-imposed limitation on absolute power which is the condition of a real exercise of the spiritual or higher springs of life is the reverse of real limitation. This is the lesson of every human responsibility. Is not every new duty, social or moral, a limitation of some kind — an obligation to others which at least in some direction appears to impose a limit on us, and yet which enlarges the whole scope of our nature? And is it not equally clear that a divine solitude would be more limited by the necessity of solitude, than by the freedom of the beings who are learning to share the divine life?

Mr. Mansel will say that all this is playing into his hands. He had desired to persuade us that all direct knowledge of God was impossible, because we cannot tell what is limitation and what is not; in other words, we can form no adequate "conception" of fulness or perfection of life. What seems to us limitation, may be, not limitation, but a mode of divine power; what we reverently think of as belonging to

God because it is included in our notion of power, may not really belong to Him, but be, in fact, a human limitation. Assuredly this is so. We have already admitted that if adequate or exhaustive notions, not of God only, but of any living being, were needful to us for direct knowledge, we should have no direct knowledge of life at all. But we have been protesting against Mr. Mansel, not for saying that we have no adequate conception of God, but for saying that we cannot be conscious of his presence with us, conscious of the life we do receive from Him, conscious of what He really is, in the same, indeed even in a far higher, sense than that in which we are conscious of what human beings are. We cannot tell whether this or that would be a limitation on the divine essence; but we can tell whether love and righteousness and power flow from Him into us. Does this give us no *knowledge* of God? Does this give us no communion with Him? "No," says Mr. Mansel; "for 'love,' and 'righteousness,' and 'power,' can be received into your minds only in *finite* parcels, which give no approximation to a knowledge of their infinite fountain." Here, again, we come upon that delusive and positive use of the word "infinite" which, in spite of Mr. Mansel's protest that "infinite" has only a negative meaning, runs through his whole book. He says we do not know what "infinite" means, and therefore cannot know that the "finite" is like the "infinite." We know God's love, and are obliged to believe that it is immeasurably deeper than we can know; and Mr. Mansel wishes to persuade us that this last faith may change the whole meaning of the first, that the very depth and truth which we assert ourselves unable to gauge ought to be a source of doubt whether we know the reality at all. A life comes into a man, the depths of which he cannot sound; and his very conviction that he has not the capacity to comprehend its fulness is to empty it of all defined meaning! Surely Mr. Mansel must see that "infinite" is a mere hollow word when used in this way. The conviction we express by that word is simply that what we know to be restraints on our highest and fullest life do not exist in God; but this conviction, instead of leading us to fear that righteousness and love change their nature in Him because He is "infinite," fills us with certainty that they do not. In short, righteousness and love are qualities which, if we are competent to know them really at all in any single act of God's, we know to be the same in all acts; and all that we mean by calling them infinite is, that we have more and more to learn about them for ever, which will not change and weaken, but confirm and deepen, the truth gained in every previous act of our knowledge. M. Mansel's notion, that because our knowing capacity is limited and God inexhaustible, we can never know directly more than such a fraction of his nature as would be rather a mockery than a personal revelation, is a mere physical metaphor. Our capacity for knowing may be limited either so that partial knowledge is *delusive* (as of one corner of a figure) if taken for the whole; or so only that it is true in kind, and extends to the whole, but utterly inadequate in depth. The latter is of course true of all direct knowledge of a *personality*, which we know to be one and indivisible. What we do not know is, then, mainly, the immeasurable range and inexhaustible depth of that which in a single act we do know. Or if there be other characteristics as yet wholly unknown, we know them to be in harmony, because belonging to the same perfect personality with those we do know.

In brief, we may sum up our differences with Mr. Mansel on this head by saying, that if "infinite" is to mean the exclusion of all definiteness of nature and character, — then we do know, and he himself admits that it has no application to God, if only because it would itself be a far greater limitation than that which it excluded; that if, on the other hand, it be admitted to be consistent with a defined character and constitution, and to mean rather "perfect," — then that we certainly have not an abstract idea of what this is, but have positive faculties for gradual conscious recognition of such a Perfect being when manifested to our Conscience and Reason, and an inextinguishable faith in his perfection even as unmanifested. Finally, that if it be maintained that what we can thus recognize is as nothing when compared with what is beyond our vision, we may admit it, provided only that what we do know is direct knowledge, and knowledge of God, not of a part of God; and that it carries with it not merely a hope, but a *certainty*, that the inexhaustible depths still unrevealed will only deepen and extend, instead of falsifying, that knowledge at which we have arrived.

We have dwelt somewhat long on what seem to us the most transparent sophisms, because it is on them that Mr. Mansel relies for his assertion that our knowledge of God cannot be direct; that Revelation cannot reveal Him, but only a finite type of Him, more or less different from the reality — how different no one can dare to say. Such a position destroys all interest in the Revelation when it comes. If it be only a working hypothesis, to keep us, while confined in the human, from blindly and unconsciously dashing ourselves against the laws of the divine; if it merely says, "Take this chart, which necessarily alters the infinite infinitely to make it finite; but nevertheless, if you steer by it, it will save you as much from the rocks as if it were true," — we do not believe any body would care much for Revelation at all. We should say, "Show us fresh realities, and whether they be finite or infinite, we will attend; but as for these magical clues, which only promise to keep us right, without showing us how or why, we would rather be wrecked against one really discovered rock, we would rather founder in the attempt to sound on our own 'dim and perilous way,' than be constantly obeying directions which are mere accommodations to our ignorance, and which will leave us, even if we obey them strictly and reach the end of our voyage in safety, as ignorant of the real world around us as when we began it." Yet Mr. Mansel's great plea for Revelation, as he understands it, is, that it provides us with *regulative* though not with *speculative* truth, — that it gives us wise advice, the wisdom of which we can test by experience; though furnishing nothing but guesses at the true grounds of that advice.

Now if any one is disposed to admire the apparent modesty of this conclusion, and to acquiesce in it as the true humility of mature wisdom, he will do well to study in Mr. Maurice's profound volume the evidence that every living movement of human thought, *religious or otherwise*, cries out against it. All regulative truth, all truth, that is, which has a deep influence on human action, all truth in which men trust, is founded in the discovery of ultimate causes, not of empirical rules. The distrust of empirical rules in science, in art, in morals, in theology, is all of the same root. It may be safest to act on probabilities where there is no certainty; to act by empirical rule where the principle of the rule is undiscovered; to follow a plausible authority where there is no satisfying truth; and by such rules, no doubt, *in the absence of all temptation to disregard them*, men are occasionally guided when they cannot reach any basis of fact. But, as Mr. Maurice very powerfully insists, there is no single region of life in which these "regulative" and approximate generalities exercise any *transforming* influence on the mind. The smallest probability will outweigh the greatest if it fall in with our wishes; the empirical rule suddenly appears specially inapplicable to the exceptional case in which it becomes inconvenient. The plausible authority is disputable where its recommendations are irritating or painful. It is quite different where we have reached a fresh certainty, a new cause, a new force, a new and self-sustaining truth, a new fountain of actual life. Actual things and persons we cannot ignore; we may struggle with or defy them, but we cannot forget to take them into account. For the lottery-prize we will pay far more than it is worth, the number of blanks scarcely affecting the imagination; the danger of detection never checks the *bonâ-fide* impulse to crime; a single certain suffering which will be independent of success or failure, — the anguish of conscience, which success rather intensifies, — will outweigh it all. Exactly in proportion to the exclusion of hypothetical and the presence of known and tested elements is the really "regulative" influence exerted on the human will. Believe with Mr. Mansel that Revelation gives us a more or less true notion of God, and it will cease to kindle us at all. Recognize in it with Mr. Maurice the direct manifestation of God to the conscience, and the life thus manifested will haunt us into war, if it do not fill us with its peace. If faith give no certainty, it is not "regulative," but itself speculative; if it does not satisfy the reason, it cannot overawe the will. Mr. Mansel appears to regard the phrase "satisfying to the reason" as applying to that sort of knowledge which can answer every query of human curiosity. He tells us that the influence of mind on matter is a regulative truth, of which we cannot give the least account, — and not, therefore, satisfying to the Reason. In this sense, clearly, no living influence in the universe is satisfying to the reason; for we cannot reason any thing into life. But this is a totally different sense from that in which he invites us to surrender our desire for a reasonable knowledge of God, as distinguished from a regulative message from Him. Reason in the highest sense does not pursue its questions beyond the point of discriminating between a real and permanent cause or substance, and a dependent consequence or a variable phenomenon. It asks "why" only till it has reached something which can justify its own existence, and there it stops. True Reason *is satisfied* when it has traced the stream of effect up to a living Origin, and discriminated the nature of that

Origin. It is not the impulse of Reason, but, as Mr. Maurice has finely said, the disease of Rationalism, which continues to make us restless questioners in the presence of those living Objects which ought to fill and satisfy the Reason, — inducing us to ask for a reason deeper than Beauty before we can admire, for a reason deeper than Truth before we can believe, for a reason deeper than Holiness before we can love, trust, and obey. But no true Reason is, or ought to be, satisfied with an echo, a type, a symbol, of something higher which it cannot reach. If it find transitory beauty in the type, it turns by its own law to gaze on the Eternal beauty beneath; if it find broken music in the echo, it yearns after the perfect harmony which roused the echo. Reason might be defined to be that which leads us to distinguish the sign from the thing signified, — which leads us back from the rule to the principle, from the principle to the purpose, from the purpose to the living character in which it originated, — which, in short, will *not* be satisfied with any image, but cries after the Original.

If this be Reason, then, to satisfy Reason is to find out truly regulative truth; for what is it which, in the passion and fever of life, truly transforms and chastens human purposes? Surely nothing but the *knowledge* of realities, — sensible realities more than spiritual abstractions, — spiritual realities most of all; mere *things* painful or delightful far more than any abstract ideas; men far more than things; men present more than men absent; but men absent more than the dream of an absent God, because we have lost our faith in God altogether when we have lost our faith in his direct presence with us. We need scarcely take more than one example of what Mr. Mansel calls regulative moral truth. It will be quite sufficient to test the utterly hollow and unregulative character of the gospel which he can alone deliver to his disciples. He tells us that our human morality, like our human objects of faith, is an adaptation to our condition; though it surely must resemble, with quite inconceivable differences, the divine morality from which it has been epitomized for us. What is his illustration? One so extraordinary, that it is difficult to believe he was not trying to prove that such reduced and "adapted" rules and types can have *no* regulative influence on the human will. He is arguing that there is not, and cannot be, "a perfect identity," or even "exact resemblances" between the morality of God and man, — that actions may be "compatible with the boundless goodness of God which are incompatible with the little goodness of which man may be conscious in himself." The case he takes is the duty of human forgiveness. It is the duty of man, he says, to forgive unconditionally a repented sin. People who argue that God cannot be less good than man, assume that God must do likewise. The fallacy lies, he maintains, in forgetting that the finite form of human duty essentially alters the moral standard in the mind of God. This he proves as follows:

"It is obvious, indeed, on a moment's reflection, that the duty of man to forgive the trespasses of his neighbor rests precisely upon those features of human nature which cannot by any analogy be regarded as representing an image of God. Man is not the author of the moral law; he is not, as man, the moral governor of his fellows; he has no authority, merely as man, to punish moral transgressions as such. *It is not as sin, but as injury, that vice is a transgression against man; it is not that his holiness is outraged, but that his rights or his interests are impaired.* The duty of forgiveness is imposed as a check, not upon the justice, but upon the selfishness of man; it is not designed to extinguish his indignation against vice, but to restrain his tendency to exaggerate his own personal injuries. The reasoner, who maintains 'it is a duty in man to forgive sins, therefore it must be morally fitting for God to forgive them also,' *overlooks the fact that this duty is binding on man on account of the weakness, and ignorance, and sinfulness of his nature:* that he is bound to forgive as one who himself needs forgiveness; as one whose weakness renders him liable to suffering; as one whose self-love is ever ready to arouse his passions and pervert his judgment."

We scarcely ever met with a passage in any thoughtful writer which seems to us to contain deeper and more disastrous misreadings of moral, to say nothing of Christian truth, than this. To us the profound and deadly falsehood lies exactly in that which constitutes its value to Mr. Mansel — the assumption that man's duty to forgive is not grounded in his likeness, but in his unlikeness, to God. But it is not to this point we wish to call attention, but to the *worth* of such a truth as regards its power to *regulate* human conduct. If there be anywhere a duty hard of performance, it is the duty of human forgiveness. If there be one which the ordinary nature of man spurns as humiliating, and almost as a wrong to his whole mind, it is that duty. Ground it in the very nature of God, in the holy living will which, ever close to us, ever able to crush, is ever receiving fresh injury, and yet, even in inflicting the supernatural anguish of divine judgment, is ever offering anew both the invitation and the power to repent, — and you open the spirit to a reality which cannot but awe and may melt it, in the hour of trial. But ground it with Mr. Mansel on the old, worn-out, lax sort of charity which is indulgent to others because it is weak itself, and it will be the least regulative, we suspect, of regulative duties. Mr. Maurice's exposure of the hollowness of this foundation is too fine to omit:

"'The duty of forgiveness is binding upon man on account of the weakness and ignorance and sinfulness of his nature.' But what if the weakness, ignorance, and sinfulness of my nature dispose me *not* to forgive? What if one principal sign of this weakness, ignorance, sinfulness of my nature is, that I am unforgiving? What if the more weak, ignorant, and sinful my nature is, the more impossible forgiveness becomes to me, the more disposed I am to resent every injury, and to take the most violent means for avenging it? It is my duty to forgive, because I am 'one whose self-will is ever ready to arouse his passions and pervert his judgment.' To arouse my passions; to what? To any thing so much as to acts of revenge? To pervert my judgment; how? In any way so much as by making me think that I am right and other men wrong, and that I may vindicate my right against their wrong? And this is the basis of the duty of forgiveness! The temper which inclines me at every moment to trample upon that duty, to do what it forbids! The obvious conclusion, then, has some obvious difficulties. Obvious indeed! They meet us at every step of our way; they are *the* difficulties in our moral progress. Forgiveness is 'to be a check on the selfishness of man.' Where does he get the check? From his selfishness. It is the old, miserable, hopeless circle. I am to persuade myself by certain arguments not to do the thing which I am inclined to do. But the inclination remains as strong as ever; bursts down all the mud fortifications that are built to confine it; or else remains within the heart, a worm destroying it, a fire consuming it. Whence, O whence, is this forgiveness from the heart to come, which I cry for? Is it impossible? Am I to check my selfishness by certain rules about the propriety of abstaining from *acts* of unforgiving ferocity? God have mercy upon those who have only such rules, in a siege or a shipwreck, when social bonds are dissolved, when they are left to themselves! All men have declared that forgiveness, real forgiveness, is *not* impossible. And we have felt that it is not impossible, because it dwells somewhere in beings above man, and is shown by them, and comes down as the highest gift from them upon man. . . . And whenever the idea of Forgiveness has been severed from this root, — whenever the strong conviction that we are warring against the nature of God and assuming the nature of the Devil by an unforgiving temper has given place to a sentimental feeling that we are all sinners, and should be tolerant of each other, — then has come that weakness and effeminacy over Christian society, that dread of punishing, that unwillingness to exercise the severe functions of the Ruler and the King, which has driven the wise back upon older and sterner lessons, has made them think the vigor of the Jew in putting down abominations, the self-assertions of the Greek in behalf of freedom, were manlier than the endurance and compassion of the Christians. Which I should think too, if, referring the endurance and compassion to a divine standard, I did not find in that standard a justification of all which was brave and noble in the Jewish protest against evil, in the Greek protest against tyranny. Submission or Compassion, turned into mere qualities which we are to exalt and boast of as characteristic of our religion, become little else than the negations of Courage and Justice. Contemplated as the reflections of that Eternal Goodness and

Truth which were manifested in Christ, as energies proceeding from him and called forth by his Spirit, — submission to personal slights and injuries, the compassion for every one who is out of the way, — become instruments in the vindication of Justice and Right, and of that Love in the fires of which all selfishness is to be consumed."

We have done our best to explain why we utterly disavow Mr. Mansel's interpretation of Revelation, as a message intended to regulate human practice without unfolding the realities of the divine mind. It is a less easy task, but not less a duty, on the part of those who are gravely sensible of the emptiness of such an interpretation, to give some exposition of the deeper meaning which the fact of revelation assumes to their own minds. We hold that it is an unveiling of the very character and life of the eternal God; and an unveiling, of course, to a nature which is capable of beholding Him. It is not, in our belief, an overclouding of divine light to suit it for the dimness of human vision, but a purification of human vision from the weakness and disease which render it liable to be dazzled and blinded by the divine light. It is, in short, the history of the awakening, purifying, and answering, of the yearnings of the human spirit for a direct knowledge of Him. It proceeds from God, and not from man. The cloud which is on the human heart and Reason can only be gradually dispersed by the divine love; no restless straining of turbid human aspiration can wring from the silent skies that knowledge which yet every human being is formed to attain. Coming from God, this method, this "education of the human race," as Lessing truly termed Revelation, has been unfolded with the unfolding capacity of the creatures He was educating to know Him. Its significance cannot be *confined* to any special series of historical facts; but it is clear that the Divine government of the Jewish race was meant to bring out, and did bring out, more distinctly the personality of God, while the history of other races brings out more clearly the divine capacities of man. Hence the co-operation of different nations was requisite for the fulfilment of the Revelation. Centuries were required for the complete evolution even of that special Jewish history that was selected to testify to the righteous will and defined spiritual character of the Creator. Centuries on centuries will be required to discipline fully the human faculties that are to grow into the faith thus prepared for them. The blindness of the greatest men, of the highest races, of wide continents, cannot shake our faith that this purpose will be fulfilled; for the term of an earthly life is adequate at best for its conscious commencement, and only under special conditions even for that; nor are there wanting indications that both in the case of men and nations the longest training and the dreariest periods of abeyance of spiritual life, are often preparations for its fullest growth. By tedious discipline, by slow Providence, by inspirations addressed to the seeking intellect of the philosopher, to the yearning imagination of the poet, to the ardent piety of the prophet, to the common reason and conscience of all men, and by the fulfilment of all wisdom in the Son of God's life on earth, has the Divine Spirit sought to drive away the mists that dim our human vision. Through its wants and powers alike human nature has been taught to know God. Its every power has been haunted by a want till the power was referred to its divine source, its very wants have become powers when they have turned to their divine object. If this, then, and nothing short of this, be Revelation, a living and direct unfolding of that divine mind in which, whether we recognize it or not, we "live and move and have our being," — an eternal growth in our knowledge of the eternal Life, — we ought not to rest satisfied with showing that Mr. Mansel's reasons for disputing the possibility of such a wonderful truth are unsound, — we ought also to show by what criteria we judge that this is the actual fact, the great reality, on which all our love of truth and knowledge rests.

The first stage in any revelation must be, one would suppose, the dawning knowledge that there is a veil "on the heart" of man, and that there is a life unmanifested behind it. In Mr. Mansel's, as in our view, this is a knowlege which can be gained by man; but he makes it the final triumph of human faith and philosophy to recognize and *acquiesce* in it; while we hold it to be the very first lesson of the personal conscience, the very first purpose of that external discipline which was intended to engrave the Divine personality on Jewish history, to teach that such a cloud may ever threaten the mind and conscience, but that it *can be dispersed.*

What, indeed, is the first lesson of the human conscience, the first truth impressed upon the Jewish nation, but this, that a presence besets man behind and before, which he cannot evade, and which is ever giving new meanings to his thoughts, new direction to his aims, new depth to his hopes, new terror to his sins? Where, then, if this haunting Presence be so overpowering, if it follow us as it followed the deepest minds among the Jewish people, till it seem almost intolerable, — where is the darkness and the veil which Revelation implies? Just in the fact that this presence does seem intolerable; that it is so far apart from that of man, that, like a dividing sword, it makes his spirit start; that he seeks to escape, and is, in fact, really able to resist it; that he can so easily case-harden his spirit against the supernatural pain; that instead of opening his mind to receive this painfully-tasking life that is not his own, he can so easily, for a time at least, set up in its place an idol carved out of his own nature, or something even more passive than his own nature, and therefore not likely to disturb his dream of rest. This, we take it, is the first stage or act of revelation, whether in the individual conscience, or in that special history which is intended to reveal the conflicts between the heart of a nation and the God who rules it. It is the discovery of a presence too pure, too great, too piercing for the natural life of man, — the effort of the mind, on one pretence or another, to be allowed to stay on its own level and disregard this presence, — the knowledge that this must end in sinking below its own level, — the actual trial and experience that it is so, — the reiterated pain and awe of a new intrusion of the supernatural light, — the reiterated effort to "adapt" that light to human forms and likings, — the reiterated idolatry which all such adaptations imply, whether physical, as in the Jewish times, or intellectual, as in our own, — and the reiterated shame of fresh degradation. If this be, as, we believe, the human conscience testifies, whether as embodied in the typical history of the Jews, or in the individual mind, the first stage in that discovery which we call Revelation, what becomes of Mr. Mansel's theory, that Revelation is the "adaptation" of the "infinite" to the "finite," of the perfect to the imperfect, of the absolute morality to the poor capacities of a sinful being? If so, — why this craving of the nature to be let alone, — this starting as at the touch of a flame too vivid for it, — this comfort in circumscribing, or fancying that we can circumscribe, the living God in some human image or form of thought, and worshipping that by way of evading the reality? Does the human spirit ever quail thus before a mere notion? If God Himself is inaccessible to knowledge, should not we find it extremely easy to adapt ourselves to any abstract or ideal conception of Him? It is the living touch of righteousness, even though human only, that makes us shrink; not the idea of righteousness, which, as all theologies testify, is found pliant enough. But if it be a righteous life and will, not merely the idea or idol of a righteous life and will, that stirs human nature thus deeply, and finds us, as it found the Jews, afraid to welcome it, awestruck at the chasm which divides us from it, fearful to surrender ourselves to its guidance, ready to adapt it in any way to us, unready to adapt ourselves to it, — if, we say, we know it to be a *living* will that thus checks, urges, and besets us, Mr. Mansel's theory as to the narrow limits of human knowledge would scarcely induce him to deny that it is God Himself; for there is nothing in his theory which is not almost as much contradicted by *any* living spiritual converse between the human spirit and a spirit of perfect holiness as by direct converse with God.

This first stage of Revelation, which we have called the Jewish, may be said to discriminate the divine personality of God *more* sharply from his own works and creatures than is possible or true in any subsequent and maturer stage of his unfolding purpose. It is, in fact, the first stage in the divine "education" of the individual conscience, as well as of the human race; and is so vividly reflected in the national history of Israel, only because that is the only history in which the appeals of God to the corporate conscience of a whole nation are recorded as fully as the actual national deeds in which those appeals were complied with or defied. In the history of other nations the divine will for the nation has been at once far less vividly interpreted, and, even when adequately interpreted, far less carefully recorded; it has been allowed to gleam forth only fitfully through the often uneducated consciences of national heroes; while in the case of the Jews, we find a succession of great men, whose spirits were more or less filled with the divine light, in order that the world might see in at least one national history some continuous record of the better purposes of God for the nation, as well as of the actual life by which those purposes were partially frustrated or fulfilled. This, we believe, is the only peculiarity of Jewish history, — that a race of prophets was permitted to proclaim, — with varying truth of insight, no doubt, but still with far clearer and more continuous vision of the divine purpose than any other nation has witnessed, — what God would have had the people do and abstain from. To the nation itself this was not always a gain; probably that which was evil in it would not have grown into so stiff and hard a subsistence but for the power inherent in divine light to divide the evil from the good (for the vision of a purpose too holy for the life of a people issues in greater guilt as well as greater goodness); but for the world at large no doubt it has been and is an immeasurable blessing, — strictly speaking, a Revelation, — to see written out, parallel with the national life of a single people, the life to which God, speaking through the purest consciences of each age of their history, had called them. But the phase of Revelation which we see in Jewish history is simply, on the scale of national life, what the first discovery of God by the individual conscience is in individual life. In both cases there is a contrast presented between God and man, between God and nature, sharper than belongs to any other stage of his unfolding purposes. The separate personality of God is engraved on Jewish history with an emphasis which indicates that to the Jew there seemed scarce any common life between God and man, — any bridge between the supernatural will and the easy flow of Nature. And is it not thus engraved on the individual conscience when first man becomes aware that the natural veins and currents of his character tend to a thousand different ends, whither the brooding Spirit of God forbids us to go, — or whither if we do go, it haunts us with throes of supernatural anguish till we turn again? Is it not simply the discovery that the actual bent of our whole inward constitution is not divine, — the despair of seeing how it is ever to become so, — which makes us, like the

Jew, separate the divine Spirit so sharply from his living works and creatures, that for a time we doubt whether the nature within us can be used by God at all — whether, much rather, its forces must not be wholly cancelled, before the will can be set free?

But this sharp contrast between the personality of God and the nature of man, and in lesser degree of the external universe, is not and cannot be final. And if the Jewish history witnesses that the Will of God is the starting-point of a new order, that the forces of human nature must be brought into subjection to that, if they can be used by God at all, — then the history of a hundred other nations, more especially of the Greeks, and in later centuries of the Teutonic races, does testify with equal explicitness that natural life is essentially divine, and requires at most remoulding by the Eternal Spirit, — a remoulding which is so far from cancelling, that it brings out the true nature in all its freshness, — in order to become the fitting organ of a Supernatural Righteousness. In other words, while man takes his stand on the level of his own motives and affections, and shrinks from the transforming influence of the Spirit of God, these motives and affections are the veil which needs taking away; but if he will permit himself to be raised above that level, and will open his heart freely to the supernatural influence at which he trembles, then it will not be *against* the voice, but *by* the voice of his own spiritualized motives and affections, that God Himself speaks. The veil itself becomes transparent; the glass that was dark, luminous. Accordingly the revelation to conscience, which is more or less Jewish, and sets all the fibres of the natural life quivering like an aspen-leaf in the wind, is necessarily partial and temporary. Even in the highest of the prophetic strains there is perhaps an undervaluing of nature, and human nature in its natural manifestations, — a disposition to anticipate something like a revolution rather than a regeneration in its constitution, to represent direct praise of God as better and more worthy than the indirect praise implied in its perfect natural development. Could God's Self-Revelation have been stayed at that point, we doubt whether Gentile nations, — the Greek for instance, — could ever have embraced it. Deep sensibility to the divine beauty of all human faculty and life was so deeply wrought into the very heart of Greece, that the Greek only recoiled at the Hebrew vision of a God before whose presence human faculty seemed to pale away like starlight in the dawn. Nor could the Hebrew faith itself have lived on permanently in that phase. Already, before the Jewish era came to a close, the danger of idolatry with which Jewish faith was first threatened, — the danger that God would be confounded with his works, — had merged in the danger that He would not be recognized as living in his works. There is an exactly parallel movement in the history of the Revelation of God to the individual conscience. When first

> "Those high instincts before which our mortal nature
> Doth tremble like a guilty thing surprised"

come upon us, we feel that man is nothing, and God every thing; but soon human nature re-asserts its dominion; and if there be no full reconciliation between the two, either the "high instincts" become ossified into dogma, and the mortal nature runs a fouler course in their presence than it would in their absence, or they fade away again altogether.

There is a natural and legitimate revolt in man against any Supernaturalism which does not do full justice to nature: and the opposite risk of a deification of nature, such as Greece and the Gentile nations were prone to, produces perhaps less fearful, certainly less unlovely results than the error which divorces nature from God, and by disclaiming in the name of piety any trace in Him of the life of the world, strips that world bare of all trace of God. Judaism taught us for ever that Nature must be interpreted by our knowledge of God, not God by our knowledge of Nature; but it was only the perversion of Judaism which completely dissolved the tie between the two. The Greek shuddered, and with reason, at the sacrilege of ignoring the breath of divine life in the harmony of the world; but it was but a perversion of Hellenism when the Pantheist sought to identify the two, — to multiply his delight in natural organisms until their influences fell into a kind of musical harmony in his mind, which he called the Divine Whole. Both of these opposite tendencies are equally perversions. And both alike witness to the expectation in the human mind of some Revelation of the true tie between the life of God and the life of his creatures, — the yearning to know, not only what God is in his essential character, but what seed of his own life He has given to us, and what power it is by which that seed may be guarded through its germination from the extinction or corruption with which it is threatened. Accept with the Greek the capacity for a divine order in man and the universe; accept with the Jew the reality of the "Lord's Controversy" with man; and how are the two to be reconciled? how is the supernatural righteousness to avail itself of the perverted growths of human capacity? how is the "Lord's Controversy" to be set at rest?

This was a question which the Jewish Revelation never solved for the questioner, — except so far as it taught him that God could *conquer* the most rebellious nature. But even then he recognized the Supernatural will as *triumphing over* the poverty of human and natural life, rather than as revealing itself actually *through and in* the divine springs of that life. The "Controversy" was solved for him rather by the power of God over nature than by the power of God in nature. But what was it that the Gentile nations craved? Some new conviction that the supernatural was not at war with the constitution of nature, but the eternal source of it; that the gradual growth, the seasonal bloom, the germinating loveliness of the natural and visible universe, culminating in the wonderful life of man, is itself not a veil but a revelation, a harmony of voices addressing us from the Divine life, and claiming our allegiance to One higher than themselves. They too saw, what the Jew had been taught, that in fact this was not really so, that there was a jar, a discord somewhere; but if they saw far less clearly whence came the power which could command the discord to cease, they saw far more clearly that, if it could cease, the *true* nature would be restored and not conquered, vindicated and not extinguished, strengthened not exhaled.

The human condition of this revelation, as of all

other Revelation, is born with the human mind. The Supernatural and Righteous Will, who besets and confronts on every side the unruly impulses of our lower self, is revealed to the Conscience, and without the Conscience could not be revealed at all. But besides this, there is another experience of man's which renders him capable of another revelation. Quite apart from the conscience and the sense of guilt and the law, — quite apart from the living Will, who looks into our hearts and searches out their evil, — there is, we suppose, in every man a more natural and genial experience of the spontaneous growth and unfolding, or it may be only the *effort* to unfold, of the true nature as it ought to grow, — a gentle spontaneous resistance to the shapes into which our faults and imperfections force or try to force it, — the effort of the true man within us to grow into his right and perfect state in spite of the resistance of frailty, incapacity, and sin. What we are now speaking of is not an experience merely of the moral life, but of the whole nature. Does not every man feel that there are unused capacities of all kinds within him, gently pressing for their natural development? — that a living tendency urges us to grow, not merely in moral but in physical and intellectual constitution, towards the individual type for which we were made? — that the various frictions of evil, moral or merely circumstantial, which prevent this, when it *is* prevented, distort the true divine growth, and leave us less than what we might have been? It was this experience which the religion of Greece has preserved so vividly, — the faith that, beneath the deformity of real life, there is a formative plastic power that is ever urging us towards our truest life; beneath ungainliness, a growth, or effort to grow, of something more harmonious; beneath ignorance, a growth, or effort to grow, of the true understanding; beneath impurity and evil, the growth, or effort to grow, of the true moral beauty.

It was, we believe, to this experience in every man's mind, — an experience which cannot be called moral so much as the true instinct of *life*, — that the unveiling of God in Christ appealed, and which fitted the Christian revelation to include the Greek as well as the Jew. There at last was the harmony of the Supernatural and the Natural, — the divine effort at harmonious growth which seemed to be in every man, unfolding from the germ to the full fruit without the canker or the blight, and yet at the same time revealing to all of us exactly what the Supernatural vision reveals to the conscience, the absolute will of good, the divine anger against sin, the infinite chasm between evil and good, the power and holiness of God. What was this life, in which the unity of God and man was at length vindicated? Did it not utter in clearer accents the awful Will which had spoken within the Jew? Did it not image in living colors the perfect nature which had stirred so gently and breathed so deep a sense of divinity into the finer folds of Grecian life? Was it not at once the answer to that craving for a true vision of the moral nature of God which had haunted the Hebrew conscience, and the answer to that craving for a true vision of the undistorted life of man which had haunted the Grecian imagination? True, it was a vision of the Father only as He is seen in the Son, of the filial and submissive Will, not of the original and underived Will; but as it is the perfection of the filial Will to rest in the Will of his Father, the spiritual image is perfect, though the personal life is distinct. And this was, in fact, exactly what answered the yearning of the Greek for an explanation of that living germ of divine life within him. Was it not a perfect *nature*, filial like his own, — the very nature into which he was capable of growing, — that had thus been pushing against the weight of deformity, stirring the sources of *natural* perfection, and warning him that his mind was growing in wrong directions, and not blossoming into the beauty for which it was designed? He was ready to recognize as the divine Word, which had grown into perfect humanity in Christ, the very same higher nature which had been in him but not of him; which had filled his mind with those faint longings after something that he might have been and was not; which was still stirring within him whenever a new blight, or a new failure, or a new sin, threatened to divert him still further from the destiny to which he knew he was capable to attain. The secret Will of God was, according to the longing of the Jews, first fully manifest in Christ; the secret hopes of man were, according to the "desire of all nations," there first fulfilled.

If Christ, then, was to the Jew mainly the Revelation of the Absolute Will as reflected in the perfect filial will; to the Greek mainly the revelation of that perfect human nature which had been so long stirring within him, we might expect to find acts in which he especially revealed the living Ruler of the Universe, and acts in which he especially revealed the inward influences which were to restore order to the human heart; — acts in which he manifested the Father, and acts in which he unsealed the eternal fountains of purity in human life. Mr. Maurice, in answering Mr. Mansel's assertion that the Absolute is beyond human vision, calls attention especially to the former class. He intimates that in the miracles and the parables, for instance, we have Revelations of the spiritual source of the physical world. Mr. Wescott's thoughtful little book pursues the same track with regard to the miracles only. The tenor of both writers is the same. There had been ever in man an awe at the mighty powers of the physical universe, and the apparent recklessness with which these powers acted. The Jew, who loved to see in God the source of all power, still hardly dared to refer these crushing forces to the same national Providence which had guarded and governed his race with a personal care so express. The Greek thought them in their awful undeviating order far more sublime than he could have done had he held them to be exercises of a mere Supreme Will. But yet he would willingly have connected them with an order, spiritual as well as physical, such as he recognized in the destinies of men. Christ, by manifesting the power which controlled and upheld them, and yet manifesting it with a healing and life-giving purpose, answered both these cravings. "These powers," the miracles said, "which seem so physical, so arbitrary, sometimes so destructive, — which sometimes appear to be wielded by an evil spirit, — are in the hands of one who would heal men's miseries, restore their life, moral and physical, purify them from disease, and hush the storm into a calm: if it ever seem otherwise, be sure that the seeming destruction has a life-giving purpose, the physical disease a deeper healing influence; that the tempest is a bringer of serener peace, the blindness a preparation for diviner light. The order of the universe has a spiritual root; the purpose of love which changes, is also the purpose of love which directs it. He who can bind and loose the forces of nature, has thus revealed the eternal purposes in which they originate."

So again, Mr. Maurice, in a sermon of great beauty, claims for the parables that they were intended to reveal the spiritual significance which had been from the first embodied in the physical processes of the universe, — that the analogy between the light of the body and the light of the spirit, the sowing and reaping of the external and of the spiritual world, and the other analogies in what we usually call Christ's "figurative" language, are not really metaphorical, but exhibit the perfect insight of the divine mind of the Son into the creative purposes of the Father. If it be true that the creator of our spirits is the creator of our bodies also, we might only expect that he who revealed the true life of the one, would know and exhibit its close natural affinities with the life of the other. Is not the physical universe as a whole meant to be for man the vesture of the spiritual universe? Is not all the truest language, therefore, necessarily what we call figurative; and only false when the spiritual is interpreted by the physical, instead of the physical by the spiritual?

"But if there is this correspondence between the organs of the spirit and the organs of sense, if experience assures there is, does not that explain to us the meaning and power of the parables? May not all sensible things, by a necessity of their nature, be testifying to us of that which is nearest to us, of that which it most concerns us to know, of the mysteries of our own life, and of God's relation to us? May it not be impossible for us to escape from these witnesses? They may become insignificant to us from our very familiarity with them; nay, we may utterly forget that there is any wonder in them. The transformation of the seed into the full corn in the ear may appear to us the dullest of all phenomena, not worthy to be noted or thought of. The difference in the returns from different soils, or from the same soils under different cultivation, — the difference in the quality of the produce, and the relations which it bears to the quality of the seeds, — may be interesting to us from the effect such varieties have upon the market, from the more or less money we derive from the sale; not the least as facts in nature, facts for meditation. The relation between a landholder or farmer and those who work for him, between a shepherd and his sheep, all in like manner may be tried by the same pecuniary standard; apart from that, they may suggest nothing to us. Thus the universe becomes actually 'as is a landscape to a dead man's eye;' the business in which we are ourselves engaged, a routine which must be got through in some way or another, that we may have leisure to eat, drink, and sleep. Can any language describe this state so accurately and vividly as that of our Lord in the text? Seeing we see, and do not perceive; hearing we hear, and do not understand."

This revelation, however, through Christ, — by his life, by his miracles, by his parables, by his resurrection and ascension, — of the Supreme Will, would not have fulfilled as it did the "desire of all nations," had it not also revealed that living power in man by which human nature is wrought into his likeness. To know God has been, in all ages, but an awful knowledge, until the formative influence which is able to communicate to us his nature is revealed also. And accordingly, Christ no sooner disappears from earth than all the Christian writings begin to dwell far more on the new strength he had revealed within them than on his outward life. The interior growth of divine nature thus revealed might be called new, because now first they recognized it as a divine power, as a power they could *trust*, as a life that would grow by its own might within them if only they did not smother it and were content to restrain their own lower self from any voluntary inroads of evil. This power had been there, no doubt, in all men and all times ; the germinating life of an inward spirit of involuntary good had never been a stranger to man ; it had always pushed with gentle pressure against the limits of narrow minds and narrow hearts and of positive evil, — not, indeed, with the keen and piercing thrusts of divine judgment, but with the spontaneous movement of better life striving to cast off the scale of long-worn habit. But now this power was not only felt, but its origin was revealed. It was that same divine human nature which had been embodied in the earthly Christ that was stirring in the hearts of all men. It was he, whose life had been so strange and brief a miracle of beauty, to whom they might trust to mould afresh the twisted shapes of human imperfection, to push forward the growth of the good seed and the eradication of the tares within them. The same life which had shed its healing influence over the sick and the sinful in Galilee and Judea, was but the human form of that which fostered the true nature beneath the falsehoods of all actual life, and worked within the disciples as they preached their risen Lord. It was not they, but "Christ that worked in them." Here was the true explanation of the unity of the human race, the common life which was the source of all that was deep and good; as separative influences grew out of all that was profoundly evil. They were all members of Christ; his nature was in them all, drawing out the beauty and chastening the deformity, breathing the breath of universal charity, and kindling the flame of inextinguishable hope. This was a power to trust in, the image of the Father's will, because breathing the very spirit of that will; and fuller of hope than any vision of a holy king commanding an allegiance which they could not bend their stiff hearts to pay, or conquering their moral freedom without acting on the secret springs of their humanity. They had known this power in themselves before; but they had not read it aright, because they had not estimated aright its source and the certainty and universality of its operation. They had not before known it as directly manifested in him who opened the eyes of the blind, and cleansed the leper, and stilled the storm; who forgave sins, and wrestled with temptation; and finally passed through the grave, and trouble deeper than the grave, without being "holden" of it, because his will was freely surrendered to his Father.

Here, then, was a revelation not simply of the Absolute nature of God, but of the formative power of Christ that is at work to cancel distorted growths, and even mere natural deficiency in every human heart. But it was to do more than this, — it was to take away sin itself from those who could bring themselves to trust their hearts freely to his influence; — to reveal to them, in short, the great divine law that, as through the unity of human nature "if one member suffers, all the members suffer with it," so through the same unity a new life may spread into even the weakest and corruptest member. It was to reveal it as the highest privilege of this great central human life to purify others when once their will begins to turn towards him by entering into the very heart of their evil and reaching the very core of their inward misery; so that while new life returns to *them*, the shadow of pain inseparable from the perfect knowledge of human guilt falls back on the spirit of the great Purifier. This was the revelation of the true nature in man; a nature that not only, as the Gentile nations felt, asserted the primitive truth and goodness properly belonging to every human creature, but that is capable of restoring that truth and goodness, cancelling the sinful habit, melting the rigid heart, emancipating the sullen temper, by the mere exertion of its spontaneous fascination over any spirit which once surrenders to its control. And this, accordingly, is the great subject of Christian writers after once Christ had left the earth. It was to them a new discovery that the restorative power in every heart was *not* the power of their own wills, which they knew to be limited at most to a rejection of evil acts, but the very same power which had grown up into a perfect humanity in Christ, and only required an act of continuous trust to claim them for its own. To trust in such a power was not hard, to stifle the active rebellion of their own wills was possible; but to purge the turbid fountain of their human life, had that also been required of them, as both Jew and Gentile had often dreamed, was mere impossibility. To *know* who it was who was working in them, was to multiply infinitely the regenerating power of his life.

Such, then, we hold to be the essence of the divine Self-Revelation of God. Into the question of its exact relation to the historical narrative in the Bible, slightly touched upon both by Mr. Mansel and Mr. Maurice, we cannot here enter. While accepting gratefully the many new and brilliant lights which all Mr. Maurice's writings, and this last perhaps most of all, have cast on the deepest subject into which the human heart can enter, we should perhaps differ most from him in his biblical criticism. A mind so rich in meditative wisdom as his, so ready to snatch a religious truth from the strangest confusion of historical incident, seems scarcely able to appreciate the kind of impression which inconsistent and sometimes inconceivable statements, supported by no appreciable evidence, — such, for instance, as that of the star which is said to have guided the Magians to the manger at Bethlehem, — make on ordinary students with regard to all historical details, indeed to all the historical elements of Revelation. Mr. Maurice is as deeply persuaded as we are that the fullest and freest criticism will work out the most happy issues. For ourselves, we feel little doubt that such criticism will show a large admixture of untrustworthy elements in the narrative of both Old and New Testament; and that if it prove so, the mere emancipation of the intellect from what seems a purely literary superstition as to the truth of the Bible narratives, will probably bring far more gain to the spiritual freedom of man, and do far more to direct attention to the spiritual evidences of all divine truth, than any other result could educe. We believe Bibliolatry has been, and is likely long to be, the bane of Protestant Christianity. Spiritual realities would indeed be recognized *as* spiritual realities by few, had they had no perfect manifestation in the actual works and Providence of God, — had not the desire of the heart been embodied in the desire of the eyes. But that no minute history was needful of the earthly life of him who can interpret his own meaning, and who came that he might draw the veil from eternal power and truth, and not to fascinate men's eyes and hearts to one single illuminated point of space and time, — is sufficiently proved by the absence of all records of his life which can be called minute, or which do not rely on the faithfulness of memory even for their outlines. Human vanity, eager to guarantee its own immortality, carries laboriously about all the paraphernalia for setting down every word and action before its transient life is spent. He who is solving the agonizing problems of ages, speaking to the depths of the human spirit in generations on generations yet unborn, and uttering "the things which have been kept secret from the foundation of the world," can afford to dispense with the minute history of his life, when he has power to turn every human conscience into a new witness of his truth, and every heart into a new evangelist of his glory.

PERSONAL INFLUENCES ON OUR PRESENT THEOLOGY: NEWMAN — COLERIDGE — CARLYLE.*

"THEOLOGY," says Mr. Macaulay, in his mischievous way, "is not a progressive science." It may, however, be retrogressive; and it is sure to repay flippant neg-

* The Arians of the Fourth Century; their Doctrine, Temper, and Conduct, chiefly as exhibited in the Councils of the Church, between A.D. 325 and A.D. 381. By John Henry Newman, M.A., Fellow of Oriel College. Second edition, literally reprinted from the first edition. 8vo. London: E. Lumley. 1854.

Callista; a Sketch of the Third Century. By Dr. J. H. Newman. 12mo. London: Burns and Lambert. 1856.

The Defence of the Archdeacon of Taunton, in its complete form. Royal 8vo. London: J. Masters, and J. H. and J. Parker. 1856.

Notes, Theological, Political, and Miscellaneous. By Samuel Taylor Coleridge. Edited by the Rev. Derwent Coleridge, M.A. London: Moxon. 1853.

Charges to the Clergy of the Archdeaconry of Lewes, delivered at the ordinary Visitations in the years 1843, 1845, 1846. By Julius Charles Hare, M.A., Archdeacon. Never before published. With an Introduction, explanatory of his position in the Church with reference to the Parties which divide it. Cambridge: Macmillan and Co. 1856.

The Doctrine of Sacrifice deduced from the Scriptures. A Series of Sermons by Frederick Denison Maurice, M.A., Chaplain of Lincoln's Inn. Cambridge: Macmillan and Co. 1854.

St. Paul and Modern Thought: Remarks on the Views advanced in Professor Jowett's Commentary on St. Paul. By J. Llewelyn Davies, M.A., Fellow of Trinity College, Cambridge, and Incumbent of St. Mark's, Whitechapel. Cambridge: Macmillan and Co. 1856.

Passages selected from the Writings of Thomas Carlyle. With a Biographical Memoir. By Thomas Ballantyne. Post 8vo. London: Chapman and Hall. 1856.

National Review, October, 1856.

lect by lending its empty space to mean delusions. To its great problems *some* answer will always be attempted: and there is much to choose between the solutions, however imperfect, found by reverential wisdom, and the degrading falsehoods tendered in reply by the indifferent and superficial. Even in their failures, there is a vast difference between the explorings of the seeing and the blind. We deny, however, that Christian theology can assume any aspect of failure, except to those who use a false measure of success. It is not in the nature of religion, of poetry, of art, to exhibit the kind of progress that belongs to physical science. They differ from it in seeking, not the *phenomena* of the universe, but its *essence*, — not its laws of change, but its eternal meanings, — not outward nature, in short, except as expressive of the inner thought of God: and being thus intent upon the enduring spirit and very ground of things, they cannot grow by numerical accretion of facts and exacter registration of successions. They are the product, not of the patient sense and comparing intelligence which are always at hand, but of a deeper and finer insight, changing with the atmosphere of the affections and will. Instead of looking, therefore, for perpetual advance of discovery in theology, we should naturally expect an ebb and flow of light, answering to the moral condition of men's minds: and may be content if the divine truth, lost in the dulness of a material age, clears itself into fresh forms with the returning breath of a better time.

With hope thus moderate, in no confidence that the millennium is due at present, but certainly in no despair of larger visions than to-day's, we propose to glance at the newer characteristics of English theology; to trace their origin and deviation from the data of the antecedent generation; and to indicate any common point towards which their several lines of direction may seem to converge. Few thoughtful men, who have lived through the greater part of the present century, can fail to be more or less aware of a vast change in the religious ideas and spirit of the time,—a change surely to a higher mood of faith, and even of doubt. A rapid survey of its social conditions, and of its chief authors, living and departed, may help us to appreciate its magnitude and tendency.

Prior to the peace of 1815, the disposable activity of the English mind was bespoken for the most part by the excitement of European politics. What religious movement there was arose out of the contagion of "French principles," or the recoil from them; and was so subservient to the antagonism of parties in the state as to acquire no independent or scientific character. The disaffection of Ireland, and its threatened invasion by Napoleon, gave an anti-catholic direction to the zeal of the day, and enabled the "Clapham sect," favored by the prejudices of the king and the influence of Mr. Perceval, to attain a position disproportioned to its merits. After the close of the war, the numbers and social importance of this party continued to increase. There were large arrears of domestic politics to be dealt with; and the prominence held by the Catholic question for twelve or fourteen years made a watchword of the "Bible-cry," placed the "Evangelicals" in the van of the "Protestant interest," and Irish zealots in the van of the Evangelicals. This temporary leadership was not favorable to their permanent power. A fatal taint of political agitation infected the system; and once committed to the keeping of Hibernian rhetoric, it was spoiled for the quiet depths of the English mind.

One by one the elements of the political struggle succeeding to the war were discharged. The disabilities were swept away; the House of Commons was reconstituted; the municipalities were reformed; slavery was abolished. These great enterprises of action and resistance being over, and the strain of conflict withdrawn, attention was free for more reflective interests, and an inner movement began to replace the outward. The several religious parties, disengaged from their civic campaign, were sent home to their spiritual husbandry, and thrown upon their intrinsic resources of genius and character. The time, ever so critical for church and doctrine, had come at last, — the time of searching thought and quiet work. Other charity than would serve upon the hustings, — a deeper gospel than was known at apocalyptic tea-tables, — a piety stimulant of no platform cheers, became indispensable in evidence and expression of the Christian life. Especially at the centres of intellectual light, — the Universities, where the speculative faculties are trained, — were the reigning systems sure to be tried by the severest tests. Who could abide the day of reckoning? What party, formed amid the tastes and admirations of the previous age, could prove itself equal to the larger problems of a new time? Discharged from the work of middle-class agitation, and scrutinized by academic eyes, what had Evangelicism to show? Its men of genius?—if it has higher names than Wilberforce and Martyn, we never heard them. Its literature? — its favorites were Hannah More and Robert Montgomery. Its divinity? — it attained the altitude of Scott, Romaine, and Sumner. Its art? — the accomplishments of a modern day-school go beyond it. With faint appreciation of scholarship, and entire dislike of philosophy, it seemed studiously to repel the approaches of intellectual men; and accordingly had been illustrated by the devotion of no great mind. Its preachers, imperceptive of the English standards of good taste and reverence, could hardly be distinguished from Dissenters. Its creed, an endless chain of inflexible links, could only revolve in the same technical groove, and could apply itself to no resistance that lay out of its meridian. The cold-blooded rapture with which the most dismal pictures were drawn of this redeemed world, and a divine economy sketched which tortures every moral affection, plainly showed that the scheme was no longer realized, and had passed from an inner life to an outward opinion. The ecclesiastical doctrine of the party was moreover purely Erastian, and left no intelligible barrier to separate the Anglican Church from the crowd of Nonconformists at home, and the unepiscopal Protestants abroad. These features had been little noticed while the merits which balanced them were still fresh; while the race of idle and worldly clergymen was disappearing before the new earnestness; while great philanthropic enterprises were led by the followers of Simeon; while the fact remained conspicuous, that there was a Christianity to be recovered for the land, and that these men had stepped forth to do it. But in the third decade of this century their "first works" had grown familiar; their weaknesses had become fixed; their type of character had cleared itself of its accidents and taken shape. It caught the fastidious eye of Oxford; and ere long, beneath that fine perception all the blemishes were brought out. A series of criticisms began, at first cautious and respectful; but gradually assuming a wider range and an intenser spirit, they assailed the Evangelical party with every weapon of antipathy which could be drawn from the armory of imagination or logic, Scripture or history. The weariness and distaste felt at Oxford towards the Church-Calvinists supplied the first impulse to the Tractarian movement; and it was chiefly with a view to displace them that a new theology was advanced. As its lines were filled in, and it acquired consistency and depth, a positive inspiration of genuine faith supervened and left all party passions behind. The great agent in this work was John Henry Newman; without an estimate of whose genius and influence only two-thirds of the theological history of contemporary England could be written. In him and the Oxford *ecclesiastical* re-action we have our *first* source of the modern development; not exactly first in time, or perhaps even in importance, but most conspicuous and best-defined, and therefore most tempting to begin with.

The sister University became the *officina* of no "Tracts;" and so no one talks of a "Cambridge theology." There is such a thing, nevertheless;— at least there is a theology, perfectly distinct and characteristic of the age, formed by Cambridge men, and born with the impress of Cambridge studies, though not elaborated on the spot. Coleridge taught at Highgate; but he poetized and learned at Jesus College half a century before: and the men through whom chiefly his Platonic gospel has passed into the heart of our generation, Julius Hare and Frederick Maurice, acknowledged the same *alma mater*. To those who are familiar with the writings of these eminent teachers, it will not appear fanciful if we trace the origin of the school to intellectual revolt against their academic text-books, Locke and Paley. Empirical psychology and utilitarian ethics are the permanent objects of Coleridge's hostility; and their removal is with him the prior condition of any morality or religion at all. It was reserved for Professors Sedgwick and Whewell, at a later time, to dethrone upon the spot the two established potentates in philosophy. But the murmurs against them had long been gathering. Their school had not stood still, and in its advance had become encumbered with able but inconvenient allies; betraying, in Bentham and James Mill, the tendencies full-blown which it had been often reproached with secreting. Long before the Genius of the place, starting at the shadow of its own philosophy, recoiled and took shelter with an elder faith, the sensitive and religious mind of Coleridge had not only found refuge there for himself, but opened an asylum for other wanderers, and lighted up a chain of posts to show the way. The movement, commenced in re-action from inadequate metaphysics, never rested till it found the legitimate repose of a satisfying theology. In naming the accomplished Chaplain of Lincoln's Inn as the most distinguished representative of this type of religious thought, we do not overlook the marked individuality which assigns to him a place of his own. But this very freedom and freshness in the disciple will be found characteristic, as of Plato's so of Coleridge's disciples. Mr. Maurice may well protest against the absurd classification which, under the common designation of "Broad Church," ranks him in the same series with Whately, Powell, and Williams, — men whose first principles and whole method are the most precise contradictories of his own, however congenial with him they may be in resistance to unchristian narrowness and unworthy fears. But he has always affectionately claimed his affinity with the author of the *Aids to Reflection,* and cannot be displeased if we seek him, with Julius Hare, in the parlor of the Highgate sage. In the *philosophical* re-action proceeding thence to penetrate the whole substance of Christianity, we find the *second* element in the modern development.

It would be a curious problem of literary geography to trace the stream of French intellectual influence which has passed through Edinburgh, to effect its infiltration into the English mind. Certain it is that the action of continental culture on North Britain has been more immediate and conspicuous than on South; and in return, the writings of the "Scottish school" have met with a recognition in Paris and Geneva which they never obtained in England. The genius of the country inclines, on one side, to the Gallican type of Reformed theology; on the other, to the material sciences in which Paris, on the whole, has borne the palm. Playfair, Leslie, and Dugald Stewart, in their mathematical and physical expositions, have the peculiar impress of French neatness and precision. David Hume, scarcely English in his style, was still less so in the easy play of his logic, and the careless completeness of his Pyrrhonism. And the answers which his own countrymen gave to him were precisely such as the metaphysical orthodoxy of the *Faculté des Lettres* approved and reproduced. Again and again may be noticed a certain sympathetic or concurrent change in the speculative temperature of Edinburgh and Paris. During the depression of France after the Restoration, the re-action against the opinions and tastes of her revolutionary period was everywhere strong in Europe; and met in Edinburgh with no check from any fascinating system or powerful mind. The phrenology of Gall, the criticism of Jeffrey, the rhetoric of Brown, could not assuage the deeper thirst now beginning to be felt. Something else was needed than a new form of the discarded materialism, and freethinking, and sensationalism of the last age. In truth, Scottish logic and metaphysics had run dry, and by resort to them was no baptism of regeneration to be found. While many still wandered there in hope, there came out of the desert a Scottish *vates*, who had descried an unexhausted spring, and led the way to it by strange paths. Thomas Carlyle gave the first clear expression to the struggling heart of a desolate yet aspiring time, making a clean breast of many stifled unbeliefs and noble hatreds; and if unable to find any certain Saviour for the present, at least preparing some love and reverence to sit, "clothed and in right mind," for the Divine welcome, whenever it might come. Is the reader surprised that we keep a niche for the author of *Hero-Worship* in our gallery of *theologians?* Be it so. The officials of St. Stephen's were also surprised at the proposal to put

Cromwell's effigy among the statues of the kings. We will only say, that whoever doubts the vast influence of Carlyle's writings on the inmost faith of our generation, or supposes that influence to be wholly disorganizing, misinterprets, in our opinion, the symptoms of the time, and is blinded by current phraseology to essential facts. With this conviction, we must treat the *literary* reaction represented by him as the *third* element, completing the modern development.

To these three movements, distinguished by the names of Newman, Coleridge, and Carlyle, must be mainly ascribed the altered spirit, in regard to religion, pervading the young intellect of England. In proceeding to notice them one by one, we must be content with a slight glance at their most salient features. And we must wholly pass by many secondary, though far from unimportant, streams of separate influence which have swelled the confluence of change. The operation of Arnold's life, — of Whately's writings, — of Channing, — of the younger Newman, — of Theodore Parker, — of Emerson, — on the temper and belief of the age, has in each case been considerable. But we limit ourselves to the *prophetæ majores.* Moreover, it is only on the *fresh powers,* cutting into original directions, and making roadways of thought where before was the forest or the flood, that we propose to dwell. Whilst these have been working their way, of course the old tendencies have not quitted the field, or lost their hold. The elder orthodoxies, the elder scepticisms, of established type, are still alive; and now and then, during the last thirty years, have put forth startling re-assertions of their vitality. In Comte the physical, in Strauss the historical, negation of theology, may be said not only to re-appear, but to culminate. And each of these, again, has its group of related phenomena : the Logic of Mill, the hypothesis of the *Vestiges* (and, we would add, the greater part of the replies), the Psychology of Herbert Spencer, and the propaganda of Secularism, tracing the course of the Positivist tendency; while the freer hand which scriptural criticism everywhere displays, its more open feeling for the *human* element in the gospel, — qualities which, most conspicuous abroad, are yet familiar to us in Bunsen, Stanley, and Jowett, — indicate a direction from which the *Leben Jesu* has rendered it impossible to recede. These, however, are but the newest steps on beaten tracks of thought. Since the age of Bacon (nay, for that matter, from the days of Socrates), we have known that to seek only natural law, was the way to find only natural law; and since the time of Semler, there is no excuse for surprise if the critique of Scripture persists in demanding some modification of our faith. To lay down the true bridge from inductive science to the living God, — to settle the relation between the human and the divine factors in the process and monuments of revelation, — these are not new difficulties; nor is it an original device to fall into despair at them, and declare that the problems can be worked only on their finite side. Comte and Strauss, therefore, we disregard, at present, as mere *continuance-phenomena*, — rather clenching the past than opening the future. They do but modify the equilibrium of given conditions : and our purpose is to describe the dynamic elements which have introduced unexpected movement.

The marvellous results of the High-Church re-action have nearly effaced the remembrance of its local and personal beginnings. It was busy at Oxford long before the first "Tracts" appeared; under an aspect, however, which gave little promise of the *Newman-ia* (to borrow a witticism of Whately's) afterwards developed. Some thirteen years before the Tracts were advertised, two undergraduates had an epistolary controversy together on the subject of *baptismal regeneration;* and the correspondent who took the *evangelical* side was John Henry Newman. The doctrine, therefore, was in vogue ere its appointed advocate was converted. In truth, Dr. Charles Lloyd, who filled the chair of Divinity (Regius) from 1822, and the see of Oxford from 1827 till his death in 1829, was, throughout this period, obnoxious to the Evangelicals as the avowed representative of an opposite school, to which also Hawkins, Pusey, and Keble belonged. But the "Catholic" tendency of this group of friends was marked by other symptoms than the later Tractarian. Dr. Newman has remarked, that "the same philosophical elements" will "lead one mind to the Church of Rome; another to what, for want of a better word, may be called *Germanism.*" * He is pleased to add, that the determination towards the Tiber or the Rhine will depend on the person's "sensibility or insensibility to sin." Perhaps, also, a little on his knowledge or ignorance of the German language and literature; without some access to which, "*Germanism*" would seem to be impossible, and therefore, in the given case, Romanism inevitable. The *Præ-Newmanites* at Ox-

* Essay on the Development of Christian Doctrine, p. 71.

ford were not unfurnished with modern, in addition to ancient, scholarship; and, accordingly, were known to look with hope and favor on the aims of a scientific theology, and to be quite above the conventional disparagement of German research to which a blind cowardice resorts. Indeed, Dr. Pusey's first publication, dedicated to Bishop Lloyd, was a defence * of the "Theology of Germany" against the strictures of Mr. Rose in his *Cambridge University Sermons.* This little book, which, we believe, has long been suppressed, bears curious witness to the deflection of the Oxford movement from its original path. The author explains the extravagances of Rationalism by the absurd "stiffness" and intolerable "orthodoxism" which preceded and provoked them: he welcomes the aid of Kant and Schelling in transition to a higher faith: he treats the dangerous crisis as over, and the healthy renovation of theology as in progress. Nor are his particular judgments of men and books less remarkable than the general course of his argument. Of Lessing he speaks (p. 51) with warm affection, as "probably *more Christian*," despite his scepticism, than his orthodox opponent Göze; and (p. 156) as, "perhaps rightly, preferring Pantheism to the then existing systems." He recognizes (p. 177) De Wette's "really Christian faith," obscured though it might be by adherence to the philosophy of Fries. Schleiermacher receives (p. 115) the highest praise. Bretschneider is justified (p. 154) for attempting, in the *Probabilia*, to bring the Johannine question to an issue. And it is strange to hear (p. 80) from the

* An Historical Inquiry into the probable Causes of the Rationalist Character lately predominant in the Theology of Germany. By E. B. Pusey, M.A., Fellow of Oriel College, Oxford. 1828.

nominal father of "Puseyism," that the "*gratia ministerialis*,"—the efficacy of the sacraments and offices, though administered by evil men,—is "an absurd and pernicious fiction." That a book abounding in such estimates should be laid by this particular author at the feet of an Oxford bishop and Regius Professor; and that the successors to that divinity chair should be first Dr. Burton and then Dr. Hampden, are clear indications of a theological tendency, present and powerful in the early years of the anti-evangelical movement, but superseded and discharged at a later stage.

In 1829, Bishop Lloyd made his mortal exit. Superfluous German and defective "sensibility to sin" having thus withdrawn to other scenes, there was room for "the same philosophical elements," with proper "sensibility" and no German, to enter from the other side, and, slipping to the front, lead on whither that happy set of graces tends. For a while it seemed doubtful which of the two paths the Oxford High Church was to take—Germanism or Romanism—theological advance or ecclesiastical retrogression: and the events of that year curiously show how little either section of the party understood its own instincts and could take its proper attitude. It was the memorable year of Catholic emancipation and Sir Robert Peel's rejection at Oxford. At that election we find Dr. Pusey among the strenuous supporters, Dr. Newman among the vehement opponents, of the minister and his Relief-bill: the former reputed to be "one of the most liberal members of the University," the latter in close "union with the most violent bigots" of "the No-popery party;"*

* Life of Blanco White, vol. iii. p. 131.

the future Anglican in the camp of the liberals — the future Romanist in that of the Orangemen! Yet Newman had already betrayed the tendencies which ere long possessed him entirely, and become separated by them from his former associates of the same school. Not only had his private opinions opened out, from 1823–6, into something like "full-blown Popery,"* but he had evinced on their behalf that unrivalled power of personal influence which few sensitive minds can resist, and which carries with it a restless passion for its own exercise. He was, indeed, foiled in his first conflict with the Evangelical party, and in his first attempt to dictate a policy to his own; but his was not a power which depended on external success; it was a spiritual ascendency, yielding like the air to local strokes of force, but remaining circumambient and elastic still. The minute-book of the Oxford Auxiliary Bible Society probably records the earliest public evidence of his alienation from his undergraduate faith. Already remarkable for the force and fervor of his preaching, and not yet an object of theological suspicion, he had been appointed third secretary to the society in 1826, on the suggestion of Dr. Symons (present Warden of Wadham College), and with the approval of Dr. M'Bride (now Principal of Magdalen Hall), and other distinguished supporters of the Low Church. No sooner had he accepted the office than an anonymous circular appeared on the breakfast-table of sundry clergymen of the place, lamenting that the society was in the hands of the low party; urging the importance of effecting a change, and pointing out a rule which

* See F. W. Newman's Phases of Faith, p. 11.

conferred a vote on every clerical subscription of half-a-guinea. It was soon whispered that this paper was not unknown to the new secretary; though one at least of his near friends felt secure in denying his connection with it, and was proportionately disturbed to find it really his production. The design, thus commenced in secret, soon threw off all disguise. The draft of the annual report, drawn up in the usual unctuous style by the first secretary, Mr. Hill (Vice-Principal of St. Edmund's Hall), came before the committee for discussion. The new secretary moved some two hundred and fifty amendments, which would have struck out all the Scripture adaptations and "gracious" jargon from the document, and turned it into such English as he might use. He lost his amendments,—his office,—and all further confidence from the Evangelical party.

The loss, however, of his tutorship in Oriel, involving as it did a breach with Dr. Hawkins (the Provost), was more significant in relation to the subsequent course of Anglicanism. In conjunction with two out of three co-tutors (the elder Froude and Mr. [afterwards Archdeacon] Robert Isaac Wilberforce), he had requested that the Oriel men might be distributed into four separate sets; and that of these, one might be assigned to each tutor as his *pastoral charge*. The request was refused by the Provost, on the reasonable ground that, by the proposed arrangement, the students would fall, in each case, under the exclusive power of one man's mind, instead of experiencing, as was intended, the influence of the whole tutorial body. The disappointed petitioners resigned; and from that moment the preacher at St. Mary's, checked in his operations *within* his college, laid himself out for religious action *beyond* its walls, and raised his Church and Littlemore into a power of the first order in the history of English religion.

The death of Dr. Lloyd removed his chief external check at a time when his internal resources for influence were fast maturing. The Divinity chair and the episcopal office were no longer united; and scientific theology lost the shelter of the mitre. The subtle intellect and resolute will of John Henry Newman were left without a rival: not indisposed to crush as dangerous the explorations of German criticism, which probably suggested nothing but scepticisms to his outside gaze; and impelled to organize, out of the safer materials of patristic and ecclesiastical literature, where he was at home, a scheme of doctrine with clear passages between the parts, with commodious stowing-place for every doubt, and foundations buried out of sight. We presume it must be ascribed to the influence of his friend, that Dr. Pusey never followed up the direction on which he had so well entered in his "Inquiry" concerning Rationalism; and that a few years later (in 1836) he was ready, in his turn, to employ against Dr. Hampden the very same unworthy weapons which he had wrested from the hand of Mr. Rose. When *he* had succumbed, all ambiguity as to the course of the movement ceased. The assault on Evangelicism from the side of free learning was silent; the guns spiked, the batteries abandoned. All was to be done from the entrenched positions of Past Authority, and the communications surrendered with the open road of Future Truth. Though some cautious years had still to pass ere the full bearings of the new system were displayed, the absence of divided command accelerated its development, and simplify its history. The preacher of St. Mary's was undisputed *choregus:* and the analysis of his personal theology preserves the essence of the whole re-action.

Whence arises that strange mixture of admiration and of distrust, of which most readers and hearers of John Henry Newman are conscious? Often as he carries us away by his close dialectic, his wonderful readings of the human heart, his tender or indignant fervor, there remains a small dark speck of misgiving which we can never wipe out. The secret perhaps lies in this, — that his own faith is an escape from an alternative scepticism, which receives the *veto* not of his reason, but of his will. He has, after all, the critical, not the prophetic mind. He wants *immediateness* of religious vision. Instead of finding his eye clearer and his foot firmer the deeper he sinks towards the ultimate ground of trust, he hints that the light is precarious, and that your step may chance on the water or the rock in that abysmal realm. The tendency of the purest religious insight is ever to quit superficial and derivative beliefs, and seek the primitive roots where the finite draws life from the Infinite. The awfulness of that position, the direct contact of the human spirit with the Divine, the loneliness of communion when all media of church and usage are removed, do not appall the piety of noblest mood. With Dr. Newman the order is reversed. He loves to work in the upper strata of the minds with which he deals, detecting their inconsistencies, balancing their wants, satisfying them with the mere coherence and relative sufficiency of their belief, but encouraging them to shrink from the last questionings. With himself, indeed, he sometimes goes deeper, and descends towards the bases of all devout belief; but evidently with less of assurance as his steps pass down. The ground feels to him less and less solid as he penetrates from the deposits of recent experience into the inner laboratory of the world; and it is only when he stands upon the crust, and takes it as it is, that he loses the fear lest it rest upon the flood. His certainties are on the surface, and his insecurities below. With men of opposite character, often reputed to be sceptical, doubt is at the top, and is but as the swaying of water that is calm below, and sleeps in its entire mass within its granite cradle. He seems to say within himself, "There *is* no bottom to these things that I can find; we must therefore *put one there;* and only mind that it be sufficient to hold them in, supposing it to be real." He deals, in short, with the first truths of religion as *hypotheses*, not known or knowable in themselves, but recommended by the sufficient account they give of the facts, and the practical fitness of belief in them to our nature. He denies the existence for our mind of any thing ἀνυπόθετον, and treats even our highest persuasions as a provisional discipline, wholesome for us to retain, whether they be harmless errors or eternal truths. Nor is this radical scepticism merely implied at second-hand: it receives direct and repeated statement as a philosophical principle. In his History of the Arians,* the author explains the distinction drawn by the Fathers between θεολογία and οἰκονομία,

* Pages 43, 44.

between absolute and relative truth in regard to God. An "economy," we are told, is a representation not corresponding with the real nature of things, but reduced into adaptation to our faculties, and substituted for the truth in condescension to our incapacity. It is not simply the broken view which alone *we* can seize of transcendent realities, given for apprehension but not yet apprehended; it is a "pious fraud," — a benevolent cheat, — directly put upon us by the Creator himself, to stand as the moral equivalent of a missing verity. Now, what does the author include under this class of representative illusions? Does he, like the Fathers, confine the application to the doctrine of the Incarnation and historical manifestation of God in Christ, as opposed to his inner and Absolute Essence? Far from it. He reduces to the same head the revelation to us of *moral laws;* and the suggestion, by sensible phenomena, of an *external material world;* and the aspect of *design and purpose* which the cosmical order assumes in the eyes of "the multitude." Are these things, then, — these porphyry pillars on which our very life is raised, — nothing but appearance, — "shadows," "beguiling the imaginations of most men with a harmless but unfounded belief"? So does our author regard them: and in his idealism saves nothing whatever, so far as we can find, from the realm of fantasy. Alike in the world of sense and in the temple of the spirit "man walketh in a vain show." In this way the very antithesis from which he starts disappears: he gives such an extension to the system of *economy* as to swallow up the *theology* altogether, and to present God to us as never and nowhere doing any thing but "simulating" on our behalf. Not only are we kept at a distance from all realities; but the representations amid which our minds are imprisoned are, or may be, *false* representations; — false in the same way and degree as the assertion that the Mosaic dispensation was unchangeable, though all the while it was destined to be abolished. Alas! have we here no key to our author's fondness for an esoteric and exoteric presentation of doctrine? — for a mystical as well as a literal exegesis? — for a *disciplina arcani?* — for *doubling* the aspect and expression of all that is offered as truth? If the universe and God set the example of being scenical, what shall hinder religion from becoming histrionic?

The hypothetical nature of even the most fundamental propositions in theology, — their dependence on assumptions which not our vision but our blindness compels us to make, — is strongly asserted in the following paragraph of the fourteenth University Sermon; on the Theory of Developments in religious doctrine:

> "It is true that God is without beginning, *if* eternity may worthily be considered to imply succession; in every place, *if* He who is a Spirit can have relations with space. It is right to speak of His Being and Attributes, *if* He be not rather super-essential; it is true to say that He is wise or powerful, *if* we may consider Him as other than the most simple Unity. He is truly Three, *if* He is truly One; He is truly One, *if* the idea of Him falls under earthly number. He has a triple Personality in the sense in which the Infinite can be understood to have Personality at all. *If* we know any thing of Him, — *if* we may speak of Him in any way, *if* we may emerge from Atheism or Pantheism into religious faith, — *if* we would have any saving hope, any life of truth and holiness within us, — this only do we know, with this only

confession we must begin and end our worship, — that the Father is the One God, the Son the One God, and the Holy Ghost the One God; and that the Father is not the Son, the Son not the Holy Ghost, and the Holy Ghost not the Father." (p. 353.)

To a faith thus contingent on certain prior assumptions there could be no valid objection, *if* the assumptions themselves are regarded as unconditionally sure. But the fatal thing is this, that every one of them is regarded by the author as an "economy"— as referable not to our knowledge but to our nescience — as rather a πρῶτον ψεῦδος than a genuine "first truth." Reason would as soon suspect as trust them; — nay, it is reason that traces them to their seat in our feebleness and incapacity, and enables us to put the case of their being false. If, in a fit of caprice, you choose to throw them all away and substitute their opposites, no one can show rational cause against you, or dispute the philosophical adequacy of your new hypothesis. *Both* doctrines, atheism and theism, our author more than once intimates, are theories that will hold water. "It is indeed," he says, "a great question whether atheism is not as philosophically consistent with the phenomena of the physical world, taken by themselves, as the doctrine of a creative and governing Power."* In preferring the religious interpretation of the universe, we seize an hypothesis at a venture, impelled by the presumptions of a good heart.

On every account we object to this statement of the ultimate grounds of religion. The author concedes far too much to the atheistic doctrine; and by treating it

* University Sermons, chiefly on the Theory of Religious Belief, p. 186.

as an *hypothesis* puts it to a wrong test: for the question is, not whether its premises, *if true*, will cover the phenomena; but whether its premises (*e.g.* its notions of Force, Causation, Law) *are true*, or, on the contrary, confused and self-contradictory. He establishes a false variance between the rational and the moral faculties of the soul, and in consequence between philosophical and religious evidence; so that we are made to lose a truth by the one and then recover it by the other. Speculative Reason sends us to the Gazette, but Practical Reason steps in with copious assets and discharges every claim. We dislike to be made the sport of these experiments between imaginary rivals: we object to being drowned in the sea of speculation, just that the Humane Society of practical principles may rub us into life again. The intellectual and the moral functions of our nature have one and the same inspiration,—gain their vision by one and the same light; and it is only by a trick of artificial abstraction that faith can be said to suffer ruin from the one and receive rescue by the other. The postulates of morals stand, in their own right, as first principles in philosophy. But the essential fault of our author's foundation lies in his *Idealism*. That the existence and perfection of God,—that the conflict of moral law with lower nature,—should be no more certain than the reality of an outward world, we may contentedly allow, *provided* that outward world be left to us as an immediate object, positively given to our knowledge by a veracious faculty. This, however, is precisely what Dr. Newman refuses to us. He treats the notion of a material universe as an "unfounded belief," neutral at best as to truth or falsehood. Our moral faith, our religious faith, he sets on the same footing with our natural realism; and then slips that realism away as a harmless beguilement, "simulating" yet masking the inaccessible fact.* The logical consequence is evident — is probably *meant* to be evident; for sceptical desolation is found to be the best preparative for the shelter of an authoritative church.

The relation of faith to reason is traced by Dr. Newman with a fineness and general truth of discrimination that remind us of Butler.† He rejects the rationalist conceptions of faith, as either the purely intellectual act of believing on testimonial and other secondary evidence, or the purely moral act of carrying out by the will what has been acccepted by the understanding. The former confounds it with opinion; the latter with obedience. He does not narrow the term to the Lutheran dimensions, to denote a reliant affection towards a person, and imply a grace peculiar to the Christian and Jewish dispensations. It is a *moral act of reason*, believing, at the instigation of reverence and love, something which goes beyond the severe requirements of the evidence. In matters of pure science, where we have to do with mere nature, the mind simply follows the vestiges of proof. But in concerns of man and God we necessarily carry into every process of judgment antecedent presumptions which color our whole thought, and interpret for us the external signs given to direct us. To a cold intellect these presumptions will be wanting; and it will construe the spiritual

* Arians of the Fourth Century, pp. 44, 45. University Sermons, p. 350.

† See especially University Sermons, ix. x. xi. Essay on Development, ch. vi. § 2.

as if it were physical. To a bad heart they will be dark suspicions; and it will believe its own shadow. To an affectionate, faithful, humble mind they will be clear trusts; and it will "think no evil," and "hope all things." It is in this yielding of the reason to the better suggestion—this casting of one's lot with the higher possibility, that faith consists. Obedience to conscience partakes therefore of the nature of faith;* and implies, wherever found, a seed of grace and an offer of salvation. The great heathen world is thus brought within the compass of a divine probation; and faithful men, true to their gifts and guidance, are scattered through all lands and ages. It is characteristic of the judgments of faith, that they are immediate and intuitive, detached and unsystematic; whilst those of wisdom are mediate and reflective—the explicit and connected contents of implicit acts of trust. Wisdom is therefore the end of that Christian culture of which faith is the beginning,† the ἐπιστήμη of morals, as opposed to mere ἀληθὴς δόξα. It springs from the exercise of Reason on the data of Faith. The same Reason, exercised on the data of Sense and Perception, constitutes the scientific intellect; whose scrutiny, thus working *in alio genere*, can never alight upon moral discoveries, or replace what has been let slip through non-acceptance of the presumptions of Conscience. Here lies the great mistake of Protestants, who begin with inquiry, expecting to end with faith—"grapes from thorns, and figs from thistles." Catholics, on the other hand, begin with faith, and develop it by inquiry;‡ rever

* University Sermons, ii. pp. 19 et seqq.

† Ibid. xiii. p. 288.

‡ Loss and Gain, p. 103.

ently taking the divine instincts, and drawing out their hidden oracles into the symmetry of a holy philosophy. In this view the very materials of religious knowledge are present only to the tact of a pure heart; and our author is quite self-consistent when he affirms, in language curiously coinciding with his brother's, that the moral sense — the "spiritual discernment" — is the legitimate judge of religious truth; the intellect having only to prepare the case and watch it with negative and corrective function.*

In its broad features; its linking of moral with religious reverence; its separation of conscience from understanding; its distinction between implicit and explicit truth, — this theory of faith contrasts favorably both with the evangelical no-theory and the rationalist wrong theory. Did the author never quit its systematic statement, or, in quitting it for concrete application, never transgress its terms, we should thank him for removing old errors without remonstrance for introducing new. When, however, we turn from his disquisitions to his tales, and observe the use to which he puts his doctrine in practical life, we start back in dismay, and ask ourselves whether what we had so much approved in thought can issue in what we must utterly disapprove in action? In the sermons we seem to understand the statements, and with full heart assent to them that "faith must *venture something;*" that in order to finish by knowing, you must commence by trusting; that self-surrender in the dark to conscience clears up into open-eyed wisdom. Nor should we seriously object to the exhortation, "*Believe* first, and *conviction*

* University Sermons, iii. pp. 40, 44, 45.

will follow," so long as we may construe the "belief" to mean simple reliance on *instinctive* impressions of the good and true, and the "conviction," a reflective apprehension of their *ground;* and may therefore read the lesson thus: "You must *do* the right before you can *know* it." First, however, an uneasy wonder stops us when we are told that in early times men became Christians, not *because* they believed, but *in order to believe;** and that the characteristic doctrines of the Gospel were not offered to them till after they had bound themselves to the church by baptism. Next, the real meaning of these ill-favored general statements becomes shamefully apparent in a particular instance in *Loss and Gain*, where the hero, a puzzled Protestant, unsatisfied with English church-parties, but an entire stranger to the Romanist system and worship, is passionately urged by a recently "perverted" friend to take his hat and walk straight away into confession and adoption. He does not at the moment yield to the advice; but a little later he follows it, without any great advance in his mental preparation, and before ever witnessing a service in a Catholic church. Thus is the word "*faith*" degraded to the sense of "trying the experiment of an unknown religion, and obeying it at hazard;" and has no further reference to *conscience*, which stands quite neutral towards a church not yet appreciated. There is still, however, a lower step to be taken. Dr. Newman does not attempt to disguise the shock given to the moral feeling and taste of new-comers by many things inseparable from Romanism. How does he counsel them to deal with their distress?

* Arians, p. 78. Loss and Gain, p. 343.

To respect it as a sacred sign? to follow their own highest perception at all risks? No; but to suppress and smother it; to consider that they must not expect to get through without dirt, and to hope that things will look cleaner when the eye has become used to them. And this, *proh pudor!* he also calls "faith;" having at last turned it right round, and brought it to mean the *contradiction* of conscience, — the placid swallowing of what is offensive to the moral sense. In short, he makes it convertible with mere "*taking on trust*," without regard to the felt *quality* of the thing taken. Whether you yield to what commands, or to what scandalizes, your natural reverence, you equally satisfy the conditions of our author's "*faith*." The word thus becomes an engine that will work either in advance or in reverse: whether you believe your conscience or disbelieve, it keeps you on the pious track.

The practice of professing a creed "*in order to believe*" has long been a favorite with the casuistry of Oxford. Arnold, troubled with doubts about the doctrine of the Trinity, was recommended by his friend Keble to take a parish, and avow the doctrine several times per week, and multiply the meshes of his entanglement with it. Every Oxford tutor, we believe, could quote instances in which scepticism of greater extent has been met with similar advice. Without discussing the pleas advanced in defence of such counsels, we will test their character by an imaginary case, exhibiting the conditions in the simplest form. In a religious and highly accomplished family, connected on all hands with the church, an erring son, let us suppose, becomes enamored of the "doctrine of circumstances;" and passing through the mere fatalistic stage, settles into resolute and open-eyed atheism. No nobleness of character or confusion of thought beguiles him (as happier natures are beguiled) into the illusion that moral distinctions remain when divine realities are gone: and his life exhibits no violent inconsistency with a creed which disclaims responsibility. Among his numerous clerical connections, one, we will suppose, is captivated with the new formula, that men are to become members of the church not "because they believe, but in order to believe:" and, acting on this rule, addresses him to the following effect: "You say you disbelieve the existence of a God; but you are in no condition to judge, for you have never tried the hypothesis of theism. Your first step must be to grant it for experiment's sake, to act *as if* there were a God, and become a *quasi*-Christian. Join the church; diligently profess the creeds; take the sacrament; be constant in your prayers; expostulate with the heresies of others; and in due time *belief will follow*." It is easier, perhaps, to conceive such counsels offered than to imagine them accepted. For completeness' sake, however, let us suppose their influence for the moment to prevail. A sudden transformation is visible. The atheist looks up his prayer-book, and is seen twice a day at church: he audibly says, "I believe in one God, the Father Almighty, &c.;" he bows to the east at the name of the Lord Jesus Christ; he hears the warning from the altar to "search his own conscience" "*not* after the manner of *dissemblers with God*," and answers it by boldly partaking at "the holy table." He plays the Pharisee towards pure and pious friends, needing his rebuke for their "neological" tendencies. His fictitious zeal at last outstrips the pace of his spiritual counsellor; to whom he points out certain worldly-minded friends as requiring to be brought to a "sense of their condition." The clergyman declining so delicate an office, the spell of his influence is broken; his hopeful novice throws up with disgust "the hypothesis of a God," relapses into the atheism which had never really left him for an hour: and "Richard is himself again."

That we have not misconceived the natural issue of this sort of experiment, critics of human nature will perhaps allow. That the experiment itself is a legitimate offspring of the parent maxim, the logical reader will hardly question. But between logic and life, it will be said, bridges are scarce; and, in practice, these extreme cases never find the means to cross. Those who speak thus can have had little access to the inner history of the present age. When the time comes for its sincerest biographies to appear, the truth will often prove "stranger than our fiction."

The theory of Christianity which Dr. Newman's writings present deserved better at his hands than to be given as an hypothesis and an "economy." Stript of perverse adjuncts, and checked at its points of deflection, it assumes the aspect of a religious philosophy, combining, with an unusual sense of proportion, the chief truths of Christian morals and faith. In its results it concurs, of course, with the Catholic doctrines; but it brings them out in fresh connections and with reference all round to the rival teachings, from the midst of which the expositor himself has emerged into them. The briefest notice of the main features must content us.

The human soul cannot lose its essentially moral constitution. Free and responsible still in the heathen notwithstanding the fall, and in the Christian though brought under grace, it has never sunk below the capacity, and never rises above the obligation, of obedience. The sense of duty is intrinsically the highest authority, — the ultimate ground of all ecclesiastical pretensions. The "objective authority" of the church, which is peculiar to revealed religion, would have nothing to rest upon, were it not for the prior "subjective authority" of conscience, which belongs to natural religion. The dispensations of God are not, therefore, restricted to the Hebrew course of history: they are universal as the human conscience, and every man has his trust of light and grace. Even special revelation must be regarded as probably given at different times to all nations; no tribe being without traditions of supernatural events. The distinction in favor of the Jewish race is simply that with it alone have the facts been preserved by authentic records and media. And as the inspiration of God is not restricted by limits of place, so neither does it die out with time. He speaks to us still, and enables us to add to our store; not, indeed, by taking any new point of departure, but developing and applying the divine data, — by resolving the vision and concrete thought of the Son of God into the component ideas and living truths which it yields to holy reflection.

In its very nature religious truth is *self*-evidencing, — evolved from the mind rather than deposited on it: and the care of the teacher or the church must be directed less to any intellectual elaboration of proof than to prepare the temper and posture of the receiving soul, and waken into consciousness the elementary experiences of reverence and faith. Christianity itself is self-evidencing, and by its inherent power makes way where no books of evidences could carry it. Indeed, *all* its doctrines are really given, and have actually been found, in natural religion. Only they came to wise and good heathens on the vague authority of a divine *principle*, instead of a divine *agent*. The one grand gift of the Gospel to the human mind is that, by the Incarnation, it has determined the *personality* of God, and His relations of *character and affection* towards man. *This*, and not what is called the "doctrine of the Cross," is the specialty and living kernel of the Gospel.

Christianity, however, is not adequately described as a revelation of truth; or even as a saving transaction: rather is it (inclusively, indeed, of these) a divine Institute in perpetuity for helping man to "cleanse himself from sin." His fallen nature, though not ruined or bereft of its free-will, is in a state of moral infirmity, requiring supernatural aids; and these the Christian economy provides. First, the Son of God became incarnate, "*non amittendo quod erat, sed sumendo quod non erat*," reconciling infinitude with personality, and purifying the nature He adopted and through whose experiences He passed. Next, the sacrificial merits of this act are distributed by a perpetual re-incarnation in the Eucharist, and, with modifications, by the other sacraments, as vehicles of grace. But again, the spiritual purification which is thus freely given to faith for *past* evil does not close the contingencies of the *future*. Only in proportion as the grace of faith leads to works and love, is it effectual for the time to come: so that the retrospect on Redemption does not close the prospect of Retribution, and within the Gospel there is still a Law. Baptism, which washes out all prior sin, cannot be repeated: and subsequent transgressions must be cleansed away either by the penances and absolution of the church, or by the expiations of purgatory. Throughout his doctrine our author provides a responsible place for the human will, and constructs a true "*moral* theology." His antithesis between grace and nature shows itself, not by opposing faith to morality, but by importing into morals an interior contrast between the tastes of the natural and of the religious conscience; the latter going beyond the mere human rectitudes, and producing ascetic virtues, — regarding life as penitential and expiatory, if not endowed with positive and blessed promise to self-sacrifice.

On the mere Romanist appendages to this scheme, — the Invocation of saints, the Mariolatry, the Apostolic Succession, &c. — we mean to say nothing. They are chiefly remarkable for having raised up in their defence the obnoxious but highly important "doctrine of development." In the absence of any plausible support from Scripture, it became necessary, if they were to be retained at all, to widen the source of doctrine, and give an interpreting and determining power to the church. In order to reconcile Protestants to this, it was maintained that for them too, not less than for the Catholics, the letter of the Bible was insufficient, unless read by the reflected light of later ecclesiastical decisions. Neither the doctrine of the Trinity, nor the usage of Infant Baptism, could be gathered from the sacred writings alone. Such questions as those respecting an intermediate state and the remission of past-baptismal sins are raised, but not solved, by the Gospels. Nor can Scripture determine its own canon, or its own inspiration. To set it up as a self-sufficing objective authority, is to apply it to a purpose for which it is not intended or adapted. On the other hand, traces abound upon its page that it has been composed on the principle of development, that is, with a view to an ulterior determination of many things which it leaves indeterminate. The statement of the Logos-doctrine in the proem of St. John's Gospel is but the germ in which the true doctrine of Christ's higher nature lies: and till successive heresies had started the questions dormant within it, and given occasion for a verdict on them, the right solution could not disengage itself from the possible wrong ones. The prophecies quoted from the Jewish Scriptures in the Christian seem inapplicable, till we are furnished with the double meaning or non-natural sense; and to bring this fully out required the experience of a later time, when the necessary tendency of literal and historical interpretation to Arian rationalism had been made evident in the exegetical school of Antioch, and the connection of the mystical method with orthodoxy and piety had displayed itself in the catechetical school of Alexandria. From all these symptoms it is gathered, that the Christian system, not excepting its primary principles, is only implicitly given in the canonical books; that the seed of truth, once consigned to human souls as its receptacle, more and more clearly evinced its nature and discriminated its species by the growths into which it opened; that the tact of the church in recognizing the genuine characters, and in rejecting the spurious or mixed, became finer with continued exercise, and the aid of prior definitions; that instead of testing the later by the earlier, we are to interpret the earlier by the later, and import the explicit doctrines of the fourth and fifth centuries into the rudimentary expressions of the first. Protestants must either denude their creed to its mere embryo, or let it assume the proportions of full-blown Romanism.

The state of this controversy is curious. The assumption on both sides is, that *either* the Bible or the Church is impregnable, and achieves all our protection from error for us: the only question is, *which* of the two it is. To put this to the test, each party tries to discredit the favorite refuge of the other. Dr. Newman does not scruple to discharge a volley into the intrenchment of Scripture, in order to show the Protestants that it may be made too hot to hold them, and "compel them to come in" to his stronghold. They reply by a hot fire at his church-bastions, to convince him that they may be knocked about his head. Is it surprising if both are pretty well riddled; if neither is found to be designed for the purpose to which it has been applied; and if a change of the whole ground should be the clearly indicated result? By *no* documentary process, no construction of title-deeds, be they canonical or ecclesiastical, of the first century or the fourth, can you draw forth the oracular system which you seek. Rail off what plot of history you will, the human, with all its liabilities, will be there. Wander where you will on its unenclosed spaces, the divine, with its eternal teaching, will not be absent. For discriminating the true from the false, the accidental from the essential, in morals and religion, whether drawn from the special Christian data, or from the entire life of humanity, something more is needed than to draw an arbitrary line round a select group of books, or a favored series of centuries. "Objective authority" in religion there doubtless is; but vested in a Person who is eternal, and not therefore a fixture of chronology; speaking to us through *all* the media of His life in humanity, and not therefore separable from the "subjective authority" of conscience, or discoverable without it; and though uniquely manifested in the "Word made flesh," yet owned by us even there only through the same Word in hearts already tinctured with the Christian consciousness.

Looking back on the whole influence of Dr. Newman's personality and writings, we see in it a great preponderance of good. Bishop Thirlwall has justly acknowledged that the Oxford movement has given rise to more valuable writings in theology than had appeared for a long time previous to it. And though it arrested the pursuit of critical theology for a while, the postponement was amply compensated by a newly-awakened attention to the whole history of Christianity, and a far more searching look into the moral and spiritual conditions and effects of faith in the human soul. The prosecution of the critical theology will be resumed with larger, humbler, yet freer spirit, now that some deeper root has been found for Christian obedience and belief than an authority wholly external and contingent on a literary tenure. A sense of the universality and perpetuity of Divine grace, — of the sanctity of common duties and self-denials, — of the grandeur and power of historical communion and church-life, — of the true place of beauty and art in worship,— has deeply penetrated into the newer religion of England; — chiefly, it is true, among the classes within reach of academical modes of thought and feeling, but through them affecting the administration of parishes and manors out of number. For the re-union of religious and moral ends, — for the reconciliation of human admirations with holy reverence, — for the consecration of the near and temporal, — many a heart owes a debt of unspeakable gratitude to the literature of the Oxford school. The one grand sin which we must set off against these merits, is a certain want of unconditional and ultimate trust in their own principles. Their system has too often the appearance of being constructed on purpose as a refuge from doubts they dare not face. Their intellectual men have been fond of playing with fire, and flinging about brilliant scepticisms, eating into the very heart of life, for the chance of inducing flight into their protecting fold. It is hard for a proselyte of terror to become a child of trust: and the brand of *fear* deforms the forehead of this party. "To obey," they say, "is easier than to believe: so we will begin from the conscience, that we may end with assurance." Good: but see that you obey out of the belief you *have*, instead of *with a view to a belief which you have not*. Conscience has a right to you through and through, and must be served without terms: and vainly do you mount her sacred steps on knees of painful penance, if the thought of your heart be to escape from the outer exposures and threatening skies of doubt, into the shelter of a ready temple and the sympathy of a mighty throng. The deepest form of scepticism is seen in the mind which is in haste to believe; which resolves, by some violent spring, to make an end of darkness, whether the light attained be God's or not; which is not content to follow precisely and *only* where He shows, and cannot rest upon the trustful word, "My soul, wait *patiently* for Him." Something of this *un*-faith lurks in the spirit of the new Catholic party. They recognize the ambassadorial credentials of Conscience, and show you on its casket of secrets the very signet of the King of kings: — on opening the despatch-box, you find they have stuffed in all the creeds. The self-deception involved in this is not always unmixed with artifice. All such policy is a half-conscious attempt to suborn God's Spirit on behalf of our own desires and prejudices, and against the doubts and scruples which may be truly His.

Transferring ourselves now from Oxford to Cambridge, we acknowledge at the outset that the *place* has much less to do with the party, in the case of the philosophical movement led by Coleridge, than in that of the eccesiastical represented by Newman. Yet it was before the University of Cambridge that Julius Hare* first produced the fruits of his meditations at the feet of the poet-philosopher: and it was in Trinity College chapel that he preached the sermons which mark most

* Sermon on "the Children of Light," preached before the University in 1828.

clearly his theological position.* The Highgate sage had gone to his rest at the very beginning of the Oxford movement (in 1834), and left his disciples to deal with the phenomenon according to their own lights. Mr. Hare had visited the Eternal City, and witnessed there some things which indisposed him to trifle with the honest heart of Protestantism. "I saw the Pope," he used to say, "apparently kneeling in prayer for mankind: but the legs which kneeled were artificial; he was in his chair. Was not that sight enough to counteract all the æsthetical impressions of the worship, if they had been a hundred times stronger than they were? † He saw at once the part that he should take; and in his first sermon, preached before the clergy of the diocese of Chichester, he vindicated, from the words, "Lo, I am with you always, even unto the end of the world," the living presence of the invisible Word in His own Person against the sacerdotal delegation claimed, and virtually substituted, by the Tractarians. Profoundly Lutheran in his conception of "faith," and jealous of all interposed media between the Church and her Divine Head, he resisted at the outset the dangers of an official theocracy with an absent God. The offence given to some hearers by this sermon made him hesitate for a time to accept the office of Archdeacon of Lewes. But in overruling his objections, Bishop Otter rightly interpreted the character of his mind; of which the recent

* Sermon on "the Law of Self-sacrifice," 1829; and Sermon on "the Sin against the Holy Ghost," in 1832.

† See Introduction, page xxvi. (understood to be by Mr. Maurice) to the *Visitation Charges of the Archdeacon of Lewes*, in the years 1843, 1845, 1846; a charming sketch of Hare's character and position, as rich and wise as it is affectionate.

sermon was only a partial expression; and which, though impulsive and unsystematic, had too many open and susceptible sides, too rich a culture, and too real a spiritual depth, to restrict its sympathies to any exclusive party.

In fact, the polemic attitude for the moment assumed towards the Anglicans by no means expressed the characteristic of his school. A much deeper and earlier antipathy had called it into existence, and shaped it into form. Coleridge, as all his readers are aware, was in early life a preacher among the Unitarians. Though never having a permanent pastoral charge among them, he was once on the point of settling as a minister at Shrewsbury: and, in withdrawing, he assures the congregation that, while he prefers a freer mode of life, "active zeal for Unitarian Christianity, not indolence or indifference, has been the motive of my declining a local and stated settlement as a preacher of it." * His early poems, and the name of his eldest son, attest the fervor with which he embraced the philosophy of Priestley and Hartley, as well as the "Psilanthropism" of the sect. By the side of the French atheism of the day, these opinions wore a conservative aspect towards Christianity; in the presence of the political "Church-and-King" vulgarity, they seemed generous to liberty; in the total oblivion of deeper speculation, and the absolute dominance of physical method, they satisfied the demand for compactness and system in philosophy. But only the dearth of other waters, and the parching of that desert time, could detain him at this spring. His natural

* Letter, dated Shrewsbury, Jan. 19, 1798, to Mr. Isaac Wood, High Street, Shrewsbury. Christian Reformer for 1834, p. 840.

thirst was ever feeling its way to more congenial fountains. His speculative creed had never penetrated the unconscious essence of the man, but lay as a texture about him, without growing into the fibres of his heart. In 1796, he records, in a private letter, his experience under sore affliction: "My philosophical refinements and metaphysical theories lay by me in the hour of anguish as toys by the bedside of a child deadly sick." * Never, in short, was the genius of a man more out of its element. An infirm will, a dreamy ideality, a preternatural subtlety of thought, and intense religious susceptibility, were thrown among a people eminently practical and prosaic, impatient of romance, indifferent to intellectual refinements, strict in their moral expectations, scrupulous of the veracities but afraid of the fervors of devotion. The strength and the weakness of each party were vehemently antipathic to those of the other: and their inevitable divergence once begun, the alienation became rapidly complete. Coleridge was a born Platonist, who could not permanently rest content, with Locke, to seek all knowledge in phenomena, or, with Paley, all good in happiness: and on the first opening of his cage of experience, he darted out, and took to his metaphysic wing.

It was Kant who first lifted the bar and set him free; and who, with Schelling, inspired him to seize that border territory between psychology and theology, which had long been declared a dream-land. If anywhere the relationship can be really witnessed between the human spirit and the divine, it must be on the awful

* Letter to Mr. Benjamin Flower, Editor of the Cambridge Intelligencer. Monthly Repository for 1834, p. 654.

confines of the two; and by taking stand on the ground of our highest consciousness, we may perhaps be able to pass to and fro across the line, and find the breadth of any common margin there may be, and note where, on the one hand, it sinks into pure Nature, and on the other, rises into the absolute God. Here, then, he worked in both directions, — upwards and downwards, — till the two tracks met: with results which, so far as our present object is concerned, may be briefly indicated.

Dr. Newman has himself drawn attention to a remarkable concurrence between his own conceptions and Coleridge's, respecting the sources and limits of natural religion in the human mind.* They agree in seeking the germ of devout belief in the experiences of conscience; in recognizing the essentially religious character of morality; in making faith the prior condition of spiritual knowledge, and vindicating the maxim, *Credo, ut intelligam.* Newman, however, represents the moral feeling more as a blind instinctive *datum* to be accepted; Coleridge, more as cognitive power, looking on reality with open eye. And further, with Newman there is *no other* original spring of divine knowledge; while Coleridge allows us an intellectual as well as a moral organ for the apprehension of God. Beyond and above the *Understanding*, which generalizes from the data of perception, gathers laws from phenomena, frames rules from experience, traces logical consequence and adapts means to ends, he enthrones the *Reason*, which seizes a different *order* of truths — viz. the necessary and universal, — in themselves inconceiva-

* University Sermons, ii. p. 24, note.

ble, in their absence contradictory; and in a different *way* — viz. intuitively and immediately, not mediately or through a process. The former (*Verstand*) has the field of *Nature* (that which is *born*, — the originated and transient) for its *object*, and belongs to *our natural part* as its *seat;* and is therefore not peculiar to us, but shared by other animal races, — whose so-called "instinct" is not specifically distinguishable from adaptive intelligence. The latter (*Vernunft*) has the realm of *Spirit* (the *super*-natural, to which the predicates of time and space are inapplicable) for its object, and for its seat in us our spirit or supernatural part. Had we, in combination with our sentient capacity, only understanding, though in ever so eminent a degree, we should remain mere living *things*, — with an honorable place in the records of natural history, but leaving the registers of morals and religion still blank and clasped. The Reason by which a higher life becomes possible divaricates into two functions, — the cognitive and the active; the former giving the roots of all our Ontological thinking, — the ideas of Cause, of Unity, of Infinitude, &c.; the latter furnishing the postulates of all Moral action, — the ideas of Freedom, of Personality, of Obligation. Both the speculative and the practical reason have a voice in our primary religious faith. But the former, alone and by itself, would give us merely an ontological "*One*," a Spinozistic Absolute, — the residuary God of the *a-priori* demonstrations: necessitating, no doubt, a self-subsistent Infinite of which atheism can render no account, but leaving us unassured how far predicates of character may be transferred to its mysterious subject. Hence the chief application of speculative reason in theology must always be critical rather than creative; to slay in single combat each successive foe that may arise; but not to proclaim *for whom* it is that the champion stands, and for ever keeps the field. On the other hand, the practical reason or conscience reveals to us the *Holy* God, who is the proper and positive object of our faith; who is doubtless more or less clearly apprehended in proportion to the purity of our discerning and reflecting faculty, but who lurks suspected or half-perceived in the darkest hearts; — if no otherwise, at least in their fears and compunctions: for "remorse is the implicit creed of the guilty."

The will, as empowered to carry out the ideas of Reason in the realm of Sense, — to make Spirit of avail in Nature, — is by its very function *super*-natural, and cannot be entangled as a constituent in the very system which it is to influence from above. Only the divinely-free can achieve that passage. A footman will run your errand across the town; but it needs a winged Iris or a sandalled Hermes to bear the messages of gods to men. It is precisely in the *freedom of the will* that a person is distinguished from a thing, and becomes a possible subject of moral law. And so is it in the recognition of a good other than the sentient, of an authority transcending all personal preference, of a right over us and our whole cargo of "happiness," actual and potential, that the sense of Duty and the conditions of morality begin. Hence Edwards and the necessarians, Priestley and the materialists, Paley and the Epicureans, depict a universe from which all moral qualities and beings, divine or human, are excluded: and whether reasoning down from God as absolute *Sovereign*, or up from man as simply *sentient*, miss whatever is august and holy in its life.

From the distinction drawn between nature and spirit, it follows that there cannot be such a thing as "*natural* religion." All religion must be *spiritual*, springing as it does exclusively within the supernatural element of us. Nay, more; all religion must be *revealed*, if by that word we mean, "*directly given by Divine communication*," as opposed to mediate discovery of our own. For what and whence are those primary ideas of conscience which constitute or presuppose our deepest, though not our fullest, faith? Are they of our own making?—of our own finding? Have we any thing to do with their genesis? Do they not report to us of the necessary and eternal? And are they not the presence with us of that Eternal, whereof assuredly nothing temporal and finite can report? Is there not profound truth as well as piety in the couplet:

> "None but Thy wisdom knows Thy might:
> None but Thy Word can speak Thy name!"

The reason *in* us is not *personal* to us, but only the manifestation in our consciousness of the infinite reason, presenting us with its supernatural realities, and intrusting to our will their divine rights over our world. It is thus the common ground of the divine and the human, the essential base of their communion, the Logos which is at once the objective truth and the subjective knowledge of God.

These results have thus far been reached psychologically, by beginning with the data of the human soul and tracing their indications upward. But, to meet it,

Coleridge also descends, by an ontological track, from the Absolute One to His expression in the finite, — a Platonic Logos or Son of God; to whom we are to refer at once the physical kosmos, the divine process in history, and the intimations of reason and conscience. Through this mediator, found alike at the foot of our speculative dialectic and at the summit of our moral analytic, do God and man meet and sustain living relations.

But St. John identifies this Logos with the historical Christ; in whom, therefore, the Infinite reaches not only finite, but concrete and personal manifestation. It is the glory and joy of our humanity that He took it into Himself; and conquering sin in it, purified it, and gave it a seed of higher life. Through uttermost self-sacrifice, He reconciled its deepest sorrows with complete perfection; redeemed it and drew it to God; and made manifest in time the eternal facts of His infinite love,— His personal union with our nature, — and the law of self-sacrifice as the deliverance of His universe.

If we rightly understand the theologians of this school, they do not intend, when they speak of the divine assumption of our nature, to limit their reference to the individual life of Jesus of Nazareth. The Son is united not with this or that particular man only, but with humanity itself as a type; and constitutes, as He ever has constituted, the ground and life of all its good. The blending of the two natures is not a biographical but an "eternal" fact, belonging to the essence of their relation. The particular Incarnation of the evangelical history "*reveals and realizes*" the universal truth; to which all its exceptional and marking features, —

miraculous birth, agony and crucifixion, resurrection and ascension, — stand related as symbols to the reality, — as passing phenomena that tell the tale of an eternity. They are, indeed, more than this; because they are not, — as symbols may be, — mere signs or instruments of suggestion; but are homogeneous with the thing signified, and integrated with it as its highest momenta.

Following out this interpretation of the redemptive operation of the Son, we may conceive of it in two ways: as in reality always going on, although unrecognized; and as at length revealed in a plenary Incarnation, so as to be henceforth turned out from the unconscious to the conscious state. This last change is in itself a spiritual revolution of the highest order, — like the burst of a universe only felt, and by inches, before, on the eye touched by the finger of Christ. By ceasing to be latent, — by being given to our faith, — the redeeming agency is at once raised to a higher power. Now that we know *who* it is that pleads and strives with our evil nature, we can freely go to meet Him, and He may act from *within* our will as well as from without. His life-giving energy is quite another thing, — since not a *thing* at all, but a person, — not even a "better self," but a Divine other-than-self; and confers upon the soul a "*new birth.*" From the life of nature, conscious of only Self disturbed by an impersonal law, we emerge into the life of the spirit, set free by faith, and admitted to personal communion of trust and love. The transition into the "new birth" is the chief element in the redemptive act of the Son. The continuous power of holier life in the heart thus regenerate is the sign and function of the Holy Spirit. Both these, — the crisis of change and its spiritual sequel, — are indeed full of mystery on their objective or Divine side. But from the subjective or human side it is easy to perceive how the consciousness of a Divine Person blended with the humanity of each of us, and the source in it of whatever is higher than we, may be really a new seed of life within us, giving us a holy living Object in place of a repulsive ethical abstraction, and awakening all the powerful affections that ever seek a Personal Centre of repose.

From the whole complexion of this scheme it will be gathered, that the Original Sin countervailed by redemption is not *birth*-sin (which would be natural *disease*, not *moral* evil); and that the redemption is not an extinction of punishment, but a deliverance from sin. It is not that God is paid off, but that man emerges "a new creature." The "evil ground" there is in the human will, — the downward gravitation of self, — the need of a Diviner to draw us to any good by the sacrifice of self, — are simple facts accessible to every man's self-knowledge. And we are well aware that, co-existing with our free agency, they are not our malady, but our fault. Coleridge and his school everywhere denounce the Calvinistic doctrines of hereditary depravity and of penal satisfaction, as turning man from a person into a thing, and denying to God all moral attributes. The primary conditions of any true theory of redemption are, that the whole operation takes place on humanity; and that it both finds and leaves man a free agent. Neither of these conditions is complied with by any form of the Calvinistic scheme.

Some of the peculiarities of Coleridge most familiar to theologians, — his tetrads and pentads, his doctrine of

Church and State, his denial of the documentary inspiration of the whole Bible, — we pass by; not from any slighting estimate of their importance as parts of an organic whole, but in order to insulate the one character, — of *religious Realism*, — which is the inner essence of the system itself, and the living seed of its development in the school of Mr. Maurice. It is chiefly from inapprehension of this character, and from the inveterate training of the English mind in the opposite habit of thought, that so many readers complain of obscurity in the writings of the Chaplain of Lincoln's Inn. We do not deny that his meaning is at times difficult to reach; for it is apt to be *delayed* too long by his scrupulous candor of concession, his modest shrinking from self-assertion, his preference of the sympathetic to the distinctive attitude. But we venture with some confidence to assert, that for consistency and completeness of thought, and precision in the use of language, it would be difficult to find his superior among living theologians. It is the old question, — what do you mean by a *clear* or *distinct* thought? Do you mean a mental *image* or *representation* of something, like your conception of a perceptible object or of a finite portion of space or time? Then certainly you will not cease to complain of Mr. Maurice's indistinctness; for he speaks and thinks of Spirit, and Righteousness, and God, as realities without mental picture and yet closely known; and he treats the notions of Infinitude and Eternity as something else than "negative ideas," — the finite and the temporal with all the meaning emptied out. If, however, by "clearness of idea" you mean, not "*the idea of a limit*," but "*a limit to the idea*," — if your conditions are satisfied, provided thought does not run into thought, but each keeps its own place and function with exactitude, — then you might as reasonably charge indistinctness on Mr. Mill or Archbishop Whately as on Mr. Maurice. Many parts of his doctrine we are unable to follow with assent; but we see no excuse for the absurd distortions of his peculiar Christianity, with which the party-organs of Church and Sect have long abounded. Critics who have read any one of his practical or historical essays, with some feeling of its clear and life-like charm, ought surely to know that if his theology seems difficult to them, it cannot be from his want of practised thought and literary skill, and must arise from their not having at present found his latitude.

Coleridge, commencing in re-action from a scheme of materialistic necessity, gave great prominence to his assertion of free-agency. Not till he had effectually set humanity on its feet again, did he proceed to identify the intimations of its moral reason with the indwelling life of the Divine Word. Mr. Maurice is caught up by this last thought, and has become its organ to the present age; and so intensely does it possess him, that we fear his losing sight too much of the prior truth from which the start was made, and reducing man into a mere prize, to be contended for between the Satan and the God within him. Pushing the claims of a diabolical being far into the evil phenomena of our nature, and those of a Divine Being over the whole of the good, he thins away the space for the free human personality till it becomes at times quite evanescent. This is a danger ever incident to the wish of humility, that nothing should be claimed for self, — that all should be referred to God. But it must be restrained from reaching its ultimate limit; or else the ground of morals sinks again away, and, in pantheistic guise, universal necessity absorbs us all once more. We say, "in pantheistic guise;" for, be it observed, the two personalities — the Human and the Divine — must ever appear and disappear *together:* they are the two terms of a relation which wholly vanishes on the merging of either; and though, with safety to both, there is room for considerable variety in the theory of their respective functions, yet should an eye of reverential caution be kept (especially in our day) on the limits of the problem where the foci fall into each other. If, however, Mr. Maurice has too nearly approached this danger, it is under the inspiration of a truth than which there is no greater. The assumption of humanity by the Eternal Word may be construed from above downwards, so as to illustrate the character and agency of God; or from below upwards, so as to throw light on the spiritual experiences of man. In the former view, it gives to our trust and worship One whose chosen life is in our spirits, who moulds us into unities not our own, — of family, of nation, of church, — who is not wearied by our perverseness, but, still pressing His righteousness upon us, is ever redeeming what else were lost. In the latter view, a singular sanctity is imparted to the inner facts of our own existence and the invisible springs of the world's history. All that we inadequately call our *ideals*, the gleaming lights of good that visit us, the hopes that lift again our fallen wills, the beauty which Art cannot represent, the holiness which life does not realize, the love which cannot die with death, — what are they? Not *our* higher, but a *higher than we* — the living Guide Himself, pleading with us and asking for our trust. The actual and concrete, on the other hand, which falls so immeasurably short of these fair types, — the false fact that lies ashamed beneath the true vision, — *that* is our poor *self;* in which is nothing but failure, disappointment, and negation. One simple and only thing is asked from us: to cease trusting this delusive self and go freely into the Hand that waits for us, — to exchange the tension of volition for the quiet of unreserved surrender, — to pass from the chafing mood of "works" to the still heart of "faith." The great original sin of our nature is, that we reverse this order, — that we rely on ourselves and are afraid of God, and accordingly seek, by some act of ours, to buy Him off and be rid of His terrors and persuade Him to let us alone. Whether men endeavor to propitiate Him by relinquishing something that they have, or to serve him by something that they do, they mistake their position, and measure themselves off against Him as if they had proprietary rights which they could abandon in His favor, or some availing righteousness which could satisfy His moral perception. They aim at acting upon Him: and He is wanting to act on them; and will persist till they drop their gifts, and know their failures, and freely come to Him as they are to be moulded by His thought. It was to bring about this removal of distrust towards God, to reveal the law of self-abnegation as Divine and supreme, that the Word became flesh, and passed through its grievous incidents, and entered into sympathetic pity for its sins and fears. The most alienated feeling, once apprehending this manifestation of Divine adoption, could hold out no more. Such an Incarnation, bringing to a focus the perpetual truth of the "God with us," is not a humiliation of the divine nature so much as the glory and joy of the human, and discloses to us not a fallen world but a redeemed, with whose resistance the "Spirit of holiness" will not for ever have to strive. It harmonizes with "the belief that man is not an animal carrying about a soul, but a spiritual being with an animal nature, who, when he has sunk lowest into that nature, has still thoughts and recollections of a home to which he belongs, and from which he has wandered." *

The same mode of thought by which the individual life is thus turned into a sanctuary exhibits human society as in its essence a theocracy; and wins for the experiences and polity of the Hebrew race, as particular embodiments of a universal method, a meaning which Lessing's hints ought long ago to have elicited. Not that we mean to press at all closely the analogy between the doctrine of the "Prophets and Kings of the Old Testament," and the "Thoughts on the Education of the Human Race." They are alike in this: that they pull down the fences which had detached the Hebrew life from the great territory of human history, and find a universal function for even what is most exceptional in it. In their mode of procedure, however, they differ: Lessing seeking in the career of the Jewish people the rudiments of an *unfolding* idea; Maurice, the witness to *eternal* truths, — the manifestation by time-samples of infinite realities and unchanging rela-

* Hare's Charges, Introduction, p. xxi.

tions. And this difference touches a characteristic of the living divine, which more than any other makes him a perplexity to his contemporary critics. So strong in most Englishmen is the "natural man," as habitually to assume, till they discover whither the maxim leads, that "all we know is phenomena;" or rather they turn all they know *into* phenomena, and contemplate nothing "under the form of eternity." Even their theology is no exception. They *dramitize* it; drawing it out into an *economy* or plot, with different scenes, and progressive action, and crises of terror and of rescue, and a grand catastrophe to wind up the whole. Now the elements and incidents of this plan Mr. Maurice takes out of series, and redistributes in synchronous (or rather in timeless) relations. States of *humanity* which we are apt to represent as successive, and to string together as passages of an historical process, he treats as always co-existent in all men, — as abiding attributes or affections of their being. "Original sin," for instance, is not, in his view, a *prior* condition giving way to "reconciliation" as a *posterior;* but both exist together in all men. And so too *Divine* states, which we are commonly taught to dispose chronologically, cease with him to be separate. Christ the Saviour is usually believed to have first come at the "advent," and to be identical in date with Jesus of Nazareth. But, in Mr. Maurice's view, there never was a time when our race was not equally the abode of His "real presence." "Man, according to his original constitution, was related to Christ;" * who was *in* the heathen world while they were bowing to gods of wood and stone, and *in* Saul

* The Doctrine of Sacrifice. Dedicatory Letter, p. 21.

while yet the persecutor. The conversion on Damascus' road, and the whole historical gospel, did but *reveal* a Divine person that had never been absent from our humanity. There was not — first, a lost Heathendom; and then, to replace it, a redeemed Christendom: but always, and throughout both, One who was and is redeeming; and many, alas, in each, who resist this recall of them from their outer darkness. This abolition of time-conditions, and redisposal of the same facts as essential and permanent realities, gives the true key to our author's most difficult writings. The transmutation it effects in the doctrine of "eternal punishment" is but one example of its marvellous power of rejuvenescence applied to a theology grown decrepit in routine.

The great strength of this school lies, we think, in its faithful interpretation of what is at once deepest and highest in the religious consciousness of men; and its recognition, in this consciousness, of a concrete and living Divine person, instead of mere abstractions without authority, or the dreams of unreliable imagination. And we may well be grateful for a scheme which establishes a *uniform constitution* of our nature and our world, in *steady* relation to supernatural realities, broken by no revolutionary jerks or local exemptions; and which, therefore, opens a welcome to a scientific ethic, and metaphysic, and history. Nor is its strength merely that of fair promise and earnest appeal. So long as it advances on the ground of religious philosophy, it appears to us to make its footing good: and the first questionable step is, perhaps, at the point where it enters *history*, and hands itself over from Plato to St. John. The identification of the eternal Logos with the historical Christ is at present left to rest upon external authority alone, — and *that* too the authority of a single evangelist. A thoughtful learner in this school might be brought by some Alexandrine Coleridge into a faith like Philo's in the Divine Word, and set within the spiritual forecourt of this gospel. He might next, on testimonial grounds, be led to receive the whole evangelical series of external facts from Bethlehem to the Mount of Ascension. And yet these two termini of his belief might remain in painful discontinuity: and we do not see that the links of relation have hitherto been adequately supplied. If the whole stress is to be laid on the doctrine of the fourth gospel, the question becomes an anxious one, how far the evangelist's thought has taken its complexion from the Master's discourses, — how far infused it into them. For surely, without re-opening the discussion of authorship at all, the complete equalization of tone in this gospel between the discourses and the narrative, rendering it often impossible to mark the boundary between them, is a fact of the utmost moment, — in itself accounted for in either way: and if the discourses are as *unlike* those in the other gospels as they are *like* the personal composition of St. John, the hypothesis most assuring to us respecting their historical character is at an undeniable disadvantage. Shifted from the authentication of Christ himself to that of even "the beloved disciple," the Incarnation of the Logos in Jesus (in the sense required by the theory) would rest on too doubtful a support: for who could say whether we had to do with the revelation itself, or only with the mould of thought into which the disciple threw it?

That this difficulty has not been more felt by the Coleridge divines is due, we believe, to the pre-occupation of their minds with intense convictions, thirsting for that which assimilates with them or gains a glory from them. Broad providential lights on history, genial hopes of a less selfish human world, they open to us by their wisdom and their life. And there are parts of Scripture, the Pauline Epistles eminently, and the Prophets in no slight degree, where a darkness readily breaks away at the approach of their characteristic thoughts. Mr. Maurice's *Unity of the New Testament* abounds with happy combinations possible only to a fine spiritual tact. But exegesis has work to do in which other gifts are of more avail than moral perception and religious insight: and then it is that these writers, like their favorite catechetical school of Alexandria, appear to us signally to fail. Who does not smile at Mr. Maurice's explanation of the first chapter of Genesis? And where, in addition, critical judgment and dexterity are required, the result is still worse, — as in his treatment of the genealogies of Jesus. No deficiency in the furniture of scholarship causes this phenomenon. It is simply that biblical and historical criticism never succeeds, except in striking out partial lights, when it engages minds deeply tinctured with any metaphysical or spiritual enthusiasm. The eye, accustomed to the eternal realities, loses the quick and flitting glance that best seizes the expression of nature and the phenomena of time.

After all, the real force of this school is independent of scientific imperfections. They are *believing men* — afraid of no reality, despairing of no good, and resolute to test their faith by putting it straightway into life. They set to work to realize the kingdom of God in Soho Square and other nameable localities; and in their step towards this end there is as free, confiding, joyful movement, as if with their eyes they expected to see the great salvation. There is more of the future, we suspect, contained in their gospel than in any talking theology whose cry is heard in our streets.

Hence we feel ourselves to be falling *back* a step, when we turn from the preacher of Lincoln's Inn to the prophet of Chelsea. The influence of the latter, vastly the more intense and widespread, appears to us to have reached its natural limit, and taken up the portion of believers allotted to it. As a revolutionary or pentecostal power on the sentiments of Englishmen, it is perhaps nearly spent; and, like the romantic school of Germany, will descend from the high level of a faith to the tranquil honors of literature. So long as Mr. Carlyle spoke with any *hope* to the inward reverence of men, and in giving voice to their spiritual discontents made them feel that they were emerging from mean scepticisms into nobler inspirations, he was a deliverer to captives out of number. But the early voice of hope has become fainter and fainter, first passing into an infinite pathos, and then lost in humorous mocking or immeasurable scorn: and men cannot be permanently held by their antipathies and distrusts, and cease to look for any thing from a rebellion that never ends in peace. He gets us well enough out of Egypt and all its filthy idolatries; but, alas! his Red Sea will not divide, and the promised land is far as ever, and the question presses, whether "we are to die in the wilderness?"

For a just estimate of Mr. Carlyle as an historian and man of letters the time is not yet come. But his specific action on the *religion* of the age (of which alone we speak) already belongs in a great measure to the past, and is little likely to offer new elements for appreciation.

It is difficult now to transfer ourselves back into the age, not yet faded however from living memory, when Boileau and Kames were great canonists in the world of letters, and criticism occupied the mortal form of Dr. Blair. Of what stuff the young souls of that age could be made we cannot imagine, if they really found nutriment in solemn trifles about the unities and proprieties, — the choice of diction, — the length of sentences, — the nature of tropes, — and the rhetorical temperature required for interjection and apostrophes. Mr. Carlyle, among other contemporaries, certainly rose with indignant hunger from such a table of the gods, symmetrically spread with polished covers and nothing under them. In mere analysis of the machinery of expression or even thought, in rules for the manufacture of literary effects, he could find no response to the enthusiasm kindled in him by his favorite authors. The true ambrosia of the inner life was turned into dry ash by the legislators of *belles lettres:* and he was courageous enough to ask for the missing and immortal element. The same external direction had been taken by philosophy, and produced the same consciousness of a miserable void. The searching scepticism of Hume showed the dreary results to which the mere analysis of "experience" compendiously led. And the devices of utilitarian *cuisine* for putting pleasure into the pot and drawing virtue out betrayed the loss of the very idea of morals. The very things which this desiccating rationalism flung off, were to Mr. Carlyle just the essence and whole worth of the universe: and to show that beauty, truth, and goodness, could not thus be got rid of, while impostors were hired to bear their name; that religion is not hope and fear, or duty prudence, or art a skill to please; that behind the sensible there lies a spiritual, and beneath all relative phenomena an absolute reality, — was evidently, if not his early vow, at least his first inspiration. Surely it was an authentic appointment to a noble work: and on looking back over his quarter-century, no one can deny that it has been manfully achieved.

By what providence Mr. Carlyle learned the German language, in days when the study of it was rare, we cannot tell. But through it he evidently was enabled to "find his soul;" and gained confidence to proclaim the faith which was stirring from its sleep within, and at once woke up at the sight of its reflected image without. That revolt against rationalism which Dr. Newman apparently *used*, and directed for preconceived ends and in the service of an "economy," presents itself in Mr. Carlyle with all its veracious freshness. The same positions that approve themselves to the Oxford Catholic as suitable hypotheses, and to the Highgate philosopher as rational axioms, are seized by the living intuition of the Scottish seer; — that wonder and reverence are the condition of insight and the source of strength; — that faith is prior to knowledge, and deeper too; — that empirical science can but play on the surface of unfathomable mysteries; — that in the order of reality the ideal and invisible is the world's true adamant, and the laws of material appearance only its alluvial growths. In the inmost thought of men there is a thirst to which the springs of nature are a mere mirage, and which presses on to the waters of eternity. Extinguish this thirst by stupefaction of custom, — reduce thought to work *without* wonder, — and several delusions, both doleful and ridiculous, will speedily obtain high commissions in human affairs. The true marvel of Origination being lost, a "cause-and-effect philosophy" will esteem every thing solved when it has shown how each nine-pin in the universe knocks down the next. The spiritual germ and essence of humanity being forgot or denied, "a doctrine of circumstances" will discuss the prospect of furnishing to order any required supply of poets, philosophers, or able administrators, — like so many varieties of farm-stock. The idea of a God-given freedom being dismissed with the phantoms of "the dark ages," a calculus of "motives" will be invented for finding the roots of every human problem, and raising any given sentient man to any required moral power. The genuine ground of all communion with the Infinite having sunk away within us, all sorts of logical proofs, and logical disproofs, will quarrel together about primitive certainties that shroud themselves from both. In all these complaints, the substantive concurrence of our author with Mr. Coleridge is conspicuous. And though, in his *Life of Sterling*, the humor has seized him to ridicule the "windy harangues" and dizzying metaphysics of the Highgate soirées, there was a time when he had no little faith in the same methods as well as large agreement in the same results. In his earlier essays, *he* too expounds the distinction between "Understanding" and "Reason," and sets up the latter as the organ for apprehending the ideal essence, which is the true *real* of things. He speaks with reverential appreciation of Kant's doctrine, both metaphysical and moral; and with hope as well as admiration of the several æsthetic theories developed from similar beginnings. In short, he manifestly put an early trust in the philosophical method to which Coleridge remained faithful to the last. And not less manifestly did he soon break away from this path in despair; and with characteristic vehemence thenceforth inveigh against the propensity to seek it as an illusion of disease. In 1827, he defended the *Kritik der reinen Vernunft* against ignorant objectors, as reputed by competent judges to be "distinctly the greatest intellectual achievement of the century in which it came to light;" and dwelt with approval on the rule that, in quest of the highest truth, we must look *within*, and thence work outward with the torch we have lit. Yet in 1831 he broached, in his *Characteristics*, his celebrated doctrine of "Unconsciousness:" which teaches that all self-knowledge is a curse, and introspection a disease; that the true health of a man is to have a soul without being aware of it, — to be disposed of by impulses which he never criticises, — to fling out the products of creative genius without looking at them. In a word, the *reflective* thought on which, in the former year, he had relied for the purest wisdom, had in the latter become the sin and despair of humanity. What can have befallen in the interval? Had the author meanwhile *tried* the metaphysic springs, and after due patience found them, not simply "saints wells," with no healing in them, but poison-fountains, that made the sickly soul yet sicklier? We do not believe it: for there is nowhere any trace that the first clue of entrance into the German philosophy had been followed up; and on the other hand, every indication that Mr. Carlyle's denunciation of metaphysics is the mere judgment of an intuitive genius on methods of reflection, which, however helpful to slower and more formal minds, it is not given him to take. Had he been able to retain and pursue his first hope, — had he taken the severe path of philosophical discipline, and surrendered himself to its promise of deliverance, — we hardly think that we should ever have heard that passionate cry of despair, which proclaims the distinctive glory of man to be his irremediable woe, and asserts that, in finding *himself*, he for ever falls from heaven. The preacher of this doctrine had already started problems within himself, to which no answer (as his own word declares) could be found but by faithful questioning within: and it is a serious thing to go thus far, and yet not abide long enough to hear the reply. But instead of this, he flings away the very problems with a shriek, as the fruit by which paradise is lost; repents of all knowledge of good and evil; claps a bandage round the open eyes of morals, religion, art; and sees no salvation but in spiritual suicide, by plunging into the currents of instinctive nature that sweep us we know not whither. This tragic paradox has, indeed, a generous source, and is even thrown up by a certain wild tumultuous piety. It springs from a deep sense of the hatefulness of self-worship, and the barrenness of mere self-formation. It is a stormy prayer for escape from these; only with face turned, alas! in the wrong direction—*back* towards the west, with its fading visions of Atlantic islands of Unconsciousness, instead of *forwards* to the east, where already the heavens are pale with a light, instead of a darkness, not our own.

Though this despair of the highest objective truth could not fail, in the long-run, to produce pathetic and tempestuous results, yet for a while the mere deliverance from the negations of the empirical schools sufficed for a gospel: and the new sense of divine mystery and meaning, behind all that met the common eye, was little else in effect than a revelation. A certain consecration fell on what had been quite secular before: and with this peculiarity, that its influence spread as an underground beneath the foundations of objects and pursuits previously disconnected, and became a common conductor of fresh reverence into them all. Literature, art, politics, natural knowledge, seemed to sit less apart from religion. Heave off the utilitarian incubus from above, and secret affinities begin to be felt at the roots of their life. When it is no longer "the sole aim" of poetry "to please," of science to "get fruit" for the storehouses of comfort, of government "to protect body and goods," of sculpture and painting to minister to luxury, — they obtain ideal ends, which in essence melt and merge together; and all of them — beauty, truth, and righteousness — culminate in the reality of God. Whatever the theologians may say, the age owes a debt of rare gratitude to the man who, above all others, has awakened this new sense within its soul, has touched with a strange devoutness many a class which book and surplice had ceased to awe; has taken the impertinent self-will out of the movements of pencil, pen, and chisel; and made even Mechanics' Institutions ashamed of their incipient millennium of "useful knowledge." The influence of Mr. Carlyle's writings, and especially of his *Sartor Resartus*, has been primarily exerted on classes of men most exposed to temptations of egotism and petulance, and least subjected to any thing above them, — academics, artists, littérateurs, "strong-minded" women, "debating" youths, Scotchmen of the phrenological grade, and Irishmen of the Young-Ireland school. In the altered mood of mind which has been induced in these various groups within the last five-and-twenty years we acknowledge a conspicuous good; and could even hear, with more of sadness than of condemnation, the passionate words that once burst from the lips of a believer: "Carlyle is my religion!"

The *unity*, however, which our prophet's mystic sense discerns among our human "arts and sciences" is *too* great: and we must reclaim from him a distinction which not even the fusing power of his genius can do more than blur and conceal. Not in the *human and moral* world only, but *quite similarly in the physical*, does he see the expression of the Infinite and Divine. Both are alike symbols of the one spiritual essence, which is hid from the blind, and revealed to the wise, in all. He does not, like Coleridge, separate *nature* and *spirit* into two realms, quite differently related to Him who is the source of both, — the one His moulded fabric, the other His free image, — but treats them indiscriminately as the vehicles of His manifestation, and phenomena through which the Divine force pours. This is not, indeed, done by sinking humanity into a mere object of natural history; rather by raising the objects of natural history up to the spiritual level, adding significance to them, instead of taking it from us. But still, man is not permitted to remain quite *sui generis:* he is simply the *highest* of the countless emblems woven into the universal "garment of God." The texture is one and homogeneous throughout: — in one sense all natural, as a determinate product in time; in another, all supernatural, as mysteriously issuing from eternity. The same comprehensive formula, — the appearance of the Infinite in the finite, — serves everywhere, and equally describes "the lily of the field" and the Redeemer who interpreted its meaning.

Did we want to turn human life into a mere school of Art, there might be nothing very fatal in the looseness of this doctrine. An impartial conception of some Divine idea in every thing may clear away the film of sense, and open to view the life of much that else were dead. To rend away the veil is the grand condition for enabling the eye to see: whoever does this, may talk as he pleases of the realities behind; they will vindicate themselves. Yet even for truth of *representation*, and infinitely more for faithfulness of character and action, a distinctive reverence for man as *more than natural*, as the abode of God in a sense quite false of clouds and stars, as intrusted with himself that he may surrender to a higher, — is indispensable. For want of this, Mr. Carlyle loses all ground of difference between the *natural* and the *right*, — the out-come of tendency and the free creations of conscience. He is tempted into excessive admiration of mere realizing strength, irrespective of any higher test of spiritual worth. Whatever can get upon its feet, and persist in standing on this world, is vindicated in his eyes, and exhibited as a sample of the "eternal laws:" while that which has nothing to show for itself except that it *ought to be*, — righteousness that knocks in vain at the door of visible "fact," — meets with no sympathy from him, and is even jeered for its foolish patience in still sitting on the step with unremitting prayer. True, he does not admit the rights of possession till after a pretty long term, and knows how to treat the "shams" and upstarts of to-day, the "flunkey" powers that usurp more venerable place, with withering scorn: — still, however, for a reason which would equally condemn an aspiration transcending human conditions, viz. because they are at variance with the laws of the actual, and are sure to be disowned by the baffling solidity of nature. Against the fickle multitude of momentary facts and popular semblances, he sides with the conservative aristocracy of natural laws; but recognizes no divine monarchy with prerogatives over both. The kingdom of heaven and the kingdom of nature being identical, neither transcending the other, but being related only as inner meaning and outward expression, no margin is left for an *ideal* other than the long-run of the *actual*, — for an "*ought*" beyond the "*can*," — for a will of God surpassing finite conditions. Hence Mr. Carlyle's habit of resolving all ethical evil into "insincerity" and "unveracity," — surely a most inadequate formula for the expression of even commonplace moral judgments. Extend these terms ever so much, — use them to denote *unconscious* as well as *conscious* self-variance, — nay, include in them also defiance of *nature and outward possibility*, — still, what far-fetched circuits must be taken before you can bring under such a definition the sins of envy, covetousness, resentment, and prudent licentiousness! The root of this delusive conception of human goodness lies in the pantheistic assumption, that to fly in the face of natural forces is to withstand the highest that there is; and its fruit, when fully ripe, cannot fail to be an indifference to many a natural sin, — a lowering of the ideal standard of conscience, and a derision of baffled yet trusting righteousness. Every reader of Mr. Carlyle can remember painful instances of entire abdication of all moral judgment on atrocious actions and abandoned men, — a Mirabeau and a September massacre: nay, even ridicule of the whole distinction of moral and immoral applied to actions, as "the blockhead's distinction;" and many a hint that the difference lies only in the *customariness* (*mores*) of one practice as compared with another. Did it never occur to him to ask whether it is the human usages that make the moral sense, or not rather the moral sense that makes the human usages?

Yet this questionable doctrine, often provoked into expression by some senseless prudery or ungenial rigor, is very far from representing the author's real and deepest mind. Flashes of purer light meet you not rarely, especially in his earlier writings. Who can forget how, in the hour of uttermost desolation, amid the wildest storm of unbelief, the sheet-anchor of the unhappy Teufelsdröckh was the "*infinite nature of Duty;*" and in this form never, in his utmost extremity, did the

Divine presence desert him? And are we not told, in many changing tones, that in obedience and reverence alone can any true freedom be found? that we are to recognize God in the *higher* life within us, as opposed to the pleasure-life? that we can find Him only by self-renunciation? In these ingenious days, when no one proposition is so rude as to contradict any other, some disciple of the "many-sided" poet, or some proficient in the "dialectic process," may be able to harmonize such sentiments with the assertion that "*man cannot but obey whatever he ought to obey.*" At present we do not pretend to have reached the "higher unity" in which appeals to our freedom coalesce with the assertion of universal necessity.

To pull up the fence between "nature" and "spirit" within us is to throw the Understanding and the Character into the same field. We are therefore prepared for the celebrated paradox, that intellect and goodness always go together; so that, of mental insight and moral soundness, either may be taken as the measure of the other. If by "intellect" and "insight" is meant exclusively what Coleridge calls "*reason,*" this statement not only ceases to be a paradox, but becomes almost a truism: for it is the chief function of this power to make us conscious of moral truth and obligation; and the consciousness fades when faithlessly neglected. But if these terms refer to what Coleridge calls "*understanding,*" — if the possession of this endowment constitutes a claim upon them, — then the doctrine is conspicuously false: for the "adaptive intelligence," being an *animal* faculty, is entirely separable from moral conditions; actually exists without them in many tribes of creatures; and in man simply rises to a quickness of generalization and a skill in the use of means which imply nothing respecting the wise estimate or the faithful pursuit of *ends*. Low passions and selfish impulses are quite capable of enlisting on their behalf all the resources of this mental gift; their partnership with which gives us the idea of a satanic nature. Mr. Carlyle, we believe, means to say, that *this* sort of "understanding" he will not acknowledge as intellect; it is a mere "beaver" or "fox" faculty, not to be noticed among the distinctions of man. Not till you have got beyond mechanical ingenuity and lawyer adroitness do you enter on the proper *human* territory; within which, capacity and character go together. This interpretation, throwing us upon Coleridge's upper region, reduces the maxim to an intelligible truth. But will Mr. Carlyle consent to take it with all its fair consequences? Will he, without flinching, read the truth *both* ways, — inferring *either* term of this constant ratio ("*intellectual*" and "*moral*") from the magnitude of the other? We know that, where he discovers (as in Mirabeau) great force of *mind*, he is ready to plead this in bar of all objections against *character*, and to insist that, in spite of appearances, such brightness of eye *must* carry with it soundness of conscience. But will he turn the problem round, and abide by it still? When he finds, deep hid in the retreats of private life, a goodness eminent and even saintly, a moral clearness and force great in their way as Mirabeau's keen-sightedness, will he accept the sign in evidence of mighty intellect? Will he say that, notwithstanding the meek and homely look, high genius must assuredly be there? We fear not:

at least, we remember no instance in which the inference is set with its face this way; whilst it is familiar to all his readers as an excuse for admiration startling to the moral sense. In truth, this maxim, more perhaps than any other indication, expresses the *pagan* character of our author's mind; his alienation from the distinctively Christian type of reverence, rather for the inner sanctities of self-renunciation than for the outward energies of self-assertion. His "hero-worships" certainly present us with a list far from concurrent with the "beatitudes:" nor can we fancy that he would listen with much more patience than a Lucian or a Pliny to blessings on the meek and merciful, the pure in heart, the ever-thirsty after righteousness. For him too, as for so many gifted and ungifted men, the force which will not be stopped by any restraint on its way to great achievement, — the genius which claims to be its own law, and will confess nothing diviner than itself, — have an irresistible fascination. His eye, overlooking the landscape of humanity, always runs up to the brilliant peaks of *power:* not, indeed, without a glance of love and pity into many a retreat of quiet goodness that lies safe beneath their shelter; but should the sudden lightning, or the seasonal melting of the world's ice-barriers, bring down a ruin on that green and feeble life, his voice, after one faint cry of pathos, joins in with the thunder and shouts with the triumph of the avalanche. Ever watching the strife of the great *forces* of the universe, he, no doubt, sides on the whole against the Titans with the gods: but if the Titans make a happy fling, and send home a mountain or two to the very beard of Zeus, he gets delighted with the game on any terms and cries, "Bravo!"

The *Sartor Resartus* finds the manifestation of God in the *entire life* of the universe; in visible nature; in individual man, and especially his *higher* mind; in the march and process of history; and in the organic development of humanity as a whole. The author's tendency, however, has increasingly been to retreat from all other media of Divine expression upon his favorite centre, — the genius and energy of *heroic men*. So much has he gathered-in his lights of interpretation upon this focus, as to incur the charge of setting up the personality of individuals as the single determining agency in the affairs of the world, and forgetting the larger half of the truth, that all persons, taken one by one, are but elements of a great social organism, to whose laws of providential growth they must be held subordinate. History cannot be resolved into a mere series of biographies: nor can the individual be justly estimated in his insulation, and tried by the mere inner law of his own particular nature. It would be a melancholy outlook for the world, if its courses were simply contingent on the genius and life of a few great men, without any security from a general law behind that they should appear at the right time and place, and with the aptitudes for the needful work. And, on the other hand, were the life of nations to be expended in nothing else than the production of its half-dozen heroes; were this splendid but scanty blossoming the great and only real thing it does, there would seem to be a wasteful disproportion between the mighty forest that falls for lumber and the sparse fruit that would lie upon your open hand. There is need, therefore, of some more manifest relation between individual greatness and the collective life of humanity; and to save us from egoism, from fatalism, from arbitrary and capricious morals, we must learn to recognize a divine method of development in both,—*primarily*, in race and nation, and with authority over the *secondary* functions of personal genius.

That Mr. Carlyle's "hero-worship" requires to be balanced by a supplementary doctrine of society and collective humanity, he would himself perhaps be disposed to allow. But what is this supplement to be? Is it merely to teach that the *individual* is to hold himself at the disposal of *the whole?* to correct his conscience by the general tradition or the permanent voice of humanity; to sink his egoism, to temper it by immersion in the universal element, and become the organ of the progress of the species? Far be it from us to deny that there may be men susceptible of inspiration from such a faith, — capable of dying for such abstractions as a "law of development," of being torn limb from limb out of regard for "the whole." Still less would we disparage by one word a heroism all the nobler for the faint whispers that suffice to waken it into life. Yet we cannot help feeling that in these impersonal ideas, — of "collective society," "law of the whole," "destination of mankind," &c. — there is a want of natural authority over the conscience, and, missing the conscience, over the personal impulses of individual men. In the mere notions of "whole and part," of "organism and member," of "average rule and particular case," there resides no *moral* element, no *rights over the will:* and if ever they seem to carry such functions, it is only because a deeper feeling lurks behind and lends them the insignia of a prerogative not their own. In a world of mere "general laws," it would ever remain a melancholy thing to see living heroes and saints struck down at the altar of "historical tendency" by some shadowy dagger of necessity. Love, enthusiasm, devotion, need some concrete and living object; if not to command their allegiance, at least to turn it from sorrow into joy. And you have but to translate your "progress of the species" into "Kingdom of Heaven," and the problem is solved. The ever-living God stands in Person between the "individual" and the "whole,"— by His communion mediating between them, — stirring in the conscience of the one, and constituting the tides of advancing good in the other, — and so engaging both in one spiritual life. Surrendering immediately to Him, instead of to the ultimate ratios of the world, faithful men fling themselves into Omnipotent sympathy, and find deliverance and repose. They have a trust that relieves them of every care; and can leave themselves to be applied to the great account and problem of the world by One who is in the midst, and from the first, and at the end, at once. Through Him, therefore, as the common term of all righteousness, must the collective humanity win its due rights and reverence from Each. The private conscience ceases to be private, the public claim to be merely public, when both are to us the instant pleadings of His living authority. In obeying them, we yield neither to a mixed multitude of our own kind, whose average voice is no better than our own, nor even to our mere higher self; but to the august Revealer of whatever is pure and just and true. In enforcing its traditions and inheritance of right, the Nation or Society of men is not proudly riding on its own arbitrary will, but recognizing the trust committed to it and serving as the organism of eternal rectitude.

It is for want of this deliverance from Self at the upper end, that Mr. Carlyle, resolute to break the ignoble bondage on any terms, proposes escape at the lower end; and, preaching up the glories of "Unconsciousness," sighs for relapse into the life of blind impulsive tendency. With him, we confess the curse; we groan beneath its misery; but we see from it a double path,— backward into Nature, forward into God, — and cannot for an instant doubt that the Self-consciousness which is the beginning of Reason is never to recede, but to rise and free itself in the transfiguration of Faith. Deny and bar out this hope, and who can wonder if the sharpest remedies for man's selfish security are welcomed with a wild joy; if *any* convulsion that shall strip off the green crust of artificial culture and lay bare the primitive rock beneath us, appears as a needful return of the fermenting chaos? How else are the elementary forces of instinctive nature to re-assert their rights and *begin again* from their unthinking freshness? In some such feeling as this we find, perhaps, the source, in Mr. Carlyle, of that terrible glee that seems to flame up at the spectacle of revolutionary storms, and to dart with mocking gleams of devilry and tender streaks of humanity over a background of "divine despair." Indeed we could not wish for a better illustration of the two paths of escape from Self, — back into Nature, forward into God, — than the contrast of Carlyle and Maurice in the whole coloring and climate of their spirit: the sad, pathetic, scornful humor of the one, capricious with laughter, tears, and anger, and expressive of manful pity and endurance, alike removed from fear and hope; and the buoyant, serene, trustful temper of the other, genial even in its indignation, and penetrated with the joy of an Infinite Love.

The three schools of doctrine at which we have thus rapidly glanced occupy the most distant points in the English religion of the present age; or, at least, in the new fields of tendency which it has opened. It may seem a vain quest to look for any thing common to the whole. Yet when they are interpreted by their inner spirit, rather than by their outward relations, one thought will be found secreted at the heart of all — the perennial Indwelling of God in Man and in the Universe. This is the distinct gain that has been won by the spiritual consciousness of the time; and that already enriches fiction and poetry, art and social morals, not less than direct theology. In the preceding criticisms we have said enough to show that we are not indifferent to the mode and form of doctrine in which this thought is embodied. But however threatening the mists from which it has to clear itself, it is the dawn of a truth, — a blush upon the East, — wakening up trustful hearts to thanksgiving and hope. We know well the anger and antipathy of all the elder parties towards every phase of the new sentiment. We are accustomed to their absurd and heartless attempt to divide all men between the two poles of their logical dilemma, — either absolute Atheism, or else "our" orthodoxy. But these are only symptoms that the new wine cannot go into the old bottles. They do but betray the inevitable blindness of party-life, — the increasing self-seeking, the loss of genial humility, the conceit of finished wisdom, which mark the decadence of all sects. Precisely in the middle of this pretended alternative of necessity, — far from "Atheism" on the one hand, and from most "orthodoxies" on the other, — stand at this moment the vast majority of the most earnest, devout, philosophic Christians of our time; men with trust in a Living Righteousness, which no creed of one age can adequately define for the fresh experiences given to the spirit of another. To them, and not to the noisy devotees and pharisees of party, do we look for the faith of the future.

THEOLOGY IN ITS RELATION TO PROGRESSIVE KNOWLEDGE.*

THE College which resumes its work this day professes to impart a special training for the Christian Ministry: and the Christian Minister is one who, in discipleship to Jesus Christ, aims to guide the reverence, to ennoble the conscience, and sustain the piety, of men. To treat such an office as the object of a particular discipline, not simply for the character and affections, but for the intellect too, takes for granted, what has not always been admitted, that Theology is, in some sense, a Science and admits of being methodically taught. This assumption would be false, if religious truth were simply a natural intuition, or a supernatural inspiration, in each individual mind. Just as Aristotle, in order to save Ethics for scientific treatment, dismisses the hypothesis that virtue is either a native faculty or a given feeling, and insists that it is a formed quality and developed order of preferences in the mind;† so, if our "schools of the prophets" are to have any justification, we must be prepared to show, that religion contains matter for teaching, and is neither inborn like eyesight, nor

* An Address at the Opening of the Session 1865-6 of Manchester New College, London, October the 9th, 1865.

† Eth. Nic. II. v.

an arbitrary visitant like a trance or dream: for, in the one case, training would be superfluous, and, in the other, impossible. All teaching is communication from mind to mind: it implies that one mind may know more than another, and the same mind more at a later time than at an earlier. And, using the inequality as instrument for the progress, it further assumes that teacher and taught, instead of being abandoned to lonely inspiration,—"words that cannot be uttered,"—have a common medium of thought and mutual intelligence, and can meet, when they speak together, upon the same real objects. As every Medical school takes for granted, by its very existence, that the animal body is real, and its physiological constitution permanent and cognizable; as every Law school takes for granted that human society is constant, and throws its self-regulating forces into a machinery but little variable; so does a Theological school assume that God and his relations to man are objective realities, perpetually there and approachable by human faculties. Two things therefore, with regard to the nature of religion, are denied by every such institution as this: (1) it is not a mere natural instinct; (2) it is not a mere supernatural grace. And two things about it are affirmed: (1) it presents something real and permanent for the intellect to hold by; (2) it has its undetermined and progressive lines, on which it is the business of the teacher to move and mark the fixed points as they emerge.

Without this mixed composition, of the constant and the variable, it may be doubted whether, intellectually, religion would retain its interest at all. Were it nothing but a scheme of shifting conceptions, unrelated to any thing beyond our personality, — the mere shadow of ourselves flung on the universe without, — it might remain, like any other illusion, a curious object of psychological analysis, but would lose all serious place in human life. Were it, on the other hand, a scheme of absolute knowledge, so determined and rounded off as to be, like its Object, "without variableness or shadow of a turning," it might no doubt be recited afresh to each generation, like the alphabet or the numeration table, and so far be made the business of a school: but however new to the learner, it would be old to the teacher, and become wearisome as a routine, unquickened by the real life of his mind. So repugnant is this to both the intellectual and the spiritual nature, that no effort can render it possible for long. Thought is alive, and cannot rotate like a machine; and, in its eagerness for movement, carries every science with it, if not into advance, into aberration, — at any rate into change. Still more are reverence and affection alive; and, while faithful to the same object, they are unable to rest without transporting it into a new air and investing it with fresh lights: so that a religion forbidden to improve betakes itself to degeneracy, rather than become petrified, and, instead of growing upwards into statelier proportions, breaks into lateral deformities, as the only vent for its vitality. What, for instance, are all the outrages on sense and history committed by the prophetic or allegorical interpreter, but an attempt to adjust a fixed text to a moving world, to find room within the narrow frame of the ancient letter for the grand lines and various groups of the modern picture? These cannot be left out of the scheme of faith, since they have found their way into the scheme of things: and those who seek for God, not in his own universe, but in a document about it, are obliged to stretch and distort the record to make room for what is not there. Even in the most stationary theologies, the real interest lies in the expansion of old truth to embrace and consecrate the newest births of time.

The mode, however, of dividing the constant from the variable elements in a religion is not always the same; and in the intellectual training of Christian teachers, it makes the greatest difference which of two principles we adopt as our rule.

The first assumes that the things to be taught are a determinate stock of truths given in perpetuity, susceptible of no increase, secured against all abatement. These are the divine *constants;* filling the whole sphere of religion; and throwing out all the variables into the secular sciences and arts; amid which religion is to find its application without any re-action upon its theory. Let us consider what direction is naturally impressed upon theological education by this assumption.

The primary aim will be to teach methodically the fixed scheme of positive religion, and secure on every side its hold on the student's mind. Nor is it by any means a scanty intellectual culture that may subserve this end. For the Protestant (to whom we must limit our view) the scheme is embodied in Scripture. Now to be master of Scripture is to be at home in two languages, most unlike each other, and long silent upon the earth; to have an eye and ear for their dialectic variations in time and place; to trace the literary life of the Hebrew people from its dawn to its decline, and of Christendom in its obscure beginnings; to be familiar with the history of the Eastern world till it became a province of the West. These resources are needed for entering into the interior of Scripture. But no ancient book is rightly appreciated, unless its external history is surveyed, and the witnesses examined to its origin, its travels, its transmission, the uncertainties of its text, and worth of its translations:—researches, the extent and complexity of which are sufficiently attested by the immense critical apparatus they have placed at our disposal. From the moment when the Scriptures were snatched from sacerdotal keeping and delivered over, as the new-found oracles of God, to the venerating scrutiny of reading men, the development of sacred learning was large and rapid; and, though for a time suspended by the excitement and desolation of religious wars, still showed, in Limborch and Le Clerc, how little the intellectual impulse given by Calvin and Beza had spent its force. The refinement and security which modern scholarship has gradually attained, and the compendious form into which the results of vast research are now reduced, are unfavorable to the reputation of those earlier masters of sacred criticism: the light handbook gives us what we want at a glance, and their heavy folios are left to gather the dust upon our shelves. But whoever has occasion to consult them will be disposed to wonder at the vast strides of approach already made towards the standard of learning in our own day; especially when he remembers to how great an extent the scholar of the sixteenth and even the seventeenth century had to be his own lexicographer and grammarian, to make his own index and concordance, to work out his own archæology, to construct his own maps and tables of dates, and go to the sources of history for himself. These disadvantages, which would excuse a much greater inaccuracy than we actually find, drove the man of learning out over an immense field, and gave him a range of erudition and a grasp of judgment which may well astonish the more special students of later times.

The proportions in which the religious and the simply intellectual impulse contributed to the great works of Protestant erudition, it is impossible to determine. Were it not that, at the revival of learning, precisely similar phenomena appeared on the field of secular literature, and Joseph Scaliger and Henry Stephens rivalled the greatest prodigies of theological industry, we might be tempted to say that nothing short of an overpowering reverence for the Bible as the word of God, could sustain the laborious patience of the old divines, or invest with any living interest their verbal criticisms and technical disputes. Perhaps the spell put upon the imagination in the two cases, by the undiscovered wisdom and beauty of Pagan literature, and by the spiritual depth of the sacred books, was not so dissimilar as we might suppose, and would stir the mind to the same efforts, and produce analogous results. But, when the first flush of wondering impulse had passed away, secular and sacred learning were doomed, by a single cause, to take different directions, and acquire a character ever more distinct. The Scriptures were assumed to be a continuous oracle, an unbroken authoritative record, homogeneous for all the purposes of religious guidance, a divine book in which the ever-living Author, wielding the human secretaries as his organs of communication, discloses all that is known of his will and moral government. If a critic were to treat the Iliad of Homer, the Cyropædeia of Xenophon, and the history of Thucydides, as belonging to one another, and all as components of the philosophy of Aristotle, the results could scarcely be more fatally grotesque. No doubt, the sanctity attributed to every line secured an eager and prolonged scrutiny of the text, word by word: but the gaze was too close, and the imaginary light was too intense, for clear and comprehensive vision. An exaggerated significance was seen in the simplest phrase; narrative was construed into type, and myth mistaken for history; a Hebrew ode was made to yield evangelic dogma; and whether the Elohist or the Jehovist told the story of Creation, whether Job affirmed of God or his friends denied, whether the Preacher taught Epicureanism or the later Isaiah the law of humiliation, whether Matthew presented Christ as miraculously conceived, or Paul as the pre-existing spiritual Adam, or John the evangelist as the Incarnate Logos,—it was all alike authoritative:—the various elements fused into one uniform alloy, and re-issued, as shekels of gold, to serve for coin of the temple. In the presence of such preconceptions, it is evident that all historical method, all recognition of natural growth of religious ideas, all critical appreciation of contrasted doctrines, all discharge of local and personal errors from the imperishable essence of divine truth, must remain impossible: and scholarship, kindled at first, but dizzied at last, with the monotonous glory it sees upon the page, settles into blindness and distinguishes nothing. There is an immense accumulation of theological erudition; but, under this spell, it lies dead and dark, and yields none of the brilliant results of the corresponding secular learning. There is not within it the free, sincere and healthy movement on which elsewhere the veracious instinct of the intellect insists; it is held in hand and marched about, as if to check an enemy. Are there weak places exposed and threatened? its masses are ordered up to close and hide them. Can an impression be made of reserved strength? its ranks are opened to show it and scare assault away. This is not the spirit of the true scholar; who, knowing no enemy, can leave unguarded any holy places already held, and go forth, as pilgrim and explorer, to find new ones that shall enlarge his homage and consecrate fresh points upon the world.

Not even the most rigid theologian, however, can live exclusively with what he regards as the *constants* of religion. Fix these as he may, he finds himself in a changing scene, with the *variables* of which he is in immediate contact; and the relations between the immutable data of his creed and the shifting conditions of human life have to be re-adjusted, as new ideas and wants arise. To qualify himself for this, and become a proficient in *applied religion*, he must know how the world is going on, follow in the track of the advancing sciences, listen to the tones of the younger literature, and breathe the air of other men's thought. He cannot act as trustee of the deposit committed to him, unless he looks around him and sees how it is to be administered in the altered temper of the generations as they rise; what doubts it has to meet, what repugnance to encounter; by what fresh paths of approach it must reach minds now transported into uncalculated latitudes. Theological education, therefore, however severely conservative, is far from deserving the reproach of indifference to the march of the phenomenal sciences. Its own purpose can never be fulfilled without a comprehensive knowledge, revised and filled in from time to time, of whatever the historical critic, and the inductive philosopher, and the speculative thinker, may profess to have achieved. But, under such an inflexible system, the student's specialty is this; through his wide range he sees nothing in its simply natural light, judges nothing by its own proper evidence, but carries with him a criterion foreign to the field; his stock of *constants* he uses as *regulative*, determining without appeal what shall be taken and what be left; all that falls in with them he appropriates and works in to modernize his creed; all that conflicts with them he discards and blackens as profane. By thus importing the postulates of a divinity-school as the measure of inductive truth, a hopeless breach is created between the logic of theology and that of science, and a war begun which is the more miserable, because the parties to it, always within reach of irritating challenge, move upon different lines and can never fairly meet. It is needless to say how this method spoils every thing it touches, scholarship, natural knowledge, religion, and produces the temper most alien to the genius of them all. Is it not a melancholy fact that every modern science has had to make good its footing, not only against sluggish incredulity and prejudice, but against misguided piety? that the very Sun could not find his right place in the heavens, or Man prove, by bits of pottery and flint, his long tenancy of this earth, without a clamor of devout fear and futile contradiction? Is it right that we should always know beforehand, irrespective of the evidence, what reception every physical or ethnological theory which makes large demands on time, every critical verdict which lowers the date or renames the author of a Hebrew book, will meet with from the clergy? There must be something wrong in a system which disturbs the quiet of eternal truth by dissolving in it a fermenting mass of decaying opinion; and whoever can precipitate the precarious foreign admixtures, and leave the fountains of faith pure and clear, brings the truest healing to the moral and spiritual life of men.

In order to provide for this function, and escape the evils just described, the College for which I speak today follows a different rule in drawing its line between the constants and the variables in religion. The principle is this: the things *about which we teach* are given in perpetuity; but the things *to be taught about them* are open to revision in every age. God, in his relations to the universe and to ourselves; Man, his individual and social nature, his responsible position, his history, his destination, — are the ultimate objects which we here aspire to know; and, as media of this knowledge, on the philosophical side, the intellectual, ethical and spiritual phenomena of the mind; and, on the historical, the manifestations of Divine Life in the past of our humanity, and primarily in the person and work of Jesus Christ, with whom it culminates, and from whom dates a new birth of inextinguishable faith and aspiration, a new glow, unexhausted yet, of pity and of hope. The form and spirit of an intellectual training conducted on this principle it is not difficult to trace.

It is sometimes supposed, that where so much is left open to revision, the continuity of belief must be broken, and no permanent roots be struck to feed the growth and mature the fruits of religious character. Each teacher, it is imagined, relying on his lonely fancies, and dignifying them with the name of intuitions, will begin his quest *de novo*, and think out his scheme of doctrine, as if he were floating by himself in space; owning no authority, and deriving no strength from his partnership in the heritage of humanity. Nothing can be more erroneous. No doubt it must always rest with the individual reason and conscience to pronounce the personal verdict of true or false; but the pleadings on which they decide are fetched from the gathered stores of Christian and heathen wisdom, and epitomize the thought expended on the oldest and deepest problems; and, when seeming to flow immediately from a single mind, are rendered possible there only by a traceless myriad of influences infiltrating into it from earlier time. The whole Past must rain upon the uplands, and the clouds hang on the invisible peaks, of history, to make the smallest rill of thought that winds through our own day. Even in the philosophical treatment of natural Ethics and Religion, where, as in all deductive reasoning, we seem to be independent of what predecessors have found, and to draw conclusions that would be at home in any age, the appearance is illusory; for that very human nature from whose phenomena we reason and whose affections we interpret, has expanded into new and richer forms, and presents, in its circle of Christian experience, data unknown before. And in historical theology, the very semblance of any breach with the past is simply impossible. No man can extemporize, or spin out of himself, a critical knowledge of ancient languages, literature and life; he is here absolutely dependent on forerunners for his whole outfit of original assumptions and beliefs, and must start on his own explorings from the point at which they have deposited him. The slow and gentle way in which alone the shadows can ever break from off the ancient world, and a little light steal in, now from the pages of a recovered book, now through the propylæum of a dug-up temple, and then from some happy flash of philological combination, sufficiently secures us, so long as we are simple and trustful, without fear and without guile, from any but silent and insensible changes of historical conviction. In such matters, the shocks all come from our insincerities and delays on the one hand, and from the re-action of irreverent extravagance provoked upon the other; feverish paroxysms being the inevitable retribution of long reticence and suppression.

In order to fall in with the peaceful course of theological change, to hold by what is undisturbed, and detach it from the doom of the rest, the student must be well brought up to the point already reached, the point at which he pitches his tent and raises his altar, till he is ordered to move on. This involves the whole apparatus of knowledge required, in the former case, by the stationary defender of the faith; together with an important addition, viz. an acquaintance with the *history* of theology, in the largest sense; not only with the ecclesiastical stages by which accepted dogma was formed, but with the inverse critical processes by which it has been partially dissolved, and removed from the faith of scholarly men. One who is pledged to hold a compacted scheme of belief as divine, can never recognize it as growing or declining with the changing seasons of our nature, at one time the creation, at another the victim, of human reason. He is obliged, therefore, to ignore its history, however indisputable it may be; to treat as an image fallen from heaven, some idol of doctrine which, if you are familiar with its first age, you may see gradually moulded under the pressure of the time; and to insist that it still stands as adamant, though in the dry intellectual air all its tenacity is gone, and observers wonder when the clay is to crumble into dust. Even within the memory of our own generation, how many are the determinate points of change, which it would be simply stupid not to register as past events in the history of opinion! What has become of the date which stood in our school-tables, "Creation of the World, B.C. 4004"? and what of the next, "The Universal Deluge, B.C. 2348"? Into what undreamt-of distance has Egyptian chronology retreated! yet how many such steps must we repeat, ere we alight upon the first vestiges of man! and how many more, to exhaust the relics of life and death upon this world! We have learned to recognize the composite structure and comparatively low date of the Pentateuch; the progression of religious doctrine through the Old Testament; its variety in the New; the mixture of unhistorical elements in both, and of human opinions long ago corrected, and expectations never fulfilled. In what state of mind would the scholar be who did not know these things? or the reasoner who should suppose that they left all as it was before? All that is *real*, indeed, all that is *Divine*, — God in his perfection, Christ in his filial sanctity, and for humanity the eternal law of Duty and Self-sacrifice, — they and similar changes without end, sweep past and leave more majestic than before. But he only can feel the serenity of this assurance, to whose trust no constants are essential beyond the irremovable realities.

Even he, however, must, from time to time, take careful account of the course of discovery in its bearings on the common heritage of faith, with a view to guide and resettle the piety of others. For this end, something more is needed than a knowledge of what has already been done, affecting theological belief: he must know what is *still doing*, — the inquiries that are hovering and preparing to alight, — the thoughts that are in the air, — the weather-signs that drift upon the clouds: for these, interpreted by the law of the past, will often give a serviceable presage of the future, and prevent the misplacement of sympathy and effort. If he have the tact of a tender and pious heart, he will use this foresight of the probable direction of thought, not loudly to prejudge what is yet on trial, or to hurt a reverence which time, if it does not entirely spare, may gently train another way; but to avoid lingering too long upon a precarious spot, and silently to withdraw men's worship to ground for ever sacred. But, beyond this noiseless preparation for changes that may not be far, he will guard his mind against any interest of religious partisanship in the pending problems of science or criticism. Removed alike from boastful elation at their progress and from blind repugnance to it, he will give his religion no regulative power over his scientific judgment: so that, from the tone of his devotion and the cast of his affections, you shall not be able to tell beforehand what he thinks of the origin of species, or the antiquity of man, or the date of Daniel or the authenticity of the fourth Gospel; but he will surrender himself simply to the facts as they appear in evidence; frankly going with every conclusion fairly won; pausing in every suspense; resting on what is undisturbed; deeming it the office at once of reason and of faith, not to bespeak the universe that ought to be, but humbly to accept the universe that is, and find room in it for reverence and trust.

That this enlargement of the variables in theology, so as to include the whole sphere of phenomenal knowledge, is alone consistent with the true temper of the philosopher and the scholar, will hardly be questioned. But how will it affect our religion? Does it not put Revelation at hazard? Is piety safe, when so much to which it clings is set afloat?

I reply, our rule sets nothing afloat, but only provides how we shall demean ourselves towards that which, by the decree of nature and of God, *is afloat:* and the rule is simply, not to deal with it, whilst it is in motion, as if it were fixed. Certainty is not ours to create or to annihilate; we cannot make it, by pretending it; we do not destroy it, by letting its absence speak for itself. If piety has been brought, as is too probable, to cling to many doubtful and perishable things, so far it is assuredly unsafe; but will you remedy this by declaring the doubtful to be sure, and the perishable immortal? or, by giving the affection its true Object, and carrying it to an eternal rest? If Christendom, sickly and feeble with its long disease of dogma, has got to put its trust, not so much in the living God and his own real ways, as in certain opinions about him and reports of his acts, it is a healing process to disengage its soul from the detaining veil of human notions and propositions, and deliver it straight into personal divine relations. An unreserved repose upon reality, an acceptance of it as better than any semblance and having absolute right over our ideas, is the genuine piety of the intellect, without which there is no sacredness in its exercise, no struggling refractions, no tender tints of trust and sacrifice, to mellow its dry light.

All "Revelation," by the very force of the term, must be a disclosure of *things as they are*. Every corrected conception of things as they are, sustained by scientific evidence, either concurs with the presumed revelation, or it does not. If it does not, a human error is eliminated from an aggregate which we had charged entirely on God, and what is his own stands purified: the natural has gained a light, and the supernatural has lost a darkness. If it *does* concur, then what was before known as revealed is now also known as natural: we see for ourselves what had been taken on the testimony of those who knew better; and our apprehension is unspeakably cleared and deepened. The truth no longer hangs detached, plainly seen indeed, but apart from its tissue of relations; it has found its footing and settled upon its own ground. Revealed religion, so far as it is not fancied but real, must always be undergoing this conversion into natural: if it gives us the master-thought of God, the true key to which the unopened recesses of the inner and the outer world will yield, it can hardly fail to find, or by developing to add, the experiences which conform to it and evidence it. Whatever, being found in Scripture, is refound in nature and in life, becomes an independent possession of humanity; and, except that the *history* of truth is only second in importance to truth itself, the very Scriptures might so far suffer again their mediæval disappearance, without loss of the treasure they had given to the world.

And, if the theologians could but look with a calm eye upon the past, they must see that, wherever the strife is over and the field is still, every advance of knowledge has been a gain to religion, won at the expense only of deforming fictions. As our petty schemes of the world break in pieces and fall away, diviner ones construct themselves and make us ashamed of our regrets. Who would now, in the interests of piety, wish to have back the childish little kosmos of the Hebrew legends, or the three stories of the Pauline heaven? or dare to say, that, in superseding them, Copernicus and Newton blasphemed? Who would choose to have no kosmos at all till six thousand years ago, or fling a stone at a Herschel or a Lyell for letting in light and showing life within that dark immensity? The age of the world, as it deepens, does but prolong its testimony to God, and make it worthier of his eternity: its scale, as it expands, does but place us in a temple more august, and nearer to his Infinity. Does any one, whose mind has been enlarged by ancient history and whose heart has listened to the old mythologies, want to have his sympathies reduced again to the "chosen people," and the divine communion with our race, so various and pathetic in its early struggling tones, restricted to that only channel? And if from the person of Jesus Christ the artificial dress of Messianic investiture, and some disguising shreds of Jewish fable, drop away, who that can fix an appreciating eye on the emerging form, will not say that it is diviner far, embodying in its grand and touching lineaments the essence and spirit of a new life of God in our humanity? This experience, this removal to a higher point of faith, is from the first the invariable result with the scholar who works most freely, because quite trustfully, at these problems: as, after long delay, it comes to be the result with all at last. The intermediate disturbance of religious calm, —the pious dismay on the one hand, the petulant irreverence on the other, —befall chiefly those who do not intimately commune with such researches, but, looking on, judge them by external and inapplicable standards, and not by their inner and essential relations.

Whoever, in these things, has gone deep and touched ground, is not afraid of falling into a bottomless abyss: and hence the moral importance of that thoroughness of study which we strive to cultivate here. For, may we not say, the essence of the large and liberal spirit lies in the absence of fear and the promptness of love?

THE END.

Cambridge: Printed by John Wilson and Son.

www.ingramcontent.com/pod-product-compliance
Lightning Source LLC
LaVergne TN
LVHW021142110826
845150LV00005B/1106